Newspaper–Real Estate
Schemes of the 1920s

Newspaper–Real Estate Schemes of the 1920s
Pell Lake and Other Vacation Colonies for Working Class Subscribers

Margaret B. Barker

McFarland & Company, Inc., Publishers
Jefferson, North Carolina

ISBN (print) 978-1-4766-8181-8
ISBN (ebook) 978-1-4766-4179-9

Library of Congress and British Library
cataloguing data are available

Library of Congress Control Number 2020053014

© 2021 Margaret B. Barker. All rights reserved

No part of this book may be reproduced or transmitted in any form or by any means, electronic or mechanical, including photocopying or recording, or by any information storage and retrieval system, without permission in writing from the publisher.

On the cover: The concessions area at the Pell Lake pavilion could be opened to the outside to sell snacks to bathers during the day. By 1928 the lake level had receded leaving the dance hall on dry land.

Printed in the United States of America

*McFarland & Company, Inc., Publishers
Box 611, Jefferson, North Carolina 28640
www.mcfarlandpub.com*

Table of Contents

Preface   1
Introduction   3

1. The Lake, the Farmer and the Dentist   7
2. Creating a Newspaper Colony   16
3. The Genesis of the Scheme   28
4. Closing In on the Deal   40
5. The Early Colonies and the Promotional Articles   54
6. The Later Colonies and the Display Ads   69
7. The Economic Aftermath   91
8. Hybrids and Clones   102
9. William Randolph Hearst   116
10. Environmental Factors   128
11. Legal Aspects   136
12. Racial Issues   144
13. Social Considerations   156
14. Pell Lake in Context and Comparison   171

Conclusion   187
Appendix: Resort Locator   193
Chapter Notes   199
Bibliography   221
Index   233

Preface

In the 1920s a strange phenomenon took place. Newspapers, serving as the front for developers, offered inexpensive plots of land as premiums for subscribing to the paper. This collusion between publications and real estate developers spawned a land buying frenzy and produced dozens of new waterfront summer communities.

One of these newspaper colonies is Pell Lake, in Walworth County, Wisconsin, where I spent all of my childhood summers at the cottage my father built. During those times at Pell Lake I would hear mention made of something about a newspaper giving away or selling lots to subscribers but no one, not even my parents, knew or remembered the name of the paper or anything more specific.

Intrigued, I set out to investigate these rumors about the curious origin of Pell Lake. It was soon apparent that Pell Lake was not the only resort created through a newspaper promotion scheme. Eventually more than fifty such newspaper colonies in the United States and Canada were identified, most of which are today ignorant of their oddball beginnings. It also became clear that the seemingly simple premise of selling land as a bonus to subscribers had a complex underbelly that warranted exposure.

Thus, this book was written to explain how the newspaper deal developed, how the ads were cleverly and judiciously designed, how the promotion grew into a complete blending of two very different businesses, and how the structure of the arrangement resulted in lifelong consequences for the colonies it created.

Local historians, present and former lot owners, and anyone who has ever lived in one of the newspaper colonies will find the history of how these places came into existence not only entertaining but also of value. Persons involved with managing legal, environmental, and social issues at these and other similar waterfront communities will gain helpful insights from the approaches taken by others. Those interested in the history of newspaper journalism, advertising, and real estate promotion will be energized by this example of entrepreneurialism.

Preface

My background as a lawyer and familiarity with county courthouses enabled me to locate case files, contracts, deeds, and other land records and to interpret the information they contained. Personnel at the many registrar of deeds and county clerk offices I contacted were all exceedingly helpful. Secretary of state office employees obligingly provided useful information on the registration and status of corporations. In particular the staff at the Walworth County Registrar of Deeds and the Walworth County Clerk offices graciously tolerated my frequent visits and many questions.

Experience as an amateur genealogist provided the tools to track down census records, draft registrations, and vital records containing information about the personalities involved with the scheme. State and local historical societies shared their maps and other archival materials. Volunteers at the Walworth County Historical Society were especially welcoming and helpful. Staffers in the Archives Room at the Wisconsin Historical Society went out of their way to assist by sourcing the vital Pell Lake dam correspondence and obtaining fresh films for me when their records proved unreadable due to the age of the microfilm. I also want to compliment the many graduate students whose well-resourced treatises provided valuable information and help in locating obscure documents.

Several people deserve a personalized thank you. Erik Weber, writer, news publisher, and Beachwood resident, has been researching Bertram Mayo and the history of Beachwood for many years. He generously shared all of his research material including photographs, promotional booklets, and articles I would not otherwise have been able to obtain. Long-time Pell Lake resident Art Oster gave freely of his time recounting stories about the early days of the colony. Judi K-Turkel and Franklynn Peterson, both seasoned authors, graciously provided advice on the book writing process. And then there is Carol Moseson, writer, editor, and good friend, who selflessly copyedited the manuscript and offered invaluable corrections and suggestions.

Most of all, I am indebted to John W. Barker, my beautiful and brilliant husband who sadly died before the book was completed but whose inspiration and guidance shine on every page. To John, I dedicate this book.

Introduction

It was an irresistible offer emblazoned in bold letters stretching across two full pages of the newspaper.

Greatest Subscription Offer Ever Made
Subscribe to the newspaper for six months and this is what you get for $67.50
—a building lot at Pell Lake
—use of the lake, bathhouse and beaches
—free life membership in the clubhouse
—exclusive use with other lot owners of the beautiful park

Concocted by a brazen newspaper promoter and two brothers who inherited a real estate business, this newspaper scheme resulted in the development of Pell Lake, Wisconsin, and approximately fifty other newspaper colonies in the United States and Canada. This book explains the unusual origin of these rural waterfront communities.

A "newspaper colony" is a real estate development that imposed buying a newspaper subscription as a prerequisite to buying a lot. The purchase of each additional lot mandated an additional subscription. Intended primarily as summer enclaves, these resort developments shared certain characteristics. The lots were small, very small, measuring only 2,000 square feet. They were also inexpensive, promoted as being all priced the same regardless of location, and could be paid for with an installment plan. Lot ownership came with certain standard incentives including use of the roadways, the beach and parklands and, best of all, a clubhouse.

A newspaper resort was easily accessible from the major metropolitan area where the newspaper was published. Nearly all the colonies were located near a body of water and offered fishing, boating, swimming, and other activities. Rights to use the clubhouse and common lands were part of lot ownership, but little was provided in the way of improvements or utilities other than some rough roadwork.

The advertising campaign was overly zealous. For months it employed huge ads decorated with pictures of the site, the clubhouse, and the crowds flocking to the resort to buy lots and share in the fun. In addition to the inescapable advertisements, the papers printed pseudo news stories promoting the benefits of buying lots at the development and reporting on the success of the project. The sponsoring newspaper denied making a profit or being in the real estate business, and proclaimed that it was merely providing a service to its readers to build good will and increase subscriptions. The real estate developer remained in the shadows with the publication serving as the front for all transactions.

The relationship between these two unlikely partners—a newspaper and a land developer—was so ensnarled that it was difficult to distinguish one from the other. Eventually the alliance evolved into a complete blending of print media and real estate when a newspaper formed a spin-off corporation for the purpose of developing this brand of real estate community. On the pages that follow, the layers of this unique affiliation are peeled back to reveal the creative thinking that conceived the idea, the opportunities and procedures that made it possible and profitable, and the lasting effects the structure of the arrangement had on the colonies it created.

Several major themes permeate the book. In the early chapters the background and mechanics of the scheme are explored beginning with the back story of a typical resort. Pell Lake serves as a template for the history of the ownership and utilization of the acreage. It is also a model of newspaper colony development from acquisition of the land to reconfiguration of both the land and the water to installation of structures and services.

The idea to sell land as a newspaper subscription premium originated with a wild land speculation in California. When the scheme proved effective in finding buyers for plots of substandard land the ploy was repeated and refined, even managing to maneuver around a pesky fraud investigation. The scheme was taken over by a dentist and his brother, heirs to a family real estate business. When one of their agents got into a legal spat with a sponsoring newspaper, the court, in its written decision, revealed the contractual details of the alliance agreement between the publishers and the developers.

By 1920 the scheme had fully matured just in time to coincide with the favorable economic times following World War I. The newspaper colony craze spanned roughly the same years as Prohibition, and, like Prohibition, the scheme was uniquely suited to the Roaring Twenties. The economy was flourishing and the ordinary citizen had money to spend and a free-wheeling attitude. A poor man could not afford to invest in Florida land or even to travel there for pleasure. But here was an opportunity for a factory worker to own a vacation place a short train ride away at a cost of only a few dollars a month.

The center chapters of the book delve more deeply into the construction of the alliance between the two unlikely allies. Improvements in newspaper production and advances in advertising practices influenced the scheme and, conversely, the scheme had an effect on the newspapers. Both the display ads and the promotional news stories took advantage of all the latest innovations in advertising jargon.

The partners also employed a variety of mechanisms that enabled them to alter the terrain to create suitable land where none existed, expand the alliance to involve more newspapers, create tie-ins with other businesses, transform handicaps into benefits, and profit from both publicity and lack of publicity. They found ways to automate the colony creation process to the point that it became a summer resort assembly line.

In these middle chapters most of the newspaper colonies are identified and offered as examples of these business techniques. Strewn throughout the book are the identities of additional newspaper resorts and other communities bearing a relation to the ploy. The distinctions of collateral communities, termed hybrids and clones, are examined in view of the definition of a newspaper resort. In addition, William Randolph Hearst's relationship to the scheme is examined.

The latter part of the book considers the newspaper colony concept in the broader contexts of the economy, the environment, legalities, race, and other social factors. Economic conditions were a strong influence in giving rise to the popularity of the resorts and to their decline as the economy worsened with the Great Depression. The price of the lots, the wealth of the developers, and taxation all played a role. At the end of the 1920s, when the newspaper-developer alliance flourished at first and then dried up as print media declined, new allies were sought. Additional variations on the plan were attempted by both the original developers and others.

Sanitation regulations had their effect on the scheme during the 1920s, and in more recent times, the emergence of environmental consciousness clashed with the landscape alterations made by the developers and led to drastic results for some of the resorts. Transferring legal ownership of the community property to an association of lot owners imposed permanent handicaps on the colonies. They attempted to remedy this situation in a number of different ways, some proving more effective than others.

The migration of Negroes[1] to the north seeking jobs provoked racial tensions in the early 1920s and, along with the attitudes of the developers toward race, had an impact on the newspaper colonies. Social relationships at the colonies were tied to the clubhouse, organizations, and dance halls as well as the beaches. With the passage of time the newspaper resorts endured inevitable change. Some have been drastically altered in character, some have disappeared, and a few have served as settings for literary works. Finally, Pell Lake, which still survives more or less intact, is analyzed as the archetypal example of a newspaper colony.

The book concludes by taking a look back at the ethics of the phenomenon through the eyes of its critics and its supporters. An appendix provides the year of creation and location coordinates for all of the colonies and communities discussed in the book.

Much of the history of the collusion between the real estate world and the newspaper business is told by the newspapers themselves. Display ads and accompanying promotional articles describe the resorts and detail the sales pitch. Real estate transfer listings provide information about how and when land changed hands and at what price. Obituaries reveal details about the involved individuals. News stories publicize the legal situations that engulfed some of the resorts and the environmental and economic difficulties that affected others. At times the papers even snitched on each other's participation in the scheme.

A comprehensive history of Pell Lake has not been attempted here. Rather, Pell Lake is presented as the quintessential newspaper resort. Established in 1924, it was developed just at the tipping point when the newspaper deal had been perfected but before outside pressures compromised the original plan. Its historical background is typical of the farmland canvas used for the resorts, and the process of its creation is common to all of them. The economic, environmental, and social progression of Pell Lake demonstrates the consequences set in motion by the alliance. The unfolding of the details of the Pell Lake story presents the best evidence for determining if it was all a scam.

1

The Lake, the Farmer and the Dentist

The July 16, 1924, issue of the *Chicago Evening Post* printed an article on its front page with the headline "Post Opens New Vacation Paradise at Pell Lake, Wis: Lots Offered to Paper's Readers at Beautiful Wisconsin Site." The article began with a romantic tale:

> A hundred years have passed since the day old Pell, intrepid pioneer of the early years of the last century, shifted his pack from his shoulder to a convenient rock and fell in love with the lake that bears his name.
>
> Old Pell stayed to live by the little lake that had won his regard—stayed despite the austerity and rigor of a life many miles away from his fellow men. Years passed and old Pell married—a girl of the same stern stuff as he—then he passed on to a greater adventure, and his son carried on by the shores of the beautiful little lake.

As with most fictionalized history, the actual details tell a far more illuminating story.

* * *

The history of Pell Lake begins with its formation in the Ice Age. But this is not just a history of a body of water and there is no need to go back that far. The year 1832 will do nicely as the start of the story of Pell Lake. There were no children splashing around, no piers or rafts to dive from, no dance pavilion on the lakeshore, no Model Ts lined up in a row along the beaches. All of that would have to wait for another century. The little lake was just a shallow, marshy area filled with precipitation and drainage. If it had a name no one knows what it was.

The land that encompassed the lake was occupied by the native Indians, primarily the Potawatomi. Part of the Northwest Territory, the land had legally belonged to the United States since the 1780s. The area was unknown to the seventeenth- and eighteenth-century explorers and, although perhaps traversed by some fur-traders, no records have been preserved of visits by white men before the 1830s. Until then the little lake was known only to the local Potawatomi.

The native Indians had names for most lakes and creeks. One Wisconsin historian provides the Indian names for some lakes in Walworth County including She-sheip-bess, later called Duck Lake,[1] and still later Lake Como, which would also become home to a newspaper resort. But the name of the little lake here being discussed is not among those listed by the recorder of the history of Walworth County.

At the Treaty of Chicago in 1833 several Indian nations, including the Potawatomi, ceded their land rights, encompassing all of southeastern Wisconsin, to the federal government with the Indians to remain in possession for two years from ratification. Delays in the effective date of the treaty postponed the final departure of the Indians until 1836, a year that witnessed many organizational changes in this part of the country. The distinct territory called Wisconsin came into existence on July 3, and at the end of the year, Walworth County was created.

Established after the Revolutionary War, the Public Land Survey System was devised to partition the vast western territories into reasonably sized lots that could be sold to raise funds for the government and to encourage settlement. Although Bloomfield Township would not be incorporated for another eight years, the township land was charted as part of the survey between April 25 and May 4, 1836,[2] ten years before government surveyors were instructed to preserve in their field notes the native terms for lakes and streams.[3] And so the small lake, surrounded by swamps and marshland, that ended up squarely in the middle of Bloomfield Township, was identified by the surveyors quite simply as the "Lake in Sections 15 & 22."

The federal government was anxious to open the new territory to settlement and, as soon as the charting was completed, settlers from the eastern part of the country started arriving and land transfers began. Ira Pell, an experienced farmer with both the need for virgin farmland and the means to pay for it, was exactly the sort of settler the government sought to attract.

* * *

Ira Allen Pell, born in Rutland County, Vermont, about 1801, was the youngest child of Revolutionary War soldier Thomas Pell and his wife Lydia Colvin.[4] The family moved west from Vermont and eventually settled in Centerville, Allegany County, New York, where Ira married Mary Farmer and acquired 60 acres of cropland.[5] Land was abundant and cheap, sustainable farming was not practiced, and farmland was rapidly exhausted, resulting in constant westward migration in search of unbroken soil.

1. The Lake, the Farmer and the Dentist

Pell was among several Centerville residents who relocated to Walworth County in the Wisconsin Territory, where virgin land could be bought directly from the government avoiding money-raking speculators.[6] In 1841 Ira purchased 80 acres in Bloomfield Township, north and east of the little lake. The original land patent was issued to Loren Stacy, a former Centerville neighbor who purchased the land on behalf of Pell and his wife and deeded it to them at the government price of $1.25 per acre.[7] This sequence of transactions gives rise to the suggestion that Pell, like many of the buyers of the newspaper lots eighty-plus years later, committed to the purchase of the land before seeing it or knowing its proximity to the lake.

The earliest printed map of the area, dated 1857, shows Pell's 80 acres

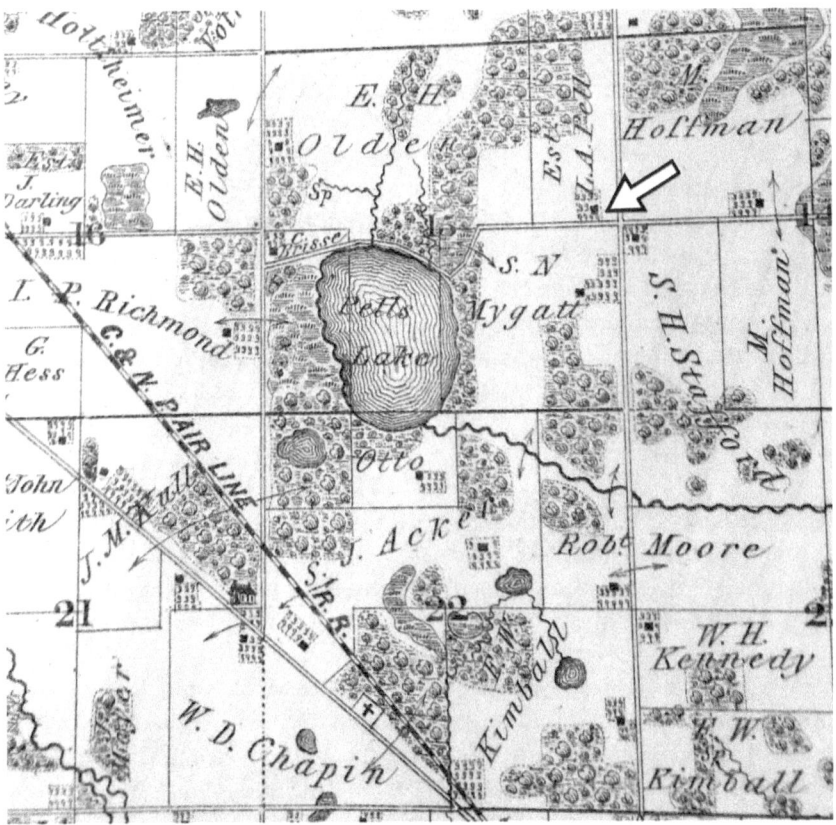

A map from 1873 is the first written record providing a name for the lake. Pell's land, then belonging to his estate, is northeast of the lake. A small black square pinpoints the location of the Pell house (see arrow) (courtesy Wisconsin Historical Society Archives).

defined by what is today known as Daisy Drive on the east and, on the west, an imaginary vertical line somewhat west of Jasmine Road. The acreage proceeded north from its southern border along the current Pell Lake Drive. A small rectangle pinpoints the approximate location of the Pell house. No name appears on the map for the little lake.[8]

How the Pell name became attached to the lake is subject to speculation. Ira Pell was clearly productive enough to feed, clothe, and otherwise sustain his family, but he was just an average farmer.[9] He was not the first to settle close to the lake, his land did not border the lake shore, nor was he one of the largest land owners in the area. He left no record of activity in local politics or government and few words are devoted to him in the histories of Walworth County.[10]

There is no conspicuous reason to name the lake after him, unless it can be attributed to the circumstances of his death. Ira Pell died on October 20, 1871,[11] and it has been reported that he drowned in the lake.[12] However, no source is cited for this assertion and no record of the cause of his death has been located.

Some local residents claim that it was a son of Ira Pell who drowned, but this is also undetermined. Ira and Mary Pell had five children including three sons. Only the cause of the death of the first son Sanford, probably occurring between 1855 and 1860, is unknown. The other two male offspring survived the naming of the lake and neither drowned, one dying of consumption and the other of heart disease.[13] When Ira's son Oren, the last surviving member of the Pell family, sold the farm to Herman Hafs in 1883[14] and moved to Iowa, the Pell family no longer had a presence in Wisconsin.

* * *

The Chicago and North Western Railway had established rail service through the area in July of 1871 and cartographers, using this as an opportunity to sell route guides for ticket agents and the touring public, published a map of Walworth County in 1873.[15] This map contains the first printed reference to "Pells Lake."[16]

Located six miles northwest of Pells Lake was the much larger and more beautiful Geneva lake, long appreciated for its clear blue water, country setting, and scenic beauty. When regular train service to Geneva commenced, the large lake became more accessible and, consequently, even more attractive. The railroad spurred the growth of Lake Geneva and secured its position as a tourist destination.

The C and NW route from Chicago to Lake Geneva proved to be one of the rail line's most successful endeavors. Traveling through Bloomfield Township on their way to Lake Geneva, the train riders passed just a stone's

1. The Lake, the Farmer and the Dentist

throw from Pells Lake, very likely never noticing it. The vision of a New York dentist would transform that view.

* * *

The ancestral and occupational path that led the dentist to the little lake contrasts sharply with that of the farmer. Ira Pell was descended from a Presbyterian Revolutionary War soldier while the lineage of Warren Smadbeck is traced back to Rabbi Koppel Freudenthal in Prussia. One of the rabbi's daughters, Henrietta Freudenthal, immigrated to the United States where she married Jacob Schmadbeck in New York City. Jacob was only 34 when he died[17] leaving Henrietta with five children including one son, Louis, born in 1855.[18]

Merchandising opportunities lured Freudenthal family members to the southwest where they became involved, not only in selling goods, but also in copper mining. At a remote Arizona hillside near Clifton, Louis' cousins, Henry and Charles Lesinsky, and his uncle Julius Freudenthal, owned and operated the rich Longfellow copper mine. Louis, with his last name now simplified from Schmadbeck to Smadbeck, was recruited by his relatives to work at the mine in the 1870s and proved himself valuable by developing an ingenious copper smelting process.

When the Longfellow was sold in 1882 Julius and the Lesinskys left the Southwest multimillionaires by today's standards. There is no direct evidence that Louis Smadbeck shared in the proceeds of the sale of the mine, but he certainly profited from his work as the chief smelter. He also owned the patent on other mine lodes.[19] Returning east with money in his pocket, a proven reputation as an innovator, and the family Germanic mercantile ideology, he was fully prepared to establish himself in a new livelihood.

Louis Smadbeck merely needed to look around at his New York surroundings to identify his next business venture—real estate was an obvious choice for speculation during the Gilded Age. Louis was not long in New York when he met and married Jennie Bach.[20] By the time their first child, a son named Warren, was born on January 13, 1885, Louis was engaged in buying and selling land and buildings in New York City. A second son, Arthur, was born in 1887, and a daughter, Evelyn, in 1889.

Louis quickly established his real estate niche zeroing in on the development of land adjacent to rail transport to the city. Beginning in 1890 he bought several large farms in Westchester County close to the Harlem Rail Road. He platted the acreage into Manhattan sized lots, 25' wide and 100' deep, and named the development Sherman Park.[21]

The small size of the lots provided many units per acre to sell and resulted in most purchasers buying two or more lots. Diminutive lots also allowed Louis to set prices at a level attractive to persons with lower incomes, enabling him to tap into a broad pool of customers. He offered an installment payment program and financing through the Sherman Park Savings and Building Association which Smadbeck operated out of his Broadway offices.[22]

In April 1891, Louis launched an aggressive advertising campaign for Sherman Park, making frequent use of the *Evening World* and *The Sun*, two New York penny papers that employed sensationalism to attract less affluent, working class readers. Using the train system to introduce prospective clients to the development, he stationed agents at depots in the city to distribute free tickets for rides to the site and even chartered special trains on Sundays. When his son Arthur grew into his teens, he was recruited to meet the chartered trains and guide the prospective purchasers around on horse drawn carriages to view what was promised to be a fashionable suburb of the future.[23]

Louis derived good mileage from the train system, incorporating under the name "Rapid Transit Real Estate Co." His display ads portrayed rail favorably with appealing cartoons of trains, while ferries and bridges, rife with fog and malaria, were to be avoided. One of his ads, warning against investment in the stock market, foreshadowed the financial downturn of 1893. In spite of the weakened market, Smadbeck continued to advertise and continued to sell building lots, even buying more land to add to the development. After four years of operation Sherman Park had reportedly sold 11,000 lots.[24]

By 1905 his oldest son Warren had graduated from New York University School of Dentistry at age nineteen and was a practicing dentist. Arthur, just out of high school, was working as a merchant.[25] A series of events beginning in late 1909 suggests that Louis' health was declining and death was looming. He executed a will in December of that year,[26] vacationed in Cuba the following April and in Europe in the fall.[27] On February 8, 1911, Louis Smadbeck died.[28]

* * *

When their father became ill, both sons began working with him to learn the real estate business. While this required Warren to abandon the practice of dentistry, he never shed the mantle of a dentist, clinging to the degree and using the title "Dr." for the rest of his life for whatever prestige it brought him in social and business networks.

Louis had developed dozens of suburban communities and had begun expanding his operations to locales near waterways such as Smithtown Lawns along the Nissequogue River in northern Long Island and Asbury Park Estates in New Jersey. Having apprenticed with their father,

1. The Lake, the Farmer and the Dentist

Before the halftone process for printing photographs came into common usage advertisements were illustrated. Some rather comical drawings appear in 1893 ads placed by Louis Smadbeck for his Sherman Park development. This ad suggests that rail transport is safer than crossing the river by aerial cable or by jumping from ice floe to ice floe (courtesy *Newspapers.com*).

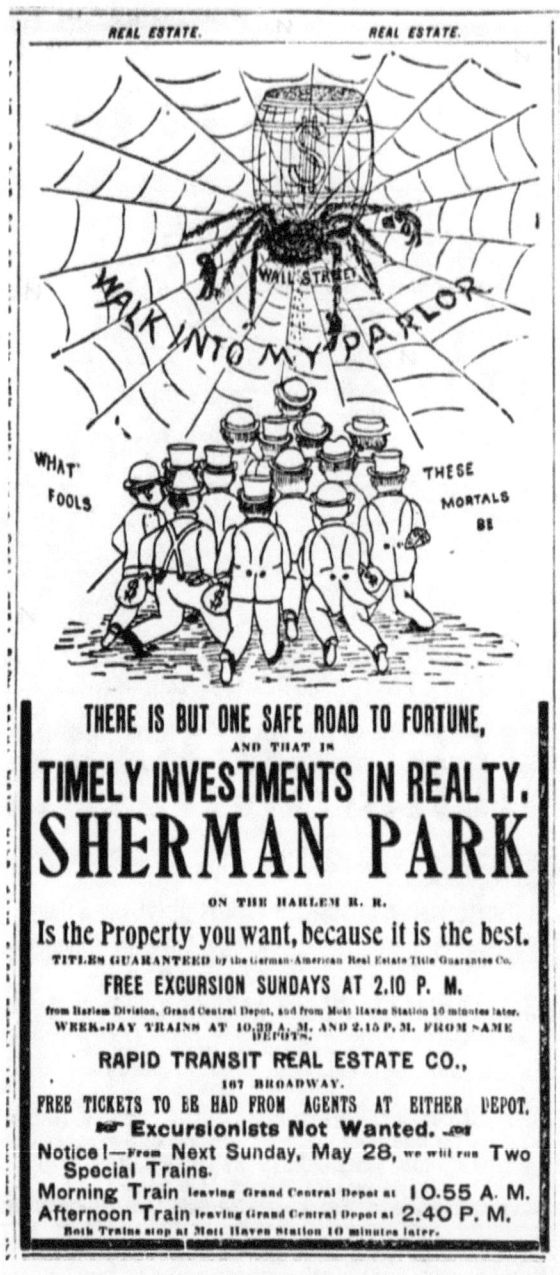

Another ad for Sherman Park makes obvious reference to the economic conditions of the Panic of 1893. Wall Street is portrayed as a spider luring foolish investors into a web while real estate is described as a safe road to fortune (courtesy *Newspapers.com*).

Warren and Arthur Smadbeck became well schooled in the basics of real estate development and in the specific elements—small, cheap lots, access to transportation, and robust salesmanship—that marked Louis' approach to the business. His instruction provided them with a solid business background and taught them the tricks of exploiting land development.

Warren and Arthur added to this foundation when they met another mentor who had devised the basic scheme of allying real estate development with newspaper promotion. With this dual tutelage the brothers fully developed the potential of the newspaper deal and eventually created a virtual assembly line producing summer resort communities for the average worker.

2

Creating a Newspaper Colony

It was an ingenious idea, and by the time the system was employed to create Pell Lake in 1924, the subscription premium real estate promotion had ripened and matured.

Pells Lake in Walworth County perfectly matched the Smadbeck template both in character and location. Covering about 100 acres, the lake was a favorable size with a partial sand bottom and two natural beaches. Surrounded by farmland for miles in every direction, it was located only a short train ride from Chicago, where a ready supply of working-class buyers resided. The abundant areas of swamp could be dealt with.

The two brothers operated through dozens of corporate entities but they also bought and sold realty in their own names as they did with the land in Wisconsin. While they worked closely together, they nevertheless handled their own projects, and Pells Lake was pursued by the dentist, Dr. Warren Smadbeck. Once he chose the location, Dr. Smadbeck began implementing the project with a sophistication that demonstrated an already well-established framework. He quickly found it convenient to drop the final "s" on the name of the lake thereby establishing "Pell Lake" as the title of his development and also altering, and solidifying, the name of the lake itself.[1]

The land was acquired using a trusted buying agent who could travel to the location and negotiate with the titleholders on Smadbeck's behalf. Ludwig B. Freudenthal, of Jersey City, New Jersey, the son of Warren's great-uncle Julius Freudenthal,[2] and a first cousin to Warren's father, was the agent employed for this purpose at Pell Lake. The first purchases, from Ed Holtzheimer and Charles Kull, took place on April 7, 1924.[3] More land was bought from Kull, James Reeves, and Harriet Hibbard in July and August, all of which was purchased by Freudenthal in his own name.[4] Ludwig then reassembled the acreage and deeded it to Warren Smadbeck in eight parcels.[5] Before the end of the year, Smadbeck had title to over 700 acres, comprising nearly all of the land immediately surrounding the lake.

Dr. Smadbeck acquired other rights to the lake as well. In the late nineteenth and early twentieth centuries surface ice was cut from southern Wisconsin lakes, especially those with access to a rail line, and Pells Lake was no exception. Ice was harvested during the winter months and stored in ice houses for shipment to Chicago in warmer times for use in the meat and produce markets.[6] But with broadening access to mechanical refrigeration and the resulting ability to artificially produce ice, the demand for harvested ice had drastically declined by 1924. This enabled Smadbeck to purchase the right to harvest ice from Pells Lake as well as riparian rights to the small parcel of waterfront property owned by the ice company, ensuring that nothing would conflict with the planned recreational usage.[7]

Smadbeck knew how to improve an imperfect body of water and Pell Lake was particularly problematical. To the north lay a swath of swamp larger than the lake itself, another wetland area to the south, and the entire western and southern shores were lined with marshes. The land around the lake would be more salable if some of these low and swampy portions could be eliminated, or at least camouflaged. Smadbeck had several tools available to accomplish this—dams, drainage, ditches, and dredging—all of which were employed at Pell Lake.

Seeking to raise the water level in the lake by three feet, he built a low dam at the southeastern end of the lake where it drained off into Nippersink Creek. Then he diverted some of the swamp drainage with ditches and conduits. When these measures did not adequately maintain the higher lake level, he engaged Davis Construction, an Iowa company, to dredge 30 acres of swamp on the south and west sides, a job that took several months.[8]

Arthur King was engaged to survey the land and prepare plat maps according to Smadbeck's specifications, subdividing the 700 acres into 9,799 lots. These plats were presented to the Bloomfield Town Board for its consideration by local attorney Sturges P. Taggart. A total of seven numbered and two lettered sections were approved at six separate sessions of the town board between July 16 and October 10, 1924, with Dr. Smadbeck present at each of the meetings.[9]

Typically, the lot pattern was a rectangle containing fifty or so lots in the center, each 20' wide and 100' deep, laid out back to back with another ten lots positioned crosswise along each end. This novel lot configuration serves to identify later resort developments as replicas of the Smadbeck plan. The plat maps were reproduced on large sheets of paper each bearing two or more sections and printed on both sides of the sheet. These maps were specifically created for use by the sales staff to assist buyers in selecting their lots.

The C and NW Railway was easily persuaded to add a stop at Pell Lake since a resort settlement would increase ridership on an already well-established route. The railway built a depot and train service to the lake began on July 5, 1924, before any of the land plats had been approved.[10] Roadways from Chicago were not yet entirely paved but with the increasing popularity of automobiles they would continue to improve.

Two lumber companies, Taggart and Zenda, established yards at Pell Lake to supply building materials and, by 1925, a third lumberyard had opened[11] along with four construction companies and three stores.[12] Smadbeck arranged for the Southern Wisconsin Electric Light Company to provide electricity to the area during limited hours.[13]

Land along the lake shore had been designated for parks and beaches and a block of lots was set aside for a clubhouse. Piers, floating rafts, beach shelters, and other structures were built for the use of the residents. In the spring of 1926 Pell Lake was sufficiently developed to justify the commissioning of a post office and 32-year-old August E. Wachtel was appointed as the first postmaster on April 3.[14] The post office was housed in Wachtel's general store located near the train station.

Two years later a Catholic church was established when Saint Mary's of the Lake opened in July of 1928.[15] Eventually a church building was constructed on land owned by George Sitterle on North Lake Shore Drive not far from Clover Road.

August Wachtel opened "Your Store" shown here in 1925. Writing on the building advertises ice cream, soft drinks, candy, and cigarettes. Wachtel and his family lived in the house next to the store. The train depot can be seen in the background.

2. Creating a Newspaper Colony

Post Office showing C. & N. W. R. R. Station in Distance, Pell Lake, Wis. 87805-nr

By 1928 the Wachtel house had been elevated on stone blocks and the store and post office moved to the newly created ground level. A blue and yellow Dixie Gas pump sits out front.

* * *

All of the careful preparation to make the site visually and functionally attractive was only part of the undertaking—equally important was the alliance with the newspaper. The interaction between these two components was carefully choreographed. Long before Smadbeck began looking for a suitable location for a summer resort in southern Wisconsin he had the promotional arrangement lined up with the *Chicago Evening Post*. The initial advertisement for Pell Lake, a two-pager, appeared in the *Post* on Wednesday, July 16, 1924, the very day that the first of the land plats was approved. It was billed as "The Greatest Subscription Premium Offer Ever Made." Readers could buy a lot for $67.50 with the purchase of a six-month subscription to the newspaper. Installment terms were $10 down and $2.50 a month. While the lot size was not mentioned, the ad emphasized that the purchase price included use of the lake, bathhouses, and beaches, lifetime membership in the clubhouse, and exclusive rights, along with the other property owners, to the parks along the lakeshore.

The advertising campaign was fashioned to generate a buying fever, a goal that was masterfully accomplished with lots in the subdivision selling at lightning speed. Several articles in the local newspaper credited Pell Lake with initiating a resort boom in Walworth County. "Twenty-Eight Subdivisions on Walworth County Lakes"[16] singled out Pell Lake as the largest

Bathing Beach, looking North, Pell Lake, Wis.   87808-8

The south beach at Pell Lake had a beach house and outdoor privies. A crude shelter and a diving board were attached to the end of the pier.

of the many summer colonies in the process of development. "Wisconsin's Land Boom"[17] predicted that the climax of the boom in Florida was causing developers to seek new areas to conquer, suggested that Walworth County presented a ripe plum, and cited Pell Lake as an example. In "Talk About Sunny Florida; Take a Look at Pell Lake Resort"[18] a direct parallel was drawn between the dramatic development of Pell Lake and land speculation in Florida.

The Pell Lake Property Owners Association (POA) was organized toward the end of 1925,[19] and two months later, the parkland and the clubhouse site were deeded to the association.[20] In February of 1927, Warren Smadbeck quietly transferred approximately 1,300 unsold lots to Matthew Jonap.[21] More than 8,000 lots had been sold to newspaper readers and the *Chicago Evening Post* had increased its subscription base by an equal number. In less than three years, from start to finish, Pell Lake was virtually complete.

* * *

Pell Lake was so successful, so quickly, it spawned copycats immediately. Farmers who either refused to sell their land or were not made an offer sought to ride on the coattails of Smadbeck by capitalizing on the extensive advertising and built up mania.

Less than a month after the final plat hearing for Smadbeck's Pell Lake,

2. Creating a Newspaper Colony

George Sitterle obtained approval for a block of lots north of the lake. He platted a second adjoining parcel in 1925 and these became Sitterle's Subdivision and Addition.[22] It consisted of a strip of land on the north side of Lake Shore Drive running west to Clover Road, and then up the hill along the right side of Clover. Sitterle offered about 100 lots of varying sizes.

Sitterle's lots were a minor adjunct compared with the Highlands and the Addition, both subdivided in the summer of 1925 by Chicago real estate men. Earl McDonald and Clifford Osborne, operating as Land O Lakes Resort Company, platted out 1,600 lots in Pell Lake Highlands creeping uphill on the other side of Clover Road from Sitterle.[23] This 125-acre tract had been used as a dairy farm by the seller, Lewis Kimball, who reserved 12 acres in the center of the section for himself including the residence and the orchard.[24] The land was disadvantaged by being at a distance from the beaches and separated from the main development by Clover Road. It was also handicapped by having no relationship with a big city newspaper other than small classified ads appearing in the *Chicago Daily Tribune*. Land O Lakes could not offer use of Smadbeck's clubhouse and so instead promoted free membership in a golf club.

Pell Lake Addition more successfully blended in with the Smadbeck development. Leon Sex[25] and Frank Sampson formed Pell Lake Development and created 1,488 lots on level land immediately east of Smadbeck's tract.[26] Sex announced that twenty lots at the corner of Daisy and Marinette

Highland Club House, Pell Lake, Wis.   87807-8

The Highland Golf Course and Tennis Courts opened to the public in July of 1926. Dances were held every Saturday night in the Highland Club House.

would be the site of a $40,000 hotel with a dining room, game rooms, and club rooms.[27] The plats also set aside an area for a golf course just off the southeast corner of the Addition.

Large display ads appearing in the *Chicago Evening Post* borrowed heavily from those of the Smadbecks with the same pricing terms and emphasizing that the Addition was adjacent to the *Post*'s development. There was no subscription tie-in but readers of the paper were told to "Follow the Blue Arrows" just as Smadbecks' ads for Pell Lake had done.[28] Both Pell Lake Highlands and the Pell Lake Addition copied the Smadbeck lot size and layout design.

Another small, but somewhat significant, addition attached itself to Pell Lake in the summer of 1925. Ira Pell's original farmland was owned by Andrew Hafs and a house located there known as the "Pell House" burned in February of 1925.[29] Hafs laid out a row of sixty-five lots along the southern edge of his property which included the site of the burned house. Christened "Pell Farm Annex to Pell Lake Summer Resort," it consumed less than three of Pell's original 80 acres and was the only part of Ira Pell's farm to be associated with the Pell Lake development.[30] While Pell Lake, an unincorporated area of Bloomfield Township, had no defined borders, the Smadbeck plats, Sitterle's lots, the Highlands, the Addition, and the Pell Farm Annex comprised the core and substance of Pell Lake for many decades.

* * *

The advertising campaign encouraged everyone to visit Pell Lake, including potential lot buyers, those who had already purchased lots at the *Post*'s office in Chicago, friends and relatives of both groups, and the general public. In the 1920s getting there was half the fun. Instead of offering free transportation to the resort, advertisements contained a full print out of C and NW's newly created schedule for trains between Chicago and Pell Lake. Those who came by rail rubbed elbows with wealthier Chicagoans before departing the train just one stop before prestigious Lake Geneva, thus giving Pell Lake a special panache.

Car travel was somewhat less reliable. The advertisements provided a map with mile by mile, turn by turn, driving directions often keyed to where concrete roads began, ended, and began again.[31] Large blue arrows were posted along the route as a further guide. The poor driving conditions and early car design caused recurrent flat tires which provided added excitement for those who reveled in the adventure. Once drivers arrived in Pell Lake they found roads that were little better than dirt trails. People packed picnic lunches and came on day outings for sun and water sports. As the promoters urged, many who visited ended up buying lots. They in

2. Creating a Newspaper Colony

turn showed them off to their friends, some of whom were also caught up in the lot-buying madness. The sale of lots took hold quickly with the lots selling at a rapid pace.

The fun-lovers made quick use of their investment, initially setting up tents for overnight stays. Outhouses were among the first structures to be built, but soon construction of cottages began. The early houses were simple structures, meant for summer living. If cottages had both inside and outside walls, the insulation between them consisted of newspapers which the lot owners had a steady supply of after buying several subscriptions to the *Post*. Most cottages were the same design—a rectangle with a kitchen, living room, two bedrooms, and a screened porch usually fitted out with hand-me-down furniture from the city dwelling. The shutters on the windows were held open with sticks in nice weather and closed and latched with bow tie turn buttons for the winter. A well dug near the kitchen door was operated by a hand water pump.

Many bungalows were built by the land owners themselves using whatever scrap materials they could find. One man, a worker in the produce market in Chicago, salvaged fruit crates and brought them out to Pell Lake piled atop his Model T. This wood became the walls of his cottage and the house never stopped smelling of citrus on hot, humid summer days.[32] Another lot buyer from the city salvaged hundreds of paving bricks when

General View of Pell Lake, Pell Lake, Wis.   19903-nc

Pell Lake is seen here at a very early stage in its development. This photograph, looking southeast, was taken from the crest of the hill on Clover Road in 1924 or 1925.

Before their cottages were built these Pel-Lakens, members of a club for young people, pitched tents and took the seats out of their cars to use as mattresses.

the streetcar tracks were removed from Cicero Avenue. These were used to create a pathway from the back door of his cottage to the outhouse at the back of the lot.

Some bungalows were precut and shipped out on the railroad in kits for the home owner to assemble. These prepackaged cottages can be

This typical cottage was shipped out in pre-cut pieces on the railroad to be assembled by the lot owner whose name was imprinted on the attic rafters. The hand pump for water can be seen just to the left of the bungalow (see arrow).

A view of the back of the cottage shows the brick path leading to the outhouse. Scythes and rakes were used to tame the tall weeds until a lawn could be established.

identified today by the names of purchasers stamped or stenciled on attic rafters. The more substantial cottages were constructed by local builders and lumberyards. A. Blackstone of Chicago had a contract to build five hundred summer homes at Pell Lake, more than a hundred of which had been constructed by June of 1925.[33]

The lake was stocked with fish, making boating and fishing popular activities with rowboats and canoes lining the shore. Children were kept occupied swimming all day in the lake while their parents chatted with new neighbors. Evenings were filled with dancing and parties. Milk, eggs, and vegetables could be bought from nearby farmers and the country air was refreshing.

Many of the lot buyers, those caught up in the mystique of getting a piece of land at a bargain price but lacking the gumption to follow through with the dream of a summer home, never even ventured to Pell Lake, buying their lots from a map with little cognizance of where the plot was in relation to the lake or the beaches. Still, enough lot buyers came, built cottages, and vacationed to cause excitement among Lake Geneva merchants. With the summer population swelling by 1,000 to 1,500 people the lumber dealers, hardware stores, furniture dealers, and dry goods merchants looked forward to increased business.[34] They were not disappointed. Grocers, meat markets, and milk dealers all reported a banner season in 1926.

Swimmers crowd the south beach at Pell Lake. Postcards of the colony provided lot owners and visitors with an easy means of writing to city friends about their happy vacations.

The railroad set a new record for summer travel averaging around 700 rail passengers a day, and on at least one occasion, handling twice that number. There was a reciprocal increase in freight shipments, especially lumber. The telegraph and post office also handled an overflow of business and the newspaper dealers reported a record year for the sale of Chicago papers.[35] Even the county benefited when its tax rolls increased by $48,000 attributable to the development of Pell Lake.[36]

With Pell Lake the newspaper deal had reached its epitome. All the resorts created before Pell Lake were a prelude to this platform of achievement and, due to changing laws and economies, none of the newspaper developments that came after it would realize the same degree of accomplishment.

The lot buying common folk were having a good time with their new adventure. Pell Lake was fun. It was the Roaring Twenties and Pell Lake was a roaring success.

3

The Genesis of the Scheme

The accomplishment of Pell Lake in 1924 resulted from a perfect harmonization of relevant factors that could only have occurred during the Roaring Twenties. There were three parties to the newspaper deal—the readers (gullible lot purchasers), the developers (primarily the Smadbeck brothers), and the newspapers themselves (the sponsors of the colonies). All were well positioned to make the newspaper deal a success at the start of the 1920s.

Primed by the rosy economic conditions, the lot buying customers were ripe for just this type of real estate contrivance. The end of the Great War launched a promising financial outlook for workers. People had more time, more money, and more new technologies to spend money on. Paid vacation time, the eight-hour work day, the five-day work week, and other gains made by the labor movement contributed to an increase in free time and leisurely pursuits. New inventions—radio, telephones, and motion pictures—were available for consumption and electricity introduced a new spectrum of labor-saving devices. Wages increased and credit was freely available. Automobiles became affordable to the masses enabling them to take driving trips into the countryside to fish, camp, or just carouse. Even swimsuit manufacturers cooperated by offering free swimming lessons to popularize the activity and sell more suits.[1] All this made the idea of owning a cottage for summer getaways an easy temptation.

Agriculture had prospered during the war as European food production declined and prices for United States farm products rose. When the war ended the foreign agricultural markets rebounded resulting in lower prices for both farm products and farmland. Farmers were more willing to sell their land just as city folks had an increased desire to own a piece of property in the country. In addition, laws had not kept pace with the energetic economy and rapidly changing society. The lack of governmental rules and regulations, especially in rural areas, afforded land developers free rein to do as they pleased.

3. The Genesis of the Scheme

* * *

In this environment the Smadbeck brothers were poised to become the major players in the creation of newspaper colonies. A variety of factors contributed to their ability to prosper from the newspaper deal and make it a success.

Warren and Arthur Smadbeck brought with them not only their real estate apprenticeship but also their father's business resources. There were many uncompleted projects when Louis Smadbeck died in 1911. A few had been ongoing for many years including Sherman Park where some lots remained unsold.[2] Other developments were in the beginning stages. Shortly before writing his will, Louis acquired acreage in Asbury Park, New Jersey, had the land platted into lots, and named his community Asbury Park Estates. It was a more upscale development, aimed at a wealthier clientele with lots, designated "villa sites" and "bungalow plots," both larger and more expensive than those at Sherman Park.

Sidestepping the *Evening World* and *The Sun*, ads were placed in the *New York Times* to reach a more sophisticated readership. The venture got off to a good start and Louis lent his endorsement to advertising in the *Times* stressing the number of sales: "Through an advertisement placed in the New York Times for three days, in response to eleven inquiries, we have sold to nine buyers.... Asbury Park Estates, L. Smadbeck, Mgr."[3] At first he followed the usual practice of frequent, prominent ads but advertising costs were expensive and needed to be paid up front. The Asbury Park Estates promotional campaign waned along with Louis' health and the task of marketing the lots was left to Warren and Arthur.

Louis Smadbeck had incorporated under various names for different purposes and his sons not only took over those corporations but created dozens more of their own. Home Guardian Company of New York, organized on March 18, 1912, was one of their earliest companies. Warren was president, Arthur was secretary and treasurer, and both were managers and directors.[4]

In 1916 Home Guardian held title to thousands of lots in Asbury Park Estates. These could have been the unsold lots from Louis' late in life venture, lots created from additional land purchased by the sons, or, perhaps, Louis' land replatted into smaller lots. Motivated to dispose of these properties for the highest possible profit, Warren and Arthur employed the newspaper deal.

* * *

Irving Rosenbaum was a sales agent, or an advertising agent, or perhaps both a sales agent and an advertising agent for Home Guardian. In the summer of 1916 he called at the offices of the *Jewish Daily News* (*Yidishes*

Tageblatt), the first daily newspaper published in New York in Yiddish. Ezekiel Sarasohn and Leon Kamaiky, operating as Sarasohn and Son, were the newspaper's copartners and publishers.

Rosenbaum approached Enoch Wolberg, the advertising manager for the *Jewish Daily News*, and made a proposition on behalf of his client that was designed to both dispose of the lots in Asbury Park Estates and increase the circulation of the newspaper. Home Guardian would deed the land to the paper in blocs of 1,000 lots. The newspaper would hold the lots as trustee and, in turn, deed them to purchasers allowing the paper to represent that it was the owner of the lots. The parcels would be priced at $32.75 each, and could be bought only with the purchase of a six-month subscription at a cost of $2. The newspaper would keep all the subscription proceeds. For each lot sold the paper would pay $30.10 to Home Guardian, retaining the difference to pay for the advertisements at regular publication rates. Home Guardian was to dictate the advertising copy and determine the amount of space to be used, guaranteeing at least $2,000 worth of advertising in the first two months of the contract.

Representatives of the paper, intrigued by the proposal, traveled to Asbury Park to view the lots, were favorably impressed, and agreed to Rosenbaum's offer on behalf of Home Guardian. The paper's circulation manager drew up the contract which also provided that *Jewish Daily News* would pay Rosenbaum a 15 percent commission on the advertising income.

Instead of the smaller ads Louis had used, Warren and Arthur opted for much more expansive displays dwarfing Louis' two-column, three-inch inserts. The *Jewish Daily News* was published almost entirely in Yiddish. Nevertheless, two pages announcing the investment opportunity, decorated with seven pen and ink drawings of notable Asbury Park features, appeared in the August 11, 1916, issue printed in English. There was also a third full-page ad in Yiddish.

It was made clear that only subscribers could take advantage of the offer—the ability to purchase a lot at Asbury Park Estates was a premium that accompanied the purchase of a six-month subscription. A limit of four lots with a two-year subscription was imposed. The ad made no mention of the lot size—20' × 100'—even narrower than the lots at Sherman Park. All lots were the same price providing an incentive for acting quickly and securing a corner or business lot.

Lot purchasers became members of the Jewish Daily News Colony Club entitling them to free bus transportation between their homes and the station, the village, and the beach for five years. The paper also offered to assist with bank loans for building costs and it was suggested that a casino was in the planning stage. A special pitch was made to take advantage of the opportunity to make parents comfortable in their old age. There was also

3. The Genesis of the Scheme

The first Smadbeck newspaper colony, Asbury Park Estates, was promoted in the August 11, 1916, issue of *Jewish Daily News* with three full pages of advertising—two pages in English and a third page in Yiddish. This is the first page of the ad in English (Historical Jewish Press website founded by the National Library of Israel and Tel Aviv University, the MaRLI Project [Manhattan Research Library Initiative], New York Public Library, Columbia University, New York University).

an appeal to the German Jewish merchant mentality with the suggestion of opening a little store.

Combining the efforts of the developers and the newspaper proved rewarding for both. In the first year of the contract 4,763 lots were sold. The *Jewish Daily News* received $9,563 in subscription money as well as $12,621.95 in advertising fees, less Rosenbaum's 15 percent. The Smadbecks reduced their inventory of lots and took in more than $138,600, and that was just in the first year of the promotion. The Smadbecks benefited in other ways. Lots could be sold to the paper in bulk rather than one by one to lot buyers. The newspaper, as purported owner, and Wolberg as its trustee, contributed to the work of deeding the lots, collecting the money, and resolving disputes with the purchasers, thus relieving the Smadbecks of much responsibility. Heavy advertising was needed but, by partnering with the newspaper, advertising costs did not have to be paid before any lots were sold.

The specifics of the newspaper deal would have remained buried had Sarasohn and Rosenbaum not disagreed over the latter's commission. In addition to the advertising percentage paid by the *Jewish Daily News*, Rosenbaum received $1 from Home Guardian for each lot sold. When Leon Kamaiky learned of this, he objected to the compensation terms as double-dipping and refused to pay Rosenbaum the percentage commission. Rosenbaum sued and, when he lost, took his case up to the New York appellate court. That court reversed the finding of the lower court and, conveniently for history, published its opinion.[5] Rosenbaum was deemed able to collect commissions from both parties to the contract proving that he, too, was well compensated by the arrangement.

* * *

Without question the newspaper deal was an ingenious innovation and Asbury Park Estates was the Smadbecks' first experiment with it. By the time Pell Lake was created in 1924 the Smadbecks had developed about a dozen communities and would go on to create several dozen more. While the Smadbecks perfected the concept, its origin can be traced to other sources.

The *Jewish Daily News* ad for Asbury Park Estates bore the headline "The Greatest, Most Wonderful Premium Ever Offered," an emphatic phrase that was common advertising parlance in the opening years of the twentieth century. This flamboyant wording was employed to offer magazines, atlases, bibles, encyclopedias, sets of chinaware, silverware, electric irons and toasters, fireworks, and even ponies as incentive to buy a newspaper subscription.

The individual deserving credit for devising the idea to offer land as a

3. The Genesis of the Scheme 33

subscription premium is not certain. An early attempt occurred in Wichita. At its debut in January of 1909 *Kansas Magazine* had a yearly subscription price of $1.50. A beginning promotional offer threw in subscriptions to another magazine and a newspaper as a bonus for subscribers. After a few months the magazine ramped up its new subscriber drive by offering a year and a half subscription to *Kansas Magazine*, a copy of *Hammond's 1909 World Atlas*, and a building lot in the latest addition to Wichita all for $18.00.

The "beautifully located" lots were southwest of the city in an area named Orienta Park after the adjacent car and locomotive shops proposed to be built by the Orient Railway. The promotion offered an initial lot, sized at a narrow 25', at the subscription rate cost with additional lots priced from $40 to $100. The proposition was multi-purposed: *Kansas Magazine* wanted to fulfill its "splendid mission" to interest the populace with facts about the Sunflower State, the developers wanted to sell land,[6] and the railroad wanted to attract a workforce with affordable housing near the shops, a goal that was furthered by ads addressed to "You Who Work for Wages."[7]

Although the lots were a premium for a magazine subscription rather than for a newspaper, ads for the promotion appeared in both. Advertisements for the Orienta Park offer were printed in several different Kansas newspapers[8] and, eventually, in 1910, in the magazine itself.[9]

* * *

In the same time frame as the Orienta Park land promotion, other real estate exploits were taking place in California under the direction of a man who would eventually become a second mentor to Warren and Arthur Smadbeck. A contemporary of their father, B.C. (Bertram Chapman) Mayo was born in Boston on March 23, 1865. The entry in the Boston birth registry lists clothing as the occupation of his father, Noah Mayo,[10] but a few years later Noah was working as a wholesale fish dealer.[11]

After completing school B.C. decided he was better suited to pursuing his father's earlier occupation and for about ten years, was engaged in the wholesale clothing business in and around Boston.[12] For one of those years, 1894, the men's furnishings company of Nickerson and Mayo is listed in a Boston Directory.[13] His friendship with Addison Doane Nickerson grew into the first of many business relationships that Mayo would engage in.

By the spring of 1904 Mayo had relocated to California[14] and was employed as business manager for the *Oakland Enquirer*.[15] He quickly penetrated elite business circles and engaged in a variety of speculative deals that exhibited both his quest for wealth and his promotional prowess.

Author, newspaperman, and lyricist William Mill Butler wrote a brief and somewhat fanciful biography of Bertram Chapman Mayo in 1924.

Butler credited Mayo with providing a box of candy as a bonus for subscribing to the newspaper, introducing the candy idea to an Oakland theater manager, and originating the idea of offering land as a subscription premium.

According to Butler, Mayo and a friend bought a piece of land in the redwoods of Sonoma County north of Oakland hoping to strike oil, but the property proved unproductive. Butler describes what happened when B.C. and some friends went to the land on a fishing trip:

> It was after the return of a jolly party with their catch to an old camp in the woods, that Mr. Mayo and his dreams and schemes were made the butt of the chaff and jokes. "B.C.," said one, "you have fed candy to the children, given theatre tickets to the mothers and clocks to the fathers, if they will only buy your daily sheet; what next to add another figure to your circulation, a house and lot?" "Just that" came back the quick reply. "I'm going to give away these red monsters of mine for a premium." Retorts were drowned in a roar of derisive laughter.

Butler goes on to report that Mayo took up the dare, and after buying out his partner, divided the property into small lots, named it "Casadero Woods," and sold the lots for $5.40 each with a subscription to the *Enquirer*.[16]

Butler knew Mayo, not at the time of these supposed events, but in later years and likely learned of his background from Mayo himself. Either Butler misremembered what he had been told or Mayo colored the story to appear more cunning. Promotion was his specialty and assuredly Mayo made use of this talent when describing his life experiences. While some elements of the biography are valid, other details are unsubstantiated by the documented evidence.

Mayo did invest in property hoping to strike oil and he also bought land in the redwoods, but these were two different locations and two very different endeavors. The oil land was near Canby in the far northeastern California county of Modoc. Mayo's partners in the Modoc Oil and Development Company were his boss, Gilbert Barber Daniels, owner of the *Oakland Enquirer*, and H.G. Betts, of Goldfield, Nevada, identified as a well-known mining man.[17] Betts confidently asserted to reporters that he would discover an immense lake of oil in the Canby basin with just a few months of drilling.[18] If Betts' predictions materialized no newspaper took notice.

The Modoc oil experiment was not the first time Mayo teamed up with Betts and Daniels in an attempted get-rich-quick venture. William B. Swears joined them in December of 1906 as incorporators of the Goldfield Diamond Drilling and Mining Company in Arizona,[19] the word "diamond" referring to a type of drill. Goldfield Diamond Drilling owned two claims near Goldfield, Nevada, a town that derived its name from the voluminous deposits of gold discovered nearby in the opening years of the twentieth century.

3. The Genesis of the Scheme

Each of the incorporators contributed to the enterprise. The claims owned by Goldfield Diamond Drilling were procured by William Swears' son, Forest J., a mining prodigy who later developed into an imposing petroleum engineer under the name F.J.S. Sur.[20] Betts managed the drilling operations and Daniels took care of business matters, handling the money, providing advertising connections, and supplying office space at the headquarters of the *Enquirer* in Oakland.

B.C. Mayo's contribution was the advertising copy offering to sell shares of the company's stock. These newspaper pronouncements had Mayo's promotional fingerprints all over them beginning with the claim "The Safest and Surest mining stock on the market today" and including a testimonial from the vice-president of a company that distributed advertising matter. The ad copy explained that drilling was required to discover the gold hidden beneath the surface and contended that the use of diamond drills was a more efficient method of locating the lodes than the sinking of shafts. The venture offered a peculiar "business feature." Rather than selling shares in gold mines the company offered shares in a drilling company that would contract to drill on the claims of others with the income from those contracts financing drilling for gold on the two mines owned by Goldfield Diamond Drilling.

In January of 1907 full-page ads offering to sell shares of the company's stock appeared in the *Oakland Tribune*. Smaller, but still good-sized ads, were printed in every issue of the Carson City, Nevada, *Daily Appeal* during the first eight months of the year. The operation discovered no gold and had limited success in contracting out its drilling services.[21] Any profits must have come from the sale of stock, sales that would have been directly attributable to Mayo's efforts. Mayo proved to be a master at composing ad copy that could sell a product no matter how questionable.

* * *

The land Mayo purchased in the Sonoma redwoods was not acquired with the expectation of striking oil. Rather, this property was bought specifically to carve up and resell at a profit. Mayo had found another resource to mine: the one-born-every-minute naive city dweller.

For this project he allied with another Oakland newspaper man, John Berkley Bartlett. Employed as an advertising manager for an Oakland newspaper,[22] probably the *Enquirer*, Bartlett also dabbled in real estate incorporating one realty business and acting as an agent for another.[23]

Between February and May of 1910, Mayo and Bartlett bought title to at least 360 acres of rugged terrain in Sonoma County from Rufus C. Chapman and Samuel R. Break, paying less than ten cents an acre.[24] Approximately two miles southwest of the town of Cazadero (Spanish for "hunting ground") the land consisted of steep stony slopes and craggy outcroppings. With a barely habitable topography, the area was used mostly for logging, an occasional rustic lodge, and camping along the rivers and streams.

As soon as they recorded their deeds, Bartlett and Mayo filed plats, sectioning out hundreds of 25' × 100' foot lots as if the ground was level.[25] The subdivision was named Cazadero Redwoods and the lots were sold for $6.50 each with a subscription to the *Oakland Enquirer*.[26] Lots were also coupled with subscriptions to *Sunset* magazine,[27] a journal created by the Southern Pacific Railroad to publicize the landscape and natural resources of the West and to attract tourists and settlers. Surveyors' markers were not installed—Cazadero Redwoods was probably not even surveyed—leaving no means of identifying the location of a particular lot. Only when, and if, buyers tried to find their lots did they discover the problematic terrain and its distance from the railway. In several instances the same lot was sold more than once.[28]

Bartlett and Mayo were not the sole perpetrators of this variety of land fraud. Between 1909 and 1913 at least a dozen such "wildcat" or "paper" subdivisions were created in the rugged country of northern Sonoma County, all platted out on paper with tiny lots and meandering streets that never materialized.[29] Cazadero Redwoods was the only one of these subdivisions that used newspaper and magazine subscriptions to sell the lots. The others, created by an array of conmen, had a different scheme for roping in unsuspecting buyers.

Moving picture houses were in their infancy in the early 1900s and silent films were shown in many small storefronts and nickelodeons. To attract customers the competing theater managers were receptive to promotional schemes such as Mayo's distribution of candy.

The wildcat subdividers paid movie house owners a few dollars to pass out tickets for a chance to win a free lot deceptively described in glowing terms and supposedly reachable by railroad or car line. Patrons provided their names and addresses on the tickets for an alleged drawing. The following day land agents would visit every theatergoer to report that his ticket won the drawing and that, while the lot was free, $5 to $10 (an inflated amount) was needed to cover the cost of the deed and abstract. Adjoining lots could be purchased for $30 to $150.

Many of the lucky winners lived as far away as Missouri, Arizona, Montana, or British Columbia. When they sought to find their land months or even years later, they discovered only valueless remote barren hillsides far from any transportation. Newspapers published articles warning against the scheme,[30] a few of which noted that some lots were peddled through a subscription "to some cheap magazine."[31] Still, the easy marks kept falling for the ploy.

3. The Genesis of the Scheme

The Sonoma County Recorder became so overburdened with processing the many deeds and fielding inquiries about the location of lots that, in 1914, the land encompassed by these subdivisions was declared worthless and removed from the assessment rolls.[32] In 1913 the California legislature made it a misdemeanor to offer tickets to win real property and collect fees to transfer the parcel. This law, still part of the California Penal Code,[33] stopped the promotions in California but the scam continued to be advertised in other states. The law also failed to have any effect on the sale of lots tied to a subscription premium. Today what had been Cazadero Redwoods is part of Little Black Mountain Preserve, a land conservancy owned and managed by the Sonoma Land Trust.[34]

* * *

Ads in *Sunset* for Cazadero Redwoods allowed as many as four subscriptions and four lots to be obtained at the same low price. In this regard Cazadero was a step closer to the newspaper deal than Orienta Park where only one lot could be purchased at the reduced subscription premium cost.

Selling all the lots at the same price nevertheless produced profits for Mayo and his partner. What made the difference between the pennies per acre that they paid for the land and the more than $100 per acre they sold it for was the way the lots were advertised and promoted. Mayo was honing in on the newspaper deal and would come closer with his next project.

Mayo reaped two significant benefits from his Modoc Oil, Goldfield Diamond Drilling, and Cazadero Redwoods ventures. They provided him with some capital but, more importantly, with business and political connections that would cause a pivotal real estate opportunity to be laid at his feet.

Gilbert Daniels, Mayo's boss and good friend, was a familiar figure in political circles as indicated by the various state positions he was appointed to after selling the *Enquirer* in 1917: superintendent of motor vehicles, market director, head of the board of control, and member of the prison board.[35] Daniels was closely associated, both personally and politically, with George Pardee, governor of California from 1903 to 1907. Mayo was introduced to Pardee by Daniels and the three men, together with their families, often socialized together.[36]

George Pardee had a fickle association with the Southern Pacific Railroad, one that spanned most of his career and put him in a position to have backdoor information about the company. William Swears, one of Mayo's business partners in the Goldfield Diamond Drilling escapade, was a private shipping commissioner in San Francisco and was familiar with issues affecting water transport. Mayo's association with these men, together with his contacts in the world of publishing, exposed him to a broad range of insider knowledge and resulting opportunity.

The Southern Pacific owned a strip of rail right-of-way through Brown Canyon on the outskirts of Los Angeles, and planned to use it to link the port at Santa Monica with inland train routes. But when the federal government opted to construct the necessary breakwater elsewhere, deflecting shipping farther south, Southern Pacific abandoned its efforts. The railroad was left with rights to a swath of land it could no longer use.[37]

Mayo obtained a managerial position with Southern Pacific's *Sunset* magazine[38] in 1911 and took over disposing of the railroad's right-of-way. He managed to obtain full title to the land by purchasing it, according to Butler, from a reluctant seller, a man named Smith.

Section by section Mayo platted a subdivision named Beverly Glen, incorporated the Beverly Glen Land Company, and hired surveyors, salesmen, office staff, and 200 Hindu laborers. Some of the land was suitable for building and these lots were advertised in the *Los Angeles Herald* with no tie-in to newspaper or magazine subscriptions.[39] But with the rocky lots higher up in the canyon he repeated the game plan used at Cazadero Redwoods and disposed of these problematic lots as premiums for subscriptions to *Sunset*, hiring a specific gang of salesmen for this aspect of the project.[40]

Mayo also initiated a feature at Beverly Glen that would become a staple of the newspaper colony. He established a construction and sales headquarters at the main intersection of the development. After the building served its initial purpose, he gave it to the community for use as a clubhouse.

Lot sales were swift and Mayo showed off his project to former governor Pardee and Gilbert Daniels when Mayo invited his friends to Beverly Glen in June of 1911.[41] Perhaps Mayo bragged to them about his method to save costs and produce profits by failing to provide needed services. Descriptions of the area in advertisements played up nature with the phrase "In the Hills Among the Trees," and frequent mention of birds, squirrels, and babbling brooks. Proclaiming that the land was presented "just as nature made it," Mayo provided no improvements at Beverly Glen other than some roads. Instead he implemented formation of an association of lot owners which he then used to organize Beverly Glen Consolidated Utilities, in effect requiring the lot buyers themselves to invest the money needed to provide transportation, water, light, telephone, and other utilities.[42]

Mayo had now twice sold small, undesirable lots as subscription premiums. If the price was right, distant buyers would purchase the lots sight unseen. He had recognized that he could avoid providing much in the way of improvements by emphasizing nature and promoting the tract as a casual summer resort. He formed a homeowners' group to take over responsibilities, and he made himself look good by donating the abandoned sales office for use as a community center. It was 1911 and most of the basic elements of the newspaper deal had been identified. Bertram Mayo could now proceed to refine his scheme.

4

Closing In on the Deal

Bertram Mayo had discovered a gold mine in California, a movable gold mine that could be transported anywhere he could find available land and eager customers. Louis Smadbeck found that developing land adjacent to water made real estate even more attractive to buyers. Mayo also came to this realization and with his next project began to combine proximity to water with the elements of the newspaper deal.

Inexpensive farmland near water and trees could be found in the vast, and still largely rural, center of the country. Mayo purchased just such land on Fox Lake twelve miles north of Muskegon, Michigan, and presented his idea to offer lots as a subscription premium to the *Chicago Evening Post* in 1912. The proposal was destined for success. The *Post* was a big city newspaper with a working-class readership and a thirst for building up its subscriber base. The Michigan land was ideal for summer homes, camping vacations, and weekend bungalows, and the lake would attract swimmers, boaters, and fishermen. Combining the geographical features of a lake and woodlands, Mayo coined the name "Lakewood" for this newest venture.

In spite of the subscription tie-in, large advertisements in the newspaper were not used. Rather, mention of Lakewood in the *Chicago Evening Post* took the form of announcements. The first appeared on May 22, 1912, proclaiming that Decoration Day would herald the opening of Lakewood where carpenters and road men have been hard at work. A tent city and a lunch room were promised to be ready.[1] Subsequent notices tell of special train and boat arrangements on Sundays in June to provide owners the opportunity to visit their lots.[2]

None of these announcements mention the terms of the subscription offer. Instead those details were contained in a circular mailed to potential subscribers and lot purchasers. The terms were also revealed by the *Post* in an article headlined "'On to Lakewood!' Slogan of Fire Fans,"[3] describing a group of Chicago friends who shared the excitement of chasing fires. Seventeen of the group bought adjoining lots at Lakewood, comprising nearly an entire block, and were making plans to share in the expense of building a jointly owned private clubhouse on their land. There were hints that a group of Chicago city employees and officials, having been caught up in the fad, were thinking of doing the same thing. The report explains that the property was carved up into lots 25' × 100' selling for $11 each with a six-month subscription to the Chicago newspaper.

Newspaper articles suggest that Mayo took great effort to upscale the development, at least on the surface. The lots were still tiny but much in the way of window dressing was employed to attract customers. The seven-foot-wide cobblestone fireplace in the spacious clubhouse, fitted with a crane, kettle, and andirons, bore an inscription, in gold lettering and old English script, reading "for you, the hearth fire burns." Numerous rocking chairs, hammocks, and swinging seats were scattered about. A tent city provided "cottage tents" furnished hotel style with a double bed renting for seventy-five cents a day. At a separate public dining room the crockery and table linens were made to order and imprinted with "Lakewood Club." Breakfast and lunch cost thirty-five cents and dinner fifty cents. An orchestra played music during the dinner hour as well as for dancing. Telephone and telegraph service was available. A variety of watercraft including launches, rowboats, canoes, punts, sail boats, and rafts, were provided. Mayo also lured the Pere Marquette Railroad to add a Lakewood stop by building a depot at his own expense and provided buses to transport visitors from the depot to the clubhouse.[4]

Lakewood then implemented a service not tackled at any other newspaper resort. This was the construction and operation of a railway to transport passengers and cargo from the Pere Marquette depot at Lakewood to the clubhouse, a distance of five and one-half miles.[5] All of the officers, directors, and shareholders for the Lakewood Street Railway Company were part of Mayo's cozy group of friends—Chicago associates engaged in real estate, the newspaper business, advertising, or else self-employed as an accountant or lawyer.[6]

Mayo's tentacles reached to all aspects of the community. In January of 1913 he formed the Lakewood Lumber and Construction Company to sell building materials and construct bungalows for the lot customers.[7] Then he hired a couple to invest in and operate a construction camp to provide living quarters for the carpenters. In addition to paying for tent space and meals, lot owners paid to rent a boat, play billiards, use the bowling alley, and patronize the barber shop and the cigar and candy counter. He set up an auto repair shop and brought in a pianist to play at the dance pavilion,[8] probably finding a way to have the piano player collect payment from the dancers. All of these add-on enterprises were structured to make money for Mayo or at least to not cost him anything.

Even as Lakewood was in its early stages, Mayo was planning his next project. In mid-1912 he began negotiations to purchase 2,000 acres of scrub pine and oak bordering on the Toms River near Barnegat Bay, New Jersey. Complications with past ownership and liens delayed the purchase of the land until 1914.

At Lakewood Mayo had become embroiled in a dispute over compensation owed to the real estate agent used to purchase the land. A lawsuit,

4. Closing In on the Deal

Left and above: Bertram Mayo created an "Extra" edition for the *New York Tribune* to promote the Beachwood colony. Vaguely dated November 1914, it was sent out by direct mail. The Smadbecks borrowed heavily from this advertisement (courtesy Erik Weber, Beachwood, New Jersey, History Archive).

a jury trial, and a court ruling were needed to resolve the matter.[9] Mayo avoided this from happening at the New Jersey tract by using the services of Addison Nickerson, his old friend from the Boston days, and now a civil engineer. Nickerson obtained the land at a sheriff's sale and almost immediately transferred title to Mayo who, in turn, deeded it to Stanley D. Brown[10] as trustee for Mayo's latest ally, the *New York Tribune*.

This venture was named Beachwood for the river front shoreline and the woods. As with Lakewood, the subscription offer was not the subject of display ads. Instead, articles extolling the virtues of the project and detailing the progress of its development, appeared in both the *New York Tribune* and the *New Jersey Courier* in Toms River.[11] The sales pitch itself was contained in a four-page "Extra" made to look like a special edition of the *Tribune*.

For both Lakewood and Beachwood Mayo created a thirty-eight-page pamphlet, also mailed to prospective subscribers and lot purchasers. The covers bore the title "The Greatest Subscription Premium Ever Offered— And the Reason Why" followed by the name and address of the respective newspaper referring to the premium department, in the case of the *Chicago Evening Post*, and the promotion department at the *New York Tribune*. These booklets are small in size and more horizontal than vertical. Each of the left-hand pages bears a photograph of a water view or a path cut through the woods and brush with dreamy, enticing captions such as "the fish are waiting for you," "wood roads wind in and out," and "bushels of blueberries here." Any structures depicted were nearby, such as the train station at Toms River, and not located on the resort property. As he had done at Beverly Glen, Mayo was promoting wilderness and nature rather than developed land.

The right-hand pages of the booklets contain a few sentences of the sales message surrounded by a linear border. The details of the wording in the two pamphlets varies but the message is consistent. The narrative begins with "A Little Plain Talk" and lays the groundwork explaining that newspapers offer premiums to obtain subscribers but, in order to do so, the premiums must be obtainable at a bargain price. The paper wanted to do something bigger and better than the household gadget items usually offered and so it came up with the idea of offering land at a ridiculously low price. The newspaper was able to do this by purchasing an entire resort, contracting for miles of road work and months of surveying, and eliminating the middle man. Of course, not all of these claims were true, especially the statement about eliminating the middle man. At this point the message is personalized as the newspaper justifies the necessary substantial outlay of money by its desire to have "you" as a subscriber.

Each pamphlet then proceeds to describe its respective resort. Both lie in the center of a resort region: for Lakewood the summer resort region of Michigan and for Beachwood the coastal resort region of New Jersey. Each is "just far enough" from Chicago (Lakewood) or New York City (Beachwood) followed by a description of the wonderful transportation facilities including the fares and schedules for boats and trains.

4. Closing In on the Deal

The particular attractions are next identified. Lakewood is surrounded by several other lakes brimming with big and little mouth bass, perch, pickerel, and muskellunge with fine duck shooting in the fall, while Beachwood is almost a part of the town of Toms River and close to the popular resort of Pine Beach with its well-known hotel. The free clubhouse, waterfront beach, and shoreline parks are touted before concluding with a promise, not to refund the purchase price if the buyer is not satisfied, but to offer assurance that the buyer's displeasure will cause the newspaper to lose what it most seeks—the reader's continued friendship and subscriptions.

A map is provided and the back cover is a mail-in postcard for requesting further details. The Lakewood booklet merely gives a phone number and encouragement to request more information. Beachwood improves on this by specifying the costs and contract terms.

* * *

Using the postal system to distribute the "Extra" edition and the informational material nearly got Mayo and the *New York Tribune* into trouble. In early 1915 Victor Watson, a journalist for the *New York American*, launched an investigation into the Beachwood promotion. The *American* was a Hearst paper and a rival of the *Tribune*. Watson visited the site several times, took photos, interviewed lot buyers, and even planted spies in the solicitation office of the *Tribune*. Apparently, anyone willing to push sales of the lots for a commission could find a job there, an opportunity that was not wasted on Watson and his staff.

When he felt that he had gathered enough evidence to make a case for mail fraud, Watson reported his findings to the U.S. attorney for the Southern District of New York, H. Snowden Marshall, who, in turn, referred the matter to postal authorities. Two postal inspectors, Oliver Schaeffer and Hugh McQuillan, met with Watson, visited Beachwood, and even traveled to Michigan to evaluate Mayo's Lakewood project. Their conclusions echoed those of Victor Watson.

The alleged fraud claims involving Beachwood had a slippery focus: the *Tribune* claimed that the land was being sold at near cost and well below actual value as a goodwill gesture to build a broader subscriber base when, in reality, the newspaper stood to make a profit of at least $300,000; the promised perquisites—clubhouse, yacht house, restaurant, hotel, and train depot—were cheaply constructed. In addition, only one road was passable, the rest being cluttered with tree stumps and unfilled depressions. Most lots were accessible only by climbing up and down railroad embankments and crossing the tracks; any improvements were concentrated in the beach area, while buyers were steered toward lots miles from the shore or offered land near the water at magnified prices.

Watson also found fault with the Lakewood promotion. He claimed that a generous area of parkland was promised along the lake but that a new map was later produced showing the parkland reduced to a narrow strip while the bulk of the recreational area was divided up into lots and sold for high prices.[12] He complained that the lot owners were given an inflated cost of the Lakewood railway, causing them to invest more than necessary while Mayo retained the controlling interest in the railway and the utility company that operated the side businesses. The lot owners had been trying to wrest control away from him without success. But when the postal authorities began their investigation, Mayo generously turned these interests over to the property owners by distributing a notice from "The Management" stating that all concessions would now be operated by the utilities company in cooperation with the lot owners' association and all profits or losses would go to the company. The notice urged patronage of the concessions to make the utilities a profitable investment.[13]

Mayo managed to head off suspicions raised by the investigation at Lakewood by sending telegrams to the press claiming, quite misleadingly, that the postal authorities deemed everything above-board and had found no evidence of wrongdoing.[14] In actuality inspectors McQuillan and Schaeffer concluded that both the Lakewood and Beachwood promotions violated the law and passed their findings on to H. Snowden Marshall, but made no recommendations to him.[15]

Both Watson and the postal inspectors anticipated a New York grand jury probe into the *Tribune*'s actions with concurrent proceedings in Chicago pertaining to Lakewood. But U.S. Attorney Marshall disappointed the accusers when he declined to take any action.

Between January and May of 1916, a Committee of the U.S. House of Representatives conducted hearings, motivated by conflicting pre–World War I political interests, investigating charges of misconduct against H. Snowden Marshall on a wide variety of issues including failure to follow up on the allegations against the *Tribune* in the Beachwood promotion.[16] A subcommittee was appointed, contempt charges were made against Marshall, and an assignment was made to a select committee, all of which became entangled in politics. In the end nothing came of the claims against Marshall, just as nothing had come of the claims against Mayo and the *Tribune*.[17]

From a positive viewpoint Beachwood was populated by some prominent people who owned yachts and built sumptuous summer homes, two of which were owned by Addison Nickerson, a man who was instrumental in establishing the resort. He negotiated the purchase of the land for Mayo, surveyed it, managed the colony, built 70 bungalows, and became the tax collector.[18] Work at Beachwood was eventually completed, the roads finished off, and most of the lots sold. A Property Owners Association was formed, with Mayo biographer William Mill Butler, one of Beachwood's earliest residents, as its president. When the colony incorporated as an independent borough in 1917, Mayo deeded the riverfront lots where the public buildings were located to the municipality and sold an additional 209 lots to the borough for a park later named Mayo Park in his honor.[19]

But Mayo's tactics left negative imprints as well. The substantial residences that Nickerson built were all near the river shore. It was the lots far from the water, those in the hinterlands, the ones on the wrong side of the tracks, those that were sold to the working-class newspaper readers, that were the subject of Watson's investigation. Butler was an enthusiastic advocate for Mayo even claiming that he refused to sell 2,000 Beachwood lots as not being good enough to meet his standards.[20] But given his past actions, it is unlikely that Mayo considered any lots, regardless of quality, to be unsaleable.

Already in mid–1915 the county clerk was having considerable difficulty identifying and preparing a list of lot owners. Between 1916 and 1918 a string of notices published in the *Tribune* encouraged property owners to apply for their tax bills if they had not been mailed to them,[21] a situation resembling that encountered by the assessor at Cazadero Redwoods and perhaps suggesting that Nickerson's service as tax collector was grounded in self-interest. Despite Butler's praise, Mayo's real estate development methods were not entirely laudatory.[22]

* * *

Browns Mills in the Pines, Mayo's last newspaper colony, offered him a different starting point. The area around Mirror Lake in Burlington County, New Jersey, was populated with cranberry bogs, blueberry fields, and poultry farms in addition to being an established resort region. Boardinghouses and hotels were in operation there at least by 1820.[23] Visitors were attracted to Browns Mills by its reputation for healing spring waters in a setting of healthful pines. By the early twentieth century it was home to tuberculosis treatment facilities as well as private nursing cottages that provided screened porches for sleeping in the fresh air.[24]

A healthy environment was a priority for Bertram Mayo. William Mills Butler claims that curative air of California was the reason Mayo moved there from the East Coast in the first few years of the 1900s[25] and more than one newspaper report noted that he was impressed with the climate of Florida.[26] Of course, the local New Jersey papers found the invigorating atmosphere of the Jersey woods where Browns Mills was situated to be superior to that of either California or Florida.[27]

Most likely, however, it was economic opportunity that drew Mayo to Browns Mills. Located a mere twenty-five miles straight west of Beachwood, and given his interest in land speculation, Mayo would certainly have been aware of the bubbling financial troubles at Browns Mills.

Mahlon W. Newton was a well known hotelier in the Delaware River valley. He began investing in and running hotels when still in his mid-twenties and achieved considerable success in renovating and updating older hotel properties. At the turn of the century he owned several large hotels, including Green's Hotel in the business center of Philadelphia, and was involved in other extensive land holdings and commercial activities.[28]

Newton first became involved with Browns Mills in 1903 when, along with former New Jersey State Senator George Pfeiffer, Jr., of Trenton, he invested in 3,100 acres of land in Burlington County with the intent of developing the property into a year-round resort.[29] A bad omen appeared a few days later when the same newspaper that reported Newton's purchase of this land expressed the opinion that the attempt to rehabilitate Browns Mills was a doubtful endeavor, suggesting it might be more successful if the name were changed and it was moved closer to the railroad.[30]

Newton soon opened bids for the construction of a hotel estimated to cost $50,000.[31] By the start of 1905 Newton was seeking $150,000 for improvements at the resort[32] and, when the new and completely equipped colonial-style inn opened on March 1, 1905,[33] the project had already defaulted on tax payments.[34] Pfeiffer, who tried his hand at operating a duck farm at Browns Mills, proved to be a poor choice for an investment partner. In December of 1905 he filed for voluntary bankruptcy, the failure of the duck venture at Browns Mills being only one of his unfortunate business experiences.[35]

An additional $100,000 investment was sought in 1910 when Mahlon W. Newton, with new partners James B. Reilly and Joseph J. Summerill, reorganized the corporate structure.[36] The Browns Mills project languished and Newton's plans to turn it into a full-time resort never materialized. Eventually, in June of 1916, the property was "sold" to Newton at a foreclosure sale. Already heavily invested in the scheme, he put up another $23,000 to maintain control of the property and protect himself against further loss in spite of the existence of other obligations pending against the land including the back taxes.[37]

Newton was ripe for an opportunity to be relieved of this fruitless endeavor. The timing of his situation could not have been better for Mayo. In August of 1916 the Marshall hearings had just concluded with no repercussions and Beachwood was winding up with the formation of the POA. Whether or not Mayo was looking for another project, the

4. Closing In on the Deal

situation presented by Browns Mills was too advantageous to ignore, and so he bought the 3,100 acres from Mahlon Newton in late September of 1916.[38]

Newton had attempted to create a hotel where people came and stayed for short periods of time. This worked for him in the cities where he could attract businessmen as repeat customers but this method did not translate well to the rural resort area of Browns Mills. Mayo's approach toward establishing a resort was different. He diced up the land into tiny pieces and sold it rapidly through his newspaper scheme. It was not an ongoing employment but rather a fast-moving operation with a defined start and a quick finish that created a miniature city rather than a grand hotel destination.

Thus far Mayo had worked with rugged, woody, undeveloped land, property that had not been developed because of its roughness, providing him with a clean slate that could be platted out and developed to suit his newspaper promotional plan. Although Browns Mills included a hotel, stables and garage, a lake, waterpower, and several miles of roadway, Mayo found no difficulty in adapting it to his formula. He teamed up with the *Philadelphia Press* and involved A.D. Nickerson in engineering and platting the lots. He put his plan into action with rapid fire precision laying out a golf course and building a large ice house, a real estate office, and a clubhouse. Carpenters from Beachwood were transferred to work at Browns Mills where over one hundred men were employed and provided with rooms and cots. It was rumored that Mayo sold 5,000 lots in just the first few months of ownership.[39]

With Beachwood and Browns Mills in the Pines Bertram Mayo had further refined the newspaper deal format. The lot size was trimmed to 20' × 100' and the ownership of the land passed through several hands making it more difficult to trace. Both the narrower lot size and the confusing chain of title holders, together with proximity to water, would become standard characteristics of the newspaper colonies.

* * *

Bertram Mayo married in 1888 and he and his wife Amy Girdler had one child, a son named Geoffrey. Mayo's varied business dealings kept the family mobile and they found it convenient to live either in apartments or hotels. In spite of his modest background, Mayo had achieved a fair degree of wealth and in 1913 began thinking about building a home.

In the fall of that year, still officially California residents, the Mayos spent the winter season in the Tampa area to make a comparison of the Florida and southern California climates. Favorably impressed, Mayo purchased property in Tarpon Springs to establish a winter residence.[40]

Curiously, the local newspaper characterized Mayo as the owner of the *Oakland Enquirer* and, as such, a gentleman of more than average intelligence and discernment, proving that Florida offered greater attractions, better climate, and larger inducements than southern California.[41] A few weeks later the paper elevated him to owner of the *Chicago Post*.[42]

The Mayo winter retreat was built on three lots at a stylish enclave known as Van Winkle Island, a piece of land projecting out into Whitcomb Bayou. An architect was engaged to design a structure that news accounts variously described as lovely, handsome, elegant, and palatial. When completed, the home included a boat house for Mayo's yacht *Amy M. II*, a name that suggests it was not his first boat.

Busy with the Beachwood project in New Jersey, Mayo spent most of his time either at the Bossert Hotel in Brooklyn or at the New Jersey resort. In addition to the clubhouse, a yacht club was built at Beachwood where the *Amy M. II* was moored in the warm summer months and used for entertaining neighbors from Florida. In November or December the Mayos would ship their car to Florida and travel south in the yacht. Friends and relatives visiting in Tarpon Springs were entertained with driving tours and boating outings including a week-long hunting trip in the Everglades that netted deer, turkey, and bear.[43]

Just as Congress was investigating the charges against H. Snowden Marshall, Mayo was entertaining former California governor George Pardee, Gilbert Daniels, and their wives at the Florida home. The guests stayed for many weeks enjoying yacht cruises and motor excursions in Mayo's big Cadillac.[44] To further compliment his friends, Mayo named streets at Browns Mills for them with Pardee Boulevard running parallel to Daniels Avenue.

* * *

Florida was not only for pleasure. Mayo also mined Tarpon Springs for commercial opportunities, intertwining the business and social worlds. In addition to property for his own home he bought land for the construction of rental cottages as well as other real estate.[45]

Early on he joined the Tarpon Springs Board of Trade and offered to pay for a carload of Florida oranges to be sent to the people of New York as a goodwill gesture by the board, suggesting that the fruit be consigned to the *New York Tribune* for distribution to the poor.[46] For the cost of a carload of oranges he ingratiated himself with both the Tarpon Springs business community and the *Tribune*.

Mayo's connections with Noah A. Van Winkle, a building contractor and president of a local bank, led to Mayo achieving a seat on the board of directors of the bank.[47] The day after being elected to the board, Mayo closed on the purchase of a strip of land adjacent to Van Winkle Island and dedicated the tract as a park, adding value to Van Winkle's subdivision and his own property.[48] These events took place just a few days before the visit from Pardee and Daniels, so Mayo had the added benefit of showing off for his friends, and Mayo actually did become owner of a newspaper when he partnered with L.L. Lucas, the editor of the *Tarpon Springs Leader*, to buy that paper in May of 1917.[49]

* * *

The business relationship that Bertram Mayo had with his son is ambiguous. Upon completing college in 1913, Geoffrey immediately became involved in the Lakewood project where he was put in charge of recruiting staff to operate the various concessions. At Beachwood he was the manager of the solicitation office at the *New York Tribune*[50] and was in partnership with his father by the time Browns Mills was developed.[51]

Mayo was still healthy when he wrote his will in December of 1914. His bequest of $100,000 to Amy was to come entirely from personal bonds and cash while he carefully delineated that his commercial interests were to pass to his son Geoffrey.[52] Once the winter home in Tarpon Springs was completed, he signed a codicil providing that the dwelling, together with its boat house, buildings, horses, carriages, and automobiles was to pass to Amy. The bequest of all his commercial assets to Geoffrey remained in place.[53]

While Mayo clearly favored his son and looked to him as heir to his professional enterprises, his asset with the most potential value, the real estate/newspaper premium idea, was transferred to Louis Smadbeck's two sons. There is nothing to suggest a cleave between Bertram and Geoffrey so perhaps the son lacked the personality or the inclination to carry on his father's profession. By 1920 Geoffrey had returned to living in California and eventually became a financial advisor and a member of the Board of Directors of Douglass Aircraft.

How Mayo crossed paths with Warren and Arthur Smadbeck and what kind of financial arrangement they had with each other is unknown, but most likely Mayo sold his promotional ideas and writings to the Smadbecks. Bertram Mayo certainly would not have just given them away.

In 1913, just one year after introducing Lakewood to Chicago residents, a new publication, *Trend Magazine*, placed ads in the *Union Postal Clerk*, the official organ of the National Federation of Post Office Clerks. *Trend* offered to sell summer home lots at Cedar Lake, Indiana, with a subscription to the magazine. The land, referred to as Post Office Colony, was located at the already established resort known as The Shades.[54] Mayo responded swiftly by filing an action seeking an injunction against *Trend* and two of its employees. Then he filed a second lawsuit asking for damages from the same parties.[55]

Court records revealing the specifics of Mayo's allegations and the judge's ruling have not been retained, but it can be safely assumed that Mayo did not prevail in the litigation. Mayo had failed to preserve copyrights to "The Greatest Subscription Premium Ever Offered—And the Reason Why" Lakewood pamphlet. A comparison of the Lakewood and Beachwood promotional booklets shows that only the latter bore the words "Copyright November, 1914 B.C. Mayo" on the inside front cover. A writer was obligated by Section 9 of the Copyright Act of 1909 to include such a statement in each copy of a published work in order to secure exclusive publication rights. Without the notice printed in the Lakewood pamphlet Mayo was precluded from relying on copyright protection.

But even if Mayo had included the required words in the booklet it still would not have helped him prosecute his claim that the magazine had usurped his promotional invention. *Trend* had used the "idea" of offering resort lots as a subscription premium. While an assemblage of wording can be copyrighted and a product can be patented, a mere idea cannot be protected with either a copyright or a patent. Six months after Mayo filed his lawsuits *Trend* was advertising in the *Chicago Daily Tribune* offering lots at The Shades with a subscription to the magazine, and pronouncing that the offer was absolutely unique, quite without precedent, and that no such proposition had ever been made to the people of Chicago before.[56] Oh, how Mayo must have recoiled at that claim!

The newspaper promoter had learned his lesson. The magic copyright words appeared in each printing of "The Greatest Subscription Premium Ever Offered—And the Reason Why" pamphlet for Beachwood. In addition, Mayo applied for and was awarded, in early 1916, copyrights for the *New York Tribune* extra edition and the Beachwood booklet.[57] Mayo could not prevent others from imitating him by selling lots as a subscription premium, but at least he alone could exploit his collection of words.

When Smadbecks' ad for Asbury Park Estates appeared in August of 1916, it was evident that a deal had been worked out between the brothers and Mayo. The *Jewish Daily News* ad copy echoes the layout and the appearance of the *Tribune* extra edition written and copyrighted by Mayo. For example the headline "Here's the Simple Proposition" in Mayo's Beachwood Extra Edition becomes "Here is Our Proposition" in Smadbecks' Asbury Park ad. However, the resemblances go far beyond that. The Smadbecks' *Jewish Daily News* ad has a box with Mayo's heading "A Little Plain Talk" and, word for word, precisely the same language as the first three pages of Mayo's Beachwood booklet, excepting only the names of the newspapers and the resorts. The Asbury Park "Plain Talk" concludes with the sentence:

4. Closing In on the Deal

"This [offer] is in line with similar offers successfully made by the New York Tribune, Chicago Evening Post, and other leading papers," obvious references to Mayo's developments of Beachwood and Lakewood.

This leads to the inescapable conclusion that Mayo shared or transferred his ideas and his copyrights to the Smadbecks almost certainly in exchange for monetary compensation.

* * *

If Mayo moved to Florida for his health, he miscalculated for it was at Tarpon Springs that he contracted tuberculosis.[58] He was probably aware of his diagnosis when World War I ended on November 11, 1918. One year later he was so ill that an airboat aviator suspended flights over Tarpon Springs because the engine noise disturbed its prominent citizen.[59]

A smattering of newspaper notices suggest that Mayo proceeded to sell off his assets in the spring of 1920. He disposed of land at Beverly Glen[60] and also at Tarpon Springs.[61] He transferred a mortgage for property on Park Avenue in New York[62] and his newspaper, the *Tarpon Springs Leader*, was also presumably sold.[63]

Exhausted by his illness, Mayo was too sick to bother with careful wording, lawyers, or formalities when he executed a holographic codicil to his will. It consisted of only two sentences. In one he increased the bequest to his wife by $250,000 and in the other expressed the hope that this change would be honored even though not in strict legal form.[64]

Mayo entered Saint Joseph's Sanitarium in Asheville, North Carolina, on June 17, 1920. By the time he died less than a month later, both his wife[65] and son[66] had obtained residences in California. The estate, with Geoffrey acting as executor, was appraised at just under $355,000. Amy received $350,000 and Geoffrey the remainder.[67]

When Bertram Chapman Mayo died on July 12, 1920,[68] Warren and Arthur Smadbeck were perfectly poised to exploit the newspaper deal. They were trained and experienced in realty, they had begun newspaper deals under Mayo's tutelage, and the economic, social, and political landscape was primed for the scheme.

5

The Early Colonies and the Promotional Articles

Bertram Mayo and the Smadbeck brothers approached the deal from opposing occupational directions. Mayo was identified as being in the newspaper advertising business[1] and his real estate development victories were a byproduct of his promotional ideas.

The Smadbecks considered themselves land developers. Warren's 1921 passport application lists real estate as his occupation,[2] and Arthur, on his World War I draft registration form, filled in "Laying out Farms & Suburban Developments."[3] For them the newspaper deal was a means of effectuating their realty aspirations.

Mayo used real estate as a tool to sell newspapers. The Smadbecks used newspapers as a tool to sell real estate. This dichotomy is at the heart of the alliance.

Resulting from a blending of the two contrasting viewpoints, the arrangement caused the newspapers and the real estate men to be interdependent and allowed each faction to achieve its goals. The Smadbeck brothers had the advantage of being a generation younger than Mayo giving them more time to fine tune the scheme. In the end it was the developers, rather than the newspaperman, who synthesized the alliance, created most of the colonies, and achieved recognition for the newspaper deal.

* * *

The relationship between newspapers and real estate was established at the very beginning of print media in the United States. In May of 1704, the first paid advertisement in a newspaper, appearing in the *Boston News-Letter*, was an ad for real estate—the sale or rental of a plantation and mill in Oyster Bay, Long Island.[4]

During the next two hundred years newspaper advertising, along with newspapers themselves, grew and changed. Several nineteenth-century developments in print media and advertising had a significant effect on the evolution of the newspaper deal.

The penny paper emerged in the mid–1830s. Technological changes allowed for mass production of these tabloids that were sold for one cent while most other papers cost six cents. Filled with gossip and crime reports and using simple vocabulary and an easily digestible format, these inexpensive papers appealed to the increasingly literate lower and middle classes, the ideal audience for the newspaper colony promotions. Even after the price increased to more than one cent, the term "penny paper" continued to be applied to publications with these characteristics.

The concept of employing premiums to sell subscriptions, another journalistic innovation, was essential to the plan. "Premium" covers a wide range of offers including a toy in a box of cereal, trading stamps awarded for the purchase of merchandise, and tote bags and tee shirts given away for donations to worthy causes. Premium use began in the 1850s and within a few years items were offered gratis as an inducement to purchase a newspaper subscription. This practice had particular importance for the penny paper press which relied in part on wide distribution to help compensate for the lower selling price of the paper.[5]

By 1915 premium usage was ubiquitous. Having both detractors and supporters, it was the subject of trade journal articles, books, legislation, and litigation. Henry Stanhope Bunting,[6] a leading proponent, devoted a chapter to the selling power of premiums in his book on advertising rules,[7] and expanded his praise for premiums in another volume entitled *The Premium System of Forcing Sales: Its Principles, Laws and Uses*.[8] Bunting championed the practice as the most effective means of persuading a buyer to part with money because a premium offer immediately appeals to self-interest. A proposal that puts a tangible prize right into the buyer's hand is automatic and self-acting, requiring no thought, reasoning, or imagination. The more open and obvious the proposition, the more readily the benefit is recognized.[9]

Beginning with Asbury Park Estates, the Smadbecks incorporated the word "premium" in their ad headlines with such phrases as "The Greatest, Most Wonderful Premium Ever Offered" and "The Most Liberal Subscription Premium Ever Offered." In doing so they implemented a modified system where the premium was not a tangible item, such as a flyswatter, but rather an "opportunity" to obtain a more costly item[10] by buying a newspaper subscription with only a modest expenditure. In order to convince buyers to part with a greater sum of money, even for the purchase of an item at a purported bargain price, Bunting's self-interest element needed reinforcement, and so another advertising invention, the "reason-why" approach, was added to the mix.

The term "reason-why" was applied to advertising in the early years of the twentieth century to describe print copy that employed reasoning to persuade a customer to buy a product. A series of articles propounding reason-why messaging appeared in the magazine *Judicious Advertising* in 1905. The compiled articles were reprinted in 1911[11] and offered, not as a book that could be purchased, but as a book available only as a premium with a subscription to *Judicious Advertising* magazine.[12] This banding together of subscription premium offer and reason-why persuasive text was irresistible to Bertram Mayo. He precisely pinpointed the combination of these two components in the title of his promotional pamphlets "The Greatest Subscription Premium Ever Offered and the Reason Why."

Yet another advertising feature that came to be used extensively in the newspaper deal traces its history to the 1880s. In order to encourage the dissemination of information, especially political intelligence, postal rates were lower for news publications. Advertisers sought to avail themselves of this favorable treatment by disguising ads to make them appear to be news reports. This gave rise to the "reading notice." This style of advertisement imitates the paper's heading and text type and uses a headline that masks its true nature as an ad.[13] Other names applied to the technique are "newshead," "advertising journalism," "sponsored content," "advertorial," or, as used on television, "infomercial." Promoted by advertising handbooks and trade journals, newsheads, along with the use of premiums, proliferated at the end of the nineteenth and beginning of the twentieth centuries.

These advances in newspaper development—penny papers, premium offers, advertorials, and reason-why verbiage—were all firmly rooted by 1920. By employing reason-why arguments in both display ads and reading notices and using them to sell lots as a premium with a subscription to a penny paper, Warren Smadbeck and his brother Arthur combined all of these developments into one package. Taking advantage of a well-timed opportunity, the Smadbecks were able to sell countless acres of real estate and became wealthy in the process.

* * *

Within days of the issuance of the indecisive report of the House subcommittee in the H. Snowden Marshall hearings, ads for the Smadbecks' Asbury Park Estates appeared in the *Jewish Daily News*. Thus, both Mayo and the Smadbecks were engaged in newspaper resort developments when the United States entered World War I in April of 1917. Mayo had begun his last project, Browns Mills, while the Smadbecks were involved with their first.

Soon after the war ended in November of 1918, the Smadbecks began creating newspaper resorts with zeal. On July 11, 1919, the plat map for Patchogue Lakes was filed in Suffolk County, New York.[14] This colony consisted of a piece of land amid three lakes located close to the south shore of Long Island, a little more than fifty miles from New York City. Lots were marketed through the *Brooklyn Citizen* at $50 each with a three-month subscription to the newspaper.

While the *Brooklyn Citizen* was the sponsoring paper, ads were not confined to that tabloid. Advertisements for Patchogue Lakes also appeared in the *Evening World*, the *Brooklyn Daily Eagle*, and the *New York Tribune*. By partnering on the premium promotion with one publication and advertising in several others, a wider audience could be reached for both lot and subscription sales. Newspapers were not likely to turn down ad money even if the content of the ads promoted a competitor, and the owners of the sponsoring papers would certainly not complain about ads for subscriptions to their paper appearing in rival publications.[15]

Another colony sold with subscriptions to the *Brooklyn Citizen* was begun the following year. Mastic Park on the Forge River was just twelve miles beyond Patchogue Lakes on the Long Island Rail Road line. With Patchogue Lakes and Mastic Park the brothers followed their father's custom of developing rural land easily accessible to big city dwellers by rail and auto. They were also operating in Louis' home territory and would return to this part of Long Island in 1926 to develop the adjoining colony of Mastic Beach.

Two other developments, also initiated in 1920, further illustrate that the Smadbecks were still experimenting with the details of the arrangement. A half page ad for Colonie Estates, north of Albany near Latham and sponsored by the *Troy Record*, is typical of the Mayo/Smadbeck display ads.[16] However, other ads for Colonie used no photos or pictures and instead emphasized the low lot price with the exclamation "What a Few Dollars Will Do,"[17] and investment in an expected land boom, "P.B.S.! Power Bill Signed, Now for a Boom."[18]

Marshfield Estates, located on the southern shore of Massachusetts southeast of Boston, was developed with the *Boston Evening Record*. Many excursions to the colony were offered, some using Louis Smadbeck's old technique of making it both inexpensive and convenient to view the site. Free train tickets were available from a representative at the city depot and an auto would meet prospective customers at the station on arrival to convey them to the resort. Bring your own lunch.[19] Excursion trips to visit the property by train or by touring car with refreshments at the clubhouse, were also available.[20] And Marshfield Estates was heavily promoted with a booth at the Home Beautiful Exposition in the spring of 1921.[21] All of these strategies would be abandoned as the Smadbecks reverted to Mayo-prescribed advertising format and wording.

* * *

As with Asbury Park Estates, both Colonie Estates and Marshfield Estates were inland and undeserving of a name that invoked an image of water or sand. Waterfront colonies proved to be more popular and sold faster, driving the Smadbecks to look farther afield for farmland that adjoined water. They sought out beaches near the Great Lakes as Mayo had done and, in the year 1922, introduced a pair of resorts consisting of strips of land along the shore of their namesake lakes, Erie and Michigan.

Lake Erie Beach enticed Buffalo residents to travel twenty-five miles southeast of the city. This promotion involved two newspapers—a lot could be had with a subscription to either the *Buffalo Courier* or the *Buffalo Enquirer*.[22] This introduced another expansion of the gimmick—one resort promoted with subscriptions to two different papers.

The Lake Erie Beach colony also provides insight into how the Smadbecks did business. Thomas Shea, the Smadbecks' buying agent, purchased much of the land for the resort from John Stocker, whose acreage included a vineyard. The contract had a specific clause reserving Stocker's right to harvest the grapes in the year of the sale. Shea turned the land over to Home Guardian before it was deeded to Eugene Murphy, business manager of the *Buffalo Courier* and trustee for the newspapers, and eventually to the individual purchasers. The vineyard land was popular with the lot buyers, but they were not informed of the claim Stocker had on the grapes and when the harvest came, they prevented the former land owner from collecting his fruit. The dispute went before a judge who, complaining that it had been a strenuous day, effectively resolved the matter by adjourning the case. No doubt the lot owners ate the grapes before the case was reconvened.[23]

The other Great Lakes colony also involved litigation over fruit and unfulfilled contractual promises. Lake Michigan Beach,[24] near Benton Harbor, was established on a former orchard. According to a lawsuit filed by Richard Casler, a deputy sheriff, he contracted with Warren Smadbeck to spray 18,000 fruit trees on the acreage. Casler alleged that, after purchasing the supplies and performing the work, Smadbeck refused to pay him thus providing a further description of the Smadbeck approach to business dealings.[25]

Lake Michigan Beach was a hundred-mile drive from the Indiana border with Chicago. It was also reachable by both rail and lake steamer although the boat across the lake arrived at Muskegon requiring a train ride from there to the colony. However clumsy it was to get there, it was close enough to Chicago to make it attractive to residents of that city and to the *Chicago Evening Post*. The *Post* was already experienced with the real estate development arrangement, having teamed with Bertram Mayo on

5. The Early Colonies and the Promotional Articles

A Lake View at Lake Michigan Beach.

The Lake Michigan Beach bathhouse was reached by a long ramp (not visible) winding down from the high ground. A single strand of electric lights was draped through the trees (barely visible; see white arrows).

Lakewood ten years earlier. Mayo had likely worked with Frank Hussey, the *Post*'s advertising manager at the time. By 1922 Hussey had assumed the added responsibilities of business manager for the paper and was actively involved in the promotion of Smadbecks' Lake Michigan Beach.

The connection between the newspaperman and the developers approached partnership status on both professional and personal levels. The *Post* consortium of papers included, in addition to the Chicago publication, the *Indianapolis Star*, *Rocky Mountain News*, the *Louisville Herald*, the *Denver Evening Times*, the *Muncie Star*, and the *Terre Haute Star*,[26] several of which sponsored or advertised Smadbeck resort developments. The Hussey-Smadbeck connection became even closer when Frank Hussey's son, R.B. (Russell Blair) Hussey, left his position with an agricultural publication in Chicago in 1923 to work for the Smadbecks, supervising the development of several newspaper colonies.[27]

* * *

The first Smadbeck project that R.B. Hussey was involved with was Knightstown Lake, developed on the heels of the two Great Lakes resorts. With Knightstown Lake the Smadbecks progressed from the Atlantic seaboard and the beaches of the Great Lakes to the interior of the country. Inland lakes opened many new possibilities. In some locations, it was feasible to acquire all of the land surrounding a lake and on occasion even the lake itself. These smaller bodies of water could be both manipulated and created and Knightstown Lake was a leading example.

Three farms were purchased about forty miles straight east of Indianapolis and a mile or two east of the city that lent its name to the lake. The property was bordered by the Big Blue River on the west and a main line of the Pennsylvania Rail Road on the south. Buck Creek ran through the center of the land which was heavily forested and studded with deep ravines. These features were promoted as picturesque and desirable but they also presented challenges to installing roads and building dwellings.

The creek was not substantial enough to be used for boating and swimming so Warren Smadbeck reconfigured the terrain. The stream was cleared of obstructions and widened in several places to make "broad,

HIGH-PERCHED COTTAGE AT LAKE.

Deep ravines at Knightstown Lake caused lot owners to be inventive in constructing their cottages. This one is mounted on cut off tree trunks. A narrow bridge suspended from other trees affords a dubious access to the front door (courtesy *Newspapers.com*).

5. The Early Colonies and the Promotional Articles 61

DREAM OF TIRED VACATIONER

REPRESENTATIVE COTTAGE AT THE STAR RESORT.

This home at Knightstown Lake, built on a rare flat stretch of land, was depicted in an advertorial as a representative cottage (courtesy *Newspapers.com*).

cool, bathing pools." A dam was constructed across the mouth of one of the woodland valleys causing the stream to spread into a lake. Star Boulevard, a broad roadway named in honor of one of the sponsoring newspapers, the *Indianapolis Star*, surmounted the embankment.[28] Reversals were described in terms of advantages so when the dam gave way a few weeks into the promotion, it was reported that the rebuilt dam would be stronger and have a "silvery waterfall" (in reality a spillway) at the center to accommodate overflow from the lake.

Knightstown Lake was introduced to the readers of the *Star* on May 6, 1923. A week later a feature story on the colony, accompanied by photos and a drawing of a couple paddling a canoe with a portable victrola on the center seat, was printed in the Sunday edition. Written by Andrew H. Hepburn, this substantial article described the resort with ornamental language designed to appeal to the emotions. A ridge of wild trees became a fringe of timbered hills, deep ravines were verdant valleys, and a jungle of wild grapevines was transformed into natural swings for the children. Hepburn painted visions of colorful sunsets reflected in the lake, blue waters simmering in the heat of the day, an unsurpassed panorama of field and forest, and hills carpeted with flowers. Pleasures for the other senses were also invoked: the sounds of trickling rivulets babbling over moss covered stones, the still hush of twilight, maple trees waiting to be tapped for syrup, and air perfumed with the "fragrance of all outdoors." Lot purchasers would enjoy tramping through a network of forest paths, canoeing to the Big Blue River, smoking a quiet evening pipe under the deep, cool shade of overarching trees, and restful sleep.

The landscape around Knightstown Lake was touted for its dramatic beauty and even a lot in a deep gully, thick with dense growth, was promoted as desirable and proven to be so with a photo of a tree top cottage accompanying another promotional article. Tree trunks had been lopped off and turned into living stilts used to support a lattice of branches as the foundation for the dwelling.[29]

Like all good hucksters, Smadbeck, Hussey, and the *Star* were selling not merely plots of land, but enjoyment, an idyllic life, happiness. The Knightstown Lake project proved that even an unwieldy piece of real estate could be transformed both physically, and, more importantly, psychologically, into a desirable, coveted product.

* * *

The Hepburn essay is a model specimen of the newshead feature—an advertisement masquerading as a news story—published by the sponsoring paper to boost the promotion. A representation of Mayo's use of this ploy is the article "Beverly Glen on Map Most Charming Region," which appeared in the *Los Angeles Herald* on May 14, 1911. This flowery news story promoted Beverly Glen in general, praised the good judgment of those who had purchased lots, and extolled their virtue in forming a corporation to establish utilities and buy its stock.

The Smadbecks made the reading notice a mainstay of the newspaper deal. While they no doubt fed the subject matter and the talking points to the publications, the wording of the articles themselves is varied enough to conclude that each paper had its own staff compose the copy. Occasionally articles bore the byline of a staff reporter as was the case with Hepburn's piece in the *Star*. The Smadbecks retained content approval and an ad fee was most likely worked into the arrangement with the paper.

Newsheads were set in a typeface that blended with the legitimate and unrelated adjacent news articles. They had a headline and a subhead, and sometimes two subheads. These extensive headings often mentioned both the name of the colony and the name of the newspaper and allowed for more of the ad message to be in a large font. Examples include "Land of Sunshine at Pell Lake Beckons to You: Don't Spend Week-Ends in Loafing; Build Home at Vacation Paradise"[30]; "Investors Seize Opportunity at Lake Erie Beach; Increase in Value of Land at New Summer Home Near Lake Shore Interests Wise Folks—Many Enjoy Beauties of Place"[31]; "Rush Starts for Star's Home Sites on Coon Lake; 250 Besiege Offices and Hurry to Select Plots at Resort."[32]

5. The Early Colonies and the Promotional Articles   63

The subject matter of these articles was predetermined, predictable, and consistent. Early articles emphasized location, value, and neighborliness. The focus would then shift to a description of the throngs of visitors coming to the site and the rush to buy lots. Reports on how fast the lots sold were designed to heighten demand and encourage a quick purchase while good lots were still available.

A story describing features of the colony would follow, perhaps the plans for a golf course or the progress on construction of the clubhouse. Then came the announcement that the popularity of the resort made it necessary to open another section and the sequence of articles emphasizing rush-to-buy and hurry-while-lots-still-available would be repeated. Interspersed among these topics were reports of the number of lots sold and the number of cottages begun and completed and, of course, reminders that owning a home in the country brought happiness.

The articles for Pell Lake in the *Chicago Evening Post* followed this pattern but some also had another emphasis. Several dramatized family stories such as "Father Visits Pell Lake and Purchases Lots," telling of a father who reluctantly visits the resort, is favorably surprised, and sneaks off to purchase lots.[33] In "Pell Lake Solves Vacation Issue; Ends Big Mutiny," there is a family disagreement over where to vacation—Dad wants good fishing, the boys want to swim, and the daughter is interested in social activities. The mother ends the family mutiny when she investigates and finds that all the family desires can be satisfied by buying lots at Pell Lake.[34] Yet another article tells of a husband who bought the maximum five lots and the couple was so impressed that the wife purchased another five lots suggesting how easy it was to get around the five-lot limit.[35]

When the majority of the lots were sold, the infomercial articles would shift to an occasional brief report on the formation of the homeowners' association and its social activities. Once the developer and the newspaper withdrew from the scene the articles ended.

* * *

Reading notices were so prolific in the first decade of the twentieth century that a law was passed to curb their abuses and protect the public from being misled. The Newspaper Publicity Act of 1912 required any reading matter for which payment was accepted, including a promise of future ads, to be marked "advertisement," and violators were subject to a monetary penalty.[36] Enforcement of the provision was imposed on the Post Office Department which had not asked for, did not want, and was ambivalent toward the law.

Postal authorities declined to issue any blanket rules, determining that each case would be judged individually. Incapable of reviewing publications to search for violations, investigations were limited to complaints, usually lodged by competitors rather than by the members of the public that the law sought to protect. The judgment standard was whether the item had "news value," a determination that was both elusive and burdensome and consequently usually left to the publisher.[37] As a result, violations were not actively pursued and within a few years the regulation came to be largely ignored.

Based on the amount of space and consistency of use devoted to articles about the colony developments it might be assumed that an agreement for payment of some kind was part of the deal between the Smadbecks and the papers. This flagrant use of newshead articles was technically illegal since they were most likely paid for but remained unidentified as advertisements. Arguably the Smadbeck reading notices were exempt from the penalties based on the news value of the articles. The newspaper was simply describing the advantages and successes of its own subscription premium offer—no product manufacturer's name or business entity was identified in the stories except that of the newspaper itself. This leads to another key factor of the deal, anonymity.

* * *

The anonymity of the developer was one of the principles established by Bertram Mayo. A chain of deeds was used to obscure the real estate operator lurking in the background. The Beachwood property was bought by Addison Nickerson and transferred to Mayo, who conveyed it to Stanley Brown, counsel for the *New York Tribune*, as trustee who then deeded the individual lots to subscribers. The Asbury Park chain was Smadbeck to Home Guardian to Enoch Wolberg, the *Jewish Daily* trustee, to the lot buyers; at Pell Lake it was Freudenthal to Smadbeck to Frank Hussey of the *Chicago Evening Post* as trustee and then the purchasers. For whom the trustees were acting was never specified in the recorded land documents.

The Smadbecks managed to avoid notoriety in other ways. Operating under the aegis of Home Guardian, the Smadbeck name is not mentioned in the *Rosenbaum v. Sarasohn* legal decision. The name was also largely kept out of the press, rarely appearing in the available ads, news headline articles, or even in the legitimate news stories about the project in either the sponsoring paper or the competing papers. The newspapers in the vicinity of Pell Lake only once mention Warren Smadbeck by name in news articles before 1930. Rather he is referred to as "the eastern interests that were in the background as silent partners of the Chicago Evening Post project."[38]

The colony of Crystal Lakes, fifteen miles northeast of Dayton, Ohio, is a rare deviation from this practice. The promotion began on July 14, 1925, with two Dayton papers, the *Journal* and the *Herald* as the sponsors.[39] A mere four months later the property owners' association was formed[40] and no ads for the colony appeared the following summer. Then, for two months in 1927, large advertisements for Crystal Lakes appeared both in the *Herald* and in another newspaper, the *Dayton Daily News*. The lots were no longer tied to a subscription and named Arthur Smadbeck as the proprietor. The decision to end the subscription promotion and use the Smadbeck name is unexplained.

The quest for anonymity was not pursued out of personal modesty but rather to further business goals including minimizing legal responsibility. The more difficult it was to trace true ownership the easier it was to avoid trouble makers. Each step in the string of land owners provided another opportunity to claim lack of knowledge of promises made. With the newspaper deal it was unnecessary to establish a nationally recognized brand name. Real estate does not easily lend itself to this advertising practice and, with a product aimed at a particular geographical audience, having a nationwide presence was no advantage. The developers instead relied on the already established reputation of the affiliated newspaper.

The publishers allowed their business image to be used in this way because they, as well as the real estate men, benefited from the duplicity. The land ownership structure—deeding the plots of land to the buyers through the newspaper trustee—allowed the paper to legitimately take credit for finding the land, developing it, and making the subscription offer, as well as to convey the land with a very official sounding "trustee's warranty deed." At the same time the newspaper could stress that it was not in the real estate business nor engaged in a commercial venture. While there was no express denial that a real estate company was involved, any mention of the shadowy developer was omitted. Similarly, the papers denied making a penny in profit on the development while avoiding reference to a profit being made by someone else.

The newspaper thus presented its goals as purely altruistic. It was establishing the colony for the benefit of its readers and for the purpose of increasing subscribers. The publication sought to render a service and give this extraordinary opportunity to its readers in order to cement the bond of friendship between the paper and its customers. It was a community project, the newspaper joining with its subscribers to establish a happy place where they could secure summer homes and solve their vacation problems.

It was a very clever ruse.

* * *

The Smadbecks streamlined the colony creating process by eliminating Mayo's practice of starting ancillary corporations for transportation and utilities. They would string a few electric lights along the beach area but otherwise they left electrical power, and all other municipal utilities, to the lot owners themselves.

Rather than operating concessions the Smadbecks referred the collateral businesses to others. While this negated the opportunity to profit from these ventures as Mayo had done, the colony creation process was faster and simpler. The less time it took to create a resort, the more colonies could be produced, and the faster money could be made.

The Smadbecks also introduced cookie cutter techniques. Naming practices fall into this category. Early on the Smadbecks established a pattern for titling the colonies: adopt a local name for the geographical area and attach "lake," "beach," or "shore," or, if not directly on a waterway, "estates" or "park." They were also consistent from the beginning in assigning the same name to the road that hugged the water's edge. As at Pell Lake, roads that curved along the lake were always called "Lake Shore Drive," or the equivalent "Shore Road" if the waterway was a river. Frequently, there was a road that bore the name of the allied newspaper, such as Star Boulevard at Knightstown Lake and Post Road in Pell Lake.

Assigning labels to the side roads was a more ominous chore. Since the Smadbecks bought undeveloped farmland and laid out the streets, they were burdened with naming the many byways. Beginning with Knightstown Lake they adopted the system Mayo used at Browns Mills, calling the roads after trees, shrubs, and flowers to buttress the image of a nature retreat for city dwellers. Using the same botanical theme, and for the most part, the same names, for the roads in all the colonies, simplified the process and was especially useful when several developments were being created simultaneously.

Major roads in Pell Lake are titled Thistle Drive, Orchid Drive, Clover Road, and Daisy Drive. Side streets have the floral names of Iris, Dahlia, Phlox, Hyacinth, Posy, Zinnia, Trumpet, Bluebell, Laurel, Violet, Moss, Jasmine, Geranium, Larkspur, Narcissus, Crocus, and even the elusive Anemone. Birds were not ignored with Flamingo, Heron, and Hawk also being used.

Developed 1924, Loveland Park, on the west bank of the Little Miami River, twenty-three miles northeast of Cincinnati, was sold through that city's *Commercial Tribune*. Loveland shared many street names with Pell Lake: Aster, Primrose, Holly and the more common tree names: Cedar, Pine, Maple, Cherry, Walnut, Birch, Elm, Mulberry, Sycamore, Chestnut, and Locust.

The Smadbecks became so repetitive in this regard that their projects can be dated by this feature: if a drive through a Smadbeck colony affords a botany lesson it is assured that the roads were platted between 1924 and 1930. This naming formula can also be used to define the borders of a Smadbeck development. The Highlands section of Pell Lake is an area adjoining, but not developed by the Smadbecks. While it includes a few tree names in its streets, it is not botanically consistent, also employing names such as Eastwood, Fairview, Hollywood and Glenwood, thereby distinguishing the Highlands section of Pell Lake as separate from the Smadbecks' original platting.

Street titles can also be used to pinpoint the location of Smadbeck colonies that no longer exist such as Lake Louisvilla, another 1924 creation. Fifteen miles northeast of the center of Louisville, Kentucky, it was a combined venture with the *Louisville Post* and the *Louisville Herald*. Consisting of only 80 acres, Lake Louisvilla was among the smallest of the colonies. Views of the roadways and lots depict the typical terrain of untamed woods and shrubbery but photographs of the lake display its appeal. The swimming beach was huddled in a cove of the boomerang-shaped lake. Paddled canoes and oared rowboats happily shared the waterway with the swimmers. It was fitted out with all the inducements: clubhouse, pavilion, bathhouse, parkland, golf course, and a boat dock. Lake Louisvilla even had a hotel, a three-tiered diving platform, and a water slide, features that never existed at Pell Lake.[41]

Although the lake itself has disappeared the location of Lake Louisvilla can still be identified by the few remaining streets bearing the names Hemlock, Peachtree, Poplar, and Catalpa, the last two also existing in both Loveland Park and Pell Lake.

* * *

There was a significant difference between Mayo's relationship with the publishers and that of the Smadbecks. Mayo seemingly operated under an employer/employee relationship and any agreement with the newspapers on the terms of the arrangement was in that context. In that sense the publishers he worked with were not allied with a real estate developer but instead had a promotions person on the staff who pursued the sale of real estate. In contrast the Smadbecks were independent agents. Their arrangement with the newspapers was a true contractual agreement between the two distinct businesses. This afforded them more freedom and opportunity.

Mayo's position restricted his activity at any given time to one promotion with one publication resulting in a limited number of projects. Between 1909 and 1917 Mayo developed only five resorts including Cazadero Redwoods and Beverly Glen. Nothing prevented the Smadbecks from conducting four or five concurrent promotions with as many different publications.

During the four-year period from 1924 to 1927 more than twenty resorts were created by the Smadbecks. In addition to Pell Lake, Loveland Park, and

Lake Louisvilla, two other colonies were formed in 1924. Lake Saint Croix Beach, twenty miles east of Saint Paul, was a venture with the *Saint Paul News*. In Rensselaer County, New York, Home Guardian purchased most of the land surrounding Nassau Lake as well as the lake bed itself. Located southeast of Albany, lots at Nassau Lake Park were marketed with subscriptions to either the *Knickerbocker Press* or the *Albany Evening News*.

The size of the developments is also subject to comparison. With more acreage, and accordingly more lots, Mayo's projects were on a grand scale: Lakewood contained 40,000 lots and Beachwood's 2,000 acres became roughly 30,000 lots. The Smadbeck developments, while greater in number, were smaller in size. Pell Lake, one of their larger colonies, had fewer than 10,000 lots. Combined with other developments initiated the same year, the Smadbecks produced an approximate total of 30,000 lots, matching the number at Mayo's Beachwood but spread out over four resorts.[42]

Bertram Mayo created colonies individually. Adding new elements with each one, he established the basic structure of the newspaper deal: small lots near a waterway sold as a subscription premium, all lots advertised at the same low price, use of newshead articles and reason-why persuasion, a chain of ownership, a clubhouse converted from the sales office, parkland given to the lot owners, and establishment of a property owners association to manage the common grounds.

The Smadbecks adopted most of these features, enhanced some, and abandoned others. They advertised more and leaned toward anonymity, while simplifying the colony creation process and making it more methodic. Letting the property owners worry about the utilities and encouraging moms and pops to operate the side businesses allowed the developers to exit the scene as soon as a POA was organized. By creating smaller colonies and using repeated patterns for such chores as street naming, they could produce more resorts in less time, shortening the time period for development of a resort to two years. As they gained experience with the promotion, repeating it over and over, the process became robotic.

Warren and Arthur Smadbeck approached the development of real estate much as Henry Ford approached the manufacture of automobiles. Using an assembly line and repetitive motions Ford was able to manufacture a car in an hour and a half. Mass production of cars lowered the price and enabled him to sell innumerable automobiles. Of course, they all looked alike, but then so did the Smadbeck lots.

Like Henry Ford the Smadbecks stamped out nearly identical products, priced them to appeal to the masses, and sold a multitude of them. The Smadbecks created an assembly line for real estate capable of mass-producing summer resorts.

6

The Later Colonies and the Display Ads

A contemporary of the Smadbecks, writing about the social history of America in the first quarter of the twentieth century, observed that mass production went hand in hand with an enormous expansion of advertising. The author credited the automobile with causing the dramatic evolution of ads from small formal announcements, providing no more than the name and address of the merchant, to large decorated displays that constituted salesmanship for the consumption of commodities. Advertisements for autos were directed to a wholly unoccupied market and were fashioned to persuade the masses of readers that they needed this new product.[1] Selling lakeside lots at a resort within easy distance of a large metropolis had similar potential with throngs of city dwellers waiting to be told that they would be happy if they owned a little piece of countryside property.

The Smadbecks were better positioned to take advantage of this opportunity than was Bertram Mayo. Mayo certainly recognized the power of display ads and made effective use of them in the Diamond Drilling project. But displays were not used in his newspaper colony ventures. For the Lakewood promotion with the *Chicago Evening Post* the promotional booklet was sent out in the mail[2] and the newspaper printed only a few minimal announcements. Beachwood was publicized with more than fifteen advertorials in the first few months of the promotion but, again, there were no display ads, just some notices providing the summer hours for the offices of the promotion department at the *New York Tribune*'s headquarters and at Beachwood.[3] The hard sell advertisements for Beachwood—the November 1914 extra edition of the *Tribune* and Mayo's pamphlet—were both distributed by direct mail rather than printed in the paper itself as advertisements.[4]

Even though the *Tribune* carried no ads for its own promotion it nevertheless sold advertising space to several builders seeking to construct bungalows at Beachwood[5] and, five years later, accepted display ads for the

Smadbeck colony of Patchogue Lakes sponsored by the competing *Brooklyn Citizen*.[6] The changing nature of journalism, fierce competition among penny papers, and a self-righteous attitude on the part of the *Tribune* provide explanations for this seeming inconsistency.

* * *

Will Irwin was a well-established author and journalist when he composed the estimable series "The American Newspaper" for *Collier's* published in the magazine between January and July 1911. Comprised of fourteen essays the compilation was subtitled "A Study of Journalism in Its Relation to the Public," and described itself as a collection of articles on "the whole subject of American journalism—the most powerful extrajudicial force in society, except religion." It was a hefty undertaking, one that was capably handled by Will Irwin.

Reflecting on the relatively brief history of journalism in America, Irwin wrote that, except for Darwin's scientific method, "no plant of thought ever grew so great in so short a period."[7] His writings traced the history of newspaper development and progressed with an analysis of the power and influence of newspapers, the rise and fall of yellow journalism, the ethics of newswriting, and the relationship of journalism to big business.

* * *

Throughout most of its history in the United States journalism flourished unfettered under the protection of freedom of speech. Newspapers evolved from the political pamphlet or broadside, an expression of opinion in written form, comprised of more editorials than news and, accordingly, appealing primarily to the intellectual classes. If news was reported at all it was presented as background for opinion. Irwin wrote that "news as we know it was not yet invented. The editorial, on the other hand, came to full perfection by the end of the eighteenth century."[8]

The purpose of these early papers was to mold public thought, promote popular causes, and speak for the people, thus providing a basis for freedom from legal restraint. This principle allowed the American press to create sentiment for independence and spurred our founders, who understood how journalism had assisted our struggle to be free, to give the fullest liberty to the press.

The Revolutionary War thus shaped journalism by ensuring freedom of the press. The Civil War changed the luxury of reading a newspaper into a necessity as residents on both sides of the divided country craved reports of the battles and lists of the dead. Both wars had an effect on molding journalism in America: the first resulted in a free press for America and the second provided a national demand for news.

6. The Later Colonies and the Display Ads

Changes in newspaper content continued to surge at an increasingly faster pace in the forty-five years following the Civil War, due both to the ideas of forward-thinking newsmen and to technological advancements. Will Irwin profiled the cognition and the practices of several eighteenth-century leaders in newspaper journalism. He credited James Gordon Bennett, Sr., publisher of the *New York Herald*, with inventing news in the modern sense by reporting on Wall Street finances, private scandals, and personal troubles. Irwin also singled out Benjamin H. Day for creating the first American newspaper for the masses, the New York *Sun*, a paper that cost only one cent with profits garnered from larger circulation and advertising.[9]

The foresight of Bennett, Day, and others like them gave rise to the penny paper, filled with news about the troubles of common people, and produced a great new body of readership, an outcome that was fueled by technology. Nineteenth-century technological advancements in production of print media, including the steam powered rotary press, wood pulp paper, and rolled paper, all contributed to making newspapers larger, cheaper, and more widely distributed. Newspapers became less costly to produce and more affordable for the average person.

* * *

But penny papers needed to sell six times as many copies as the mainstream publications to match subscription revenue. The desire to increase the number of subscribers brought about the profession of Circulation Manager,[10] newspaper men who increased circulation figures by discounting subscription rates, awarding premiums sometimes worth more than the cost of a subscription, and conducting voting contests with elaborate prizes for signing up subscribers. Copies of publications were sent to non-subscribers in numbers wildly disproportionate to paid subscriptions and "clubbing" was initiated—offering a subscription to another publication as a premium resulting in two journals adding subscribers for the purchase of only one subscription.

Maneuvers to raise circulation numbers became increasingly aggressive with many publishers resorting to outright fabrication. Some papers claimed circulation figures far in excess of the number of copies their presses were capable of printing or set the counters of their presses forward by thousands of copies before beginning a print run. Others kept two sets of books with two different figures for two different purposes or bribed paper manufacturers and freight agents to submit bogus receipts for products not ordered. Exaggeration was so blatant and figures so unbelievable that verified and sworn circulation statements were routinely regarded with suspicion.[11]

Inflating circulation by giving papers away to nonsubscribers or falsifying the figures does not add to a newspaper's income. But it does increase advertising revenue—more subscribers translate into higher advertising rates. In effect advertisers purchase circulation, that is, the privilege of using the newspaper's customers for the purpose of getting business for themselves.[12]

In exploring the question of whether journalism was a profession or a business[13] Will Irwin observed that the agendas at national publishing conventions did not include methods of news-gathering and editorial problems, but instead dealt with topics such as the price of paper and machinery, circulation, and advertising rates. Irwin portrayed advertising as a vital necessity causing the American newspaper to become a great commercial enterprise.

Taking a piercing look at the role of advertising in journalism, he noted that as the cost of newspapers fell, more were purchased, and as circulation rose, so did the amount that could be charged for advertising.[14] This resulted in advertisers replacing readers as the primary source of income for papers. As a consequence, the influence of advertising dollars altered the content of the newspapers, an observation concisely summed up as "modern business demands mutual favors."[15] It was this change in the nature of journalism that caused newspapers to slant opinion columns to attract advertising and spawned the advertorial reading notice.

Since the distribution of news was to be encouraged and fostered, publications were granted subsidized and coveted second-class mailing status. When advertisers sought to use second class mail to distribute circulars containing mostly ads to nonsubscribers, postal regulations were introduced.[16] The Newspaper Publicity Act of 1912 imposed three requirements. In addition to mandating the disclosure of the names of owners and stockholders, the law required editors to label as "advertisement" any material inserted for payment that might be mistaken for a story. This provision was aimed at the newshead articles. The act also sought to remedy the fraudulent circulation situation by tersely imposing an obligation on daily newspapers to periodically declare the number of copies sold or distributed to paid subscribers.[17]

The law was quickly challenged and affirmed by the Supreme Court in June of 1913.[18] In its decision the court, for the first time, sanctioned federal controls aimed directly at the press' profit-making activities thereby acknowledging journalism as a business.[19]

* * *

Technological and social factors were perhaps more responsible for the evolution in ads than were legal regulations. Initially considered undignified, advertising grew in acceptance as social attitudes changed and journalism transitioned away from literature and politics and toward business, police reports, rumor, scandal, and eventually, a voice for advertisers.[20] In the years before the start of World War I newspapers came to be recognized as vendors of advertising, a commodity that had become the publisher's main source of revenue.[21]

It took some time for the publishers to sort out how to cope with this new reality. The *New York Tribune*, whose stagnant circulation figures and resultant ad revenues were the lowest among comparable newspapers in New York,[22] went beyond contests and premium schemes to attract more readers by adopting a rigorous editorial policy.[23]

When the *Tribune* first publicized the Beachwood project with a news-head article on November 18, 1914, the paper was in the midst of a campaign for truth in advertising. In early August of 1913 the *Tribune* began including a statement on its masthead promoting the integrity of its advertisers and vowing to avoid publication of any misleading claims. By October of 1914 the paper had adopted the slogan "First to Last the Truth: News–Editorials–Advertisements." Two months later this assurance was turned into a money-back guarantee if a reader was dissatisfied with advertised merchandise. "No red tape. No quibbling. We make good promptly if the advertiser does not."[24]

The *Tribune* reinforced this sanctimonious effort by engaging the services of Samuel Hopkins Adams, the well-known author, campaigner against misleading advertising in the patent medicine industry, and a strong force behind the 1906 Pure Food and Drug Act. Throughout the spring of 1915 the paper ran a series of articles by Adams addressing advertising abuses. These were succeeded by a column titled "Ad-Visor" where Adams answered inquiries concerning the validity of various advertisements. The column appeared periodically between July 1915 and December 1918 and perhaps provided the newspaper with an incentive to refrain from printing display ads for the Beachwood subscription promotion.

The Ad-Visor column attracted considerable attention but was not so sacrosanct as to refrain from promoting the *Tribune*'s own interests.[25] This was openly demonstrated when a letter writer complained to the Ad-Visor that his Beachwood lot purchase was an outrage and a swindle. He expressed dissatisfaction with the location of the lots, that they were not staked out, and that the salesman on site accused him of removing the stakes. He considered himself lucky that he had not yet paid the full cost of the two lots.

Adams admitted receiving many letters about the promotion and traveled to Beachwood to view the lots purchased by the complainant. Concentrating on the bargain price of $19.60 per lot, Adams recognized that the deal appeared to be too good to be true giving rise to suspicions, but he staunchly defended the value of the land and noted that, since all lots were the same price, buyers should expect that some lot locations would be better than others. He criticized the letter writer's characterizations of outrage and swindle and advised him to hold on to his purchase.[26]

Thus, the Ad-Visor column functioned as an endorsement of the Beachwood deal by a renowned crusader for advertising honesty. Still both Mayo and the *New York Tribune* could more easily escape the money back-guarantee if there were no display ads in the paper and the premium scheme was described only in advertorials. Just to be double sure the *Tribune* clarified its policy by excepting refunds on the purchase of real estate or investments.[27] Nevertheless, the paper did make at least one refund for lots purchased at Beachwood but only after some quibbling.[28]

* * *

The newspaper deal as formulated by Bertram Mayo was far more effective in building circulation than an offer of a clock or another household item as a premium. The only way to obtain a resort lot was by purchasing a subscription to the paper whereas clocks were available from many vendors. Also, readers had a desire to own more than one lot, sometimes four or five, and as many subscriptions. Lot buyers also prompted their friends to buy lots thereby encouraging them to subscribe, something not likely to occur if the premium were a flyswatter.

Mayo capitalized on the use of the premium, his plan increased circulation, and he used advertorials to make the newspaper deal a profitable venture for a publication. But given the changing social landscape of advertising, the Smadbecks were able to take the deal a step farther.

No standard contract existed when Home Guardian approached the *Jewish Daily News* about Asbury Park Estates. The Home Guardian agent presented the basic terms of the offer, negotiated the fine points, and then had an employee of the newspaper draft the contract.[29] In addition to increasing circulation and bringing in more subscription money, the Smadbeck advertising contract increased ad revenue for the paper in a multitude of ways. The agreement most likely included remuneration for both the advertorials and the substantial display ads for the promotion, a minimum amount of which was assured by the developer. These advertorials and display ads, while being paid for by the real estate developers, had the extra bonus of praising the newspaper and promoting the sale of subscriptions. Plus, the display ads were placed in competing papers.

The colony promotion attracted advertising from other businesses as well including some targeting their products and services specifically to the resort lot buyers, such as an ad for the Town Market Furniture Company

6. The Later Colonies and the Display Ads 75

proclaiming, "We Have 6 Big Floors of Just the Kind of Furniture You Want to Furnish Your Coon Lake Cottage."[30] The additional advertising allowed the paper to raise ad rates based on the increased number of readers and on the increased demand for advertising space in the paper.

No other advertising agreement was as monetarily beneficial to a newspaper. The sponsoring papers and the developers of the newspaper colonies had achieved an epitome of mutual codependence in selling and maximizing profits for each other's products. The newspaper deal was an unequivocal business success.

* * *

Advances in printing techniques also caused changes in the appearance and content of display ads. Varied and larger type size made ads easier to read and more attractive. The increase in the physical size of papers allowed advertisements to grow in width and length and gave rise to the full-page ad, in effect a billboard adapted to newspaper space.[31] Larger ads allowed more room for fine line, detailed illustrations popularized by mail order catalogs while invention of the halftone process ushered in the use of photography.

Although the Smadbecks did make some use of direct mail, mostly fold-over postcards, they relied primarily upon display advertisements, introducing each new colony with a double full-page ad. Subtle changes demonstrate that they kept current with changing fashions in advertising trends. The 1916 Asbury Park Estates ad comprised two adjoining pages each capable of standing on its own. In comparison the 1922 ad for Lake Erie Beach was one complete ad spread out over two pages. Similarly, while the terms of the subscription offer remained unchanged, the words "Liberal" and "Premium" used in the 1919 Patchogue Lakes ad disappeared and were replaced by "Greatest" and "Offer" in the 1923 ads for Knightstown Lake.

These oversized and frequent display ads were a counterpart to the faux news articles, both often appearing in the same issue of a newspaper, although on different pages, each playing off the content of the other. The newsheads and the display ads differed primarily in appearance and configuration with both making heavy use of reason-why appeals.

The unwary reader could easily confuse the articles with news reports, but there was no mistaking the hard sell of the display ads. Advertisements for the resorts were dictated by the Smadbecks and, similar to the advertorials, were consistent from resort to resort in form, frequency, and substance.

This tandem sales approach, display ads and newshead stories, is illustrated with the promotions for two Minnesota resorts. Minnesota with its 10,000 lakes provided fertile ground for the Smadbecks. A year after

Newspaper–Real Estate Schemes of the 1920s

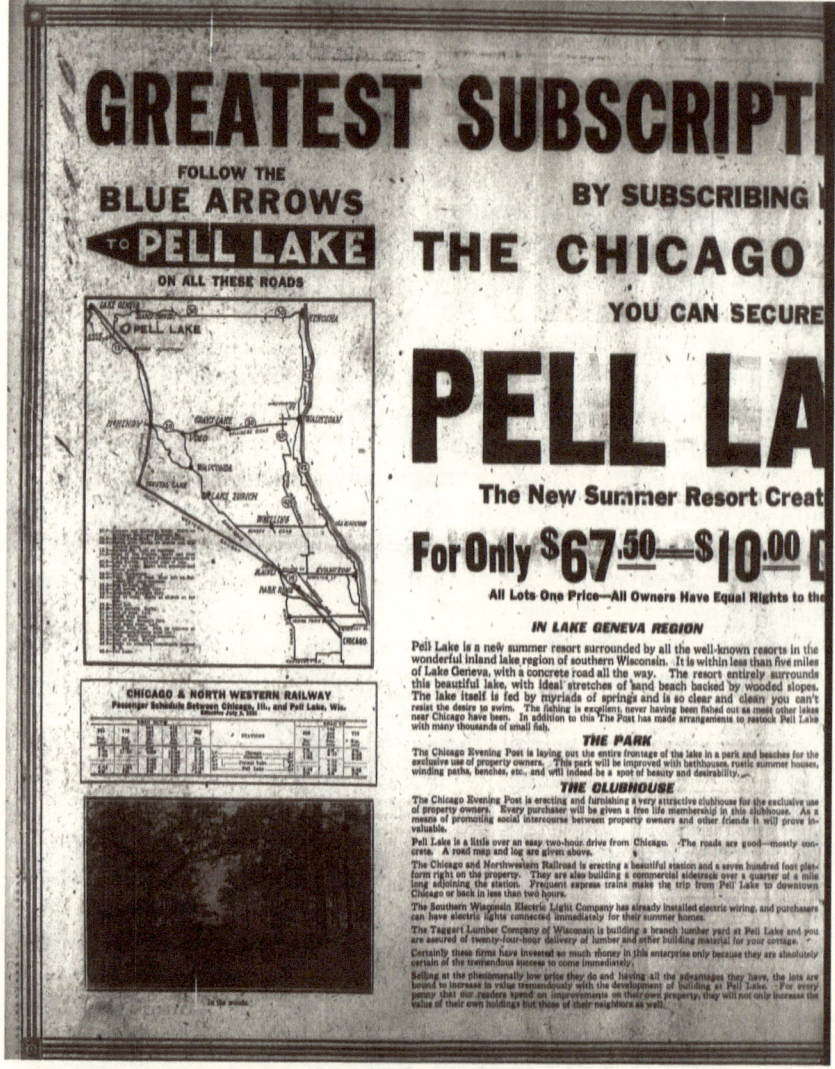

Lake Saint Croix Beach, the colony of Coon Lake Beach was begun. It was located twenty-five miles north of the Twin Cities in Anoka County and was linked with a subscription to the *Minneapolis Daily Star*. Just as the promotion of Coon Lake Beach was winding down, a second *Minneapolis Daily Star* colony was announced at Carver Beach, fifteen miles southwest of the city on the shores of Long Lake. The opening ad for Carver Beach appeared in the *Star* on Tuesday, July 19, 1927.

The ads for Carver Beach and Coon Lake Beach were typical, in layout and placement, to the display advertisements for Pell Lake and the other

6. The Later Colonies and the Display Ads

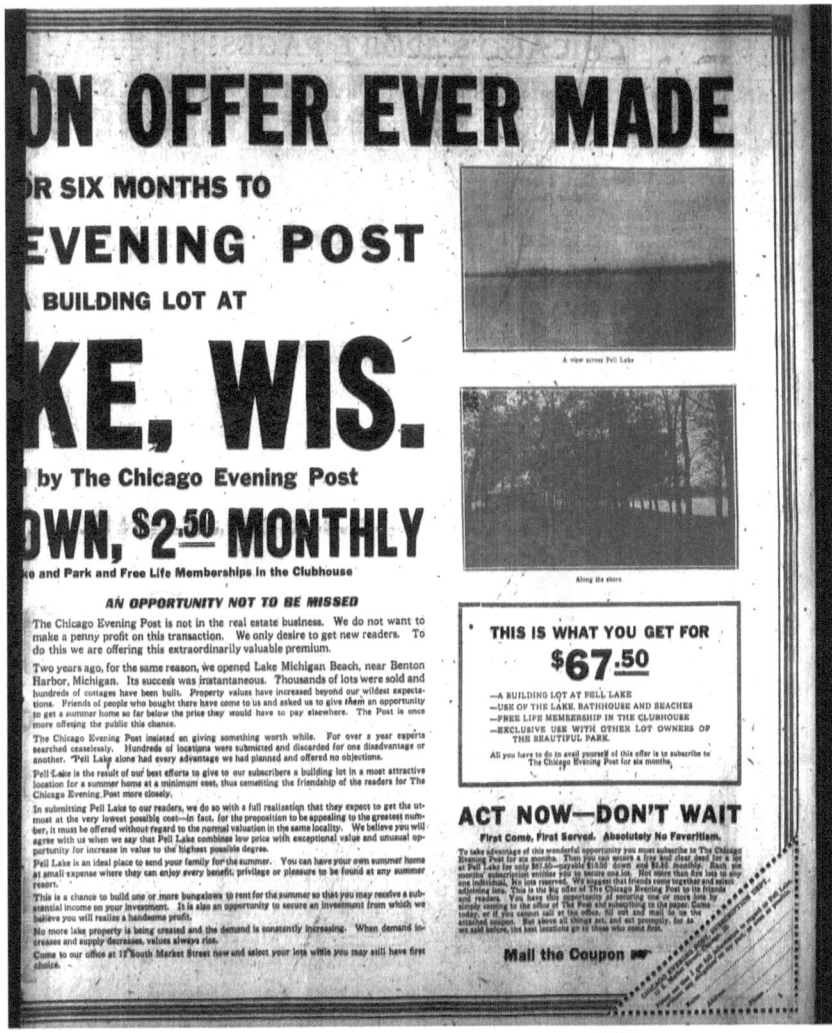

The two-page debut ad for Pell Lake exemplifies the full maturity of newspaper colony advertisement. It appeared in the *Chicago Evening Post* on July 16, 1924 (courtesy Chicago Public Library).

Smadbeck developments. The initial display ad was always two full pages, usually appearing midweek. Near full-page ads followed every day for a week or more with two-page ads in the Saturday or Sunday edition. Tailored to attract attention, their size and prevalence could not be ignored by readers.

After this initial burst of promotion, the ads would funnel down to a half-page or quarter-page, still impressive for a real estate campaign.

A month after promotion for Lake Erie Beach began the ads contracted to one-third or one-fourth page size. They continued to grow smaller, eventually eliminating all photographs. The low price of the lots was often emphasized (courtesy *Newspapers.com*).

Ads continued for five weeks or more, depending on how many lots there were, how fast they sold, and how much of the summer season remained. Typically, the total ad space purchased for a resort amounted to about fifteen full pages, an incredible amount of advertising and a big boost to the income of any newspaper. In promoting Coon Lake, the *Minneapolis Daily*

Star further augmented its revenue by tacking on a disability insurance policy for an extra $1.25.[32]

* * *

With Saint Croix, Coon Lake, and Carver Beach the Smadbeck machine had, in rapid succession, created three newspaper resorts encircling the Twin Cities. Another midwestern resort begun in this time frame was Times Beach, a collaboration with the *Saint Louis Times*. Deviating from the usual title formula, the name of the resort derived from that of the sponsoring newspaper. The 480 acres of farmland formed a fan-shaped area defined by the Meramec River curving around the northeast border, a highway running along the southern edge, and a local road on the west.[33] The resort was on a flood plain and many of the cottages built there were mounted on stilts. In future years Times Beach would gain notoriety as a victim of the environmental movement.

The Smadbecks never abandoned pursuits closer to home, along the eastern seaboard. Penn Beach in New Jersey, begun in 1925, was located on the Delaware River, only a ferry boat ride away from New Castle, Delaware. The sponsoring paper was the *Philadelphia Record* but the location of the resort attracted people from Wilmington and Baltimore as well.

Advertisements for Penn Beach employed the Smadbecks' dependably constant vocabulary, repeating certain information in every ad. This included, sensibly, the price of a lot and the terms of payment as well as the extra benefits. The clubhouse was always mentioned and photographs of the structure were often featured, first while it was under construction, then upon completion, and finally showing the furnished interior.

Additionally, the super-sized ads allowed room for many hyperbolic claims and other wordy hype employing every weapon in the advertising arsenal. The reason-why persuasive text included both pragmatic and emotional reasons for investing, made arguments to head off resistance, described the benefits of purchasing, urged fast action, and offered easy ways to pay.

While the ads claimed no profit for the newspaper, they appealed to the rationally minded by stressing the profit potential for buyers. All these phrases were used in an ad for Penn Beach: "the chance of a lifetime," "great success and long profits," "it is going to boom," "your chance to buy good land that you can hold for a profit." In addition to being a smart investment, it was pointed out that buyers could build two cottages, one for personal use and the other to rent out as a source of income.[34]

The display ads were also consistent in their omissions. They did not publicize that property owners would have the responsibility of maintaining the parkland and clubhouse, nor that the lots and any amounts paid in would be forfeited if payments were in default. Ads for a few of the earliest resorts provided lot size information but this detail soon disappeared not bothering to inform readers that the lots were so narrow that one lot was all but useless.

King Lake, begun about 1925 and named after the former property owner, was a project monitored by Arthur Smadbeck. Twenty-two miles from Omaha, Nebraska, it was among the more troublesome ventures due to its location just west of the Elkhorn River. Upon the request of the sponsoring newspaper, the *Omaha Daily News*, the health commissioner examined the shallow 20' deep wells and declared the water unfit for drinking unless boiled or chemically treated.[35] The Smadbecks were called upon to dig two deeper wells and supply the water to the cottagers through a pipe system.[36]

Then in February of 1927 a four-mile-long ice block formed in the Elkhorn River and caused severe flooding. King Lake was underwater with extensive damage to the dwellings. When the floodwaters receded about four feet of mud was deposited in the lake. It took several years before the lake bed was dredged and 40,000 cubic yards of silt removed.[37]

As the 1920s progressed more and more people owned automobiles and the advertising kept pace by providing driving route information. Mastic Beach, along with King Lake and Penn Beach were among the resorts using massive blue arrows to point the way. An ad for Coon Lake Beach advised readers to follow the route "to the big 30-foot Blue Arrow" directing drivers to turn right to the resort.[38] A Pell Lake display ad included a prominent arrow bearing the inscription "to Pell Lake."

Just how closely the symbolism of the blue arrow became identified with the newspaper resorts is shown by a 1926 classified ad in the Omaha *Evening World-Herald* offering for sale the "Blue Arrow" cafe at King Lake.[39]

* * *

Arthur Smadbeck also directed the development of Lake Como Beach, the third collaboration with the *Chicago Evening Post* and the second Smadbeck project in Walworth County, Wisconsin. The Como resort encompasses more than 1,000 acres and, in some ways, is more attractive than Pell Lake. The terrain is picturesquely hilly and filled with trees. But it lacks the cohesiveness, the oneness, that is characteristic of Pell Lake. Lake Como Beach colony runs along a portion of the northern shore of the lake while the western and southern sides were, in later years, developed with a resort at the western end and a single road with larger homes along the southern shore. There are no reliable road connections between these areas and Lake Como Beach.

Lake Como is a relatively large lake, one that is suitable for boating but

6. The Later Colonies and the Display Ads   81

not for swimming. The closest Lake Como Beach gets to having a beach is the word "Beach" in its name and a "Beach Road." There simply is no good place for sandy access to the water. All the east-west roads dead end into marshland at the eastern end of the colony while the north-south roads end at the juncture with Lakeshore Drive. The area between Lakeshore Drive and the water is a narrow grassy slope that runs down to the water's edge to house an endless string of piers and all manner of boats.

Contemporaneous with the popularity of newspaper colonies was land speculation in Florida.[40] By the time Lake Como Beach debuted with an ad in the *Post* in May of 1926, the newspaper fad had hit its peak, concurrent with the apex of frenzied land buying in Florida. But the realty boom there involved huge sums of money and rampant speculation—it was a hefty business, concentrated in one state, and it landed with a definite thud. The newspaper resort operation, far more modest in size, scattered around the country, and promoted primarily as a vacation opportunity rather than as an investment, paled by comparison and, accordingly, had a much slower, softer fall. The contrast between the status of the two land booms in 1926 is illustrated by the headlines of side-by-side news articles in the *Chicago Evening Post*: "Lake Como Beauty Appreciated by New Lot Owners" and "Florida Land Company Fails for $8,581,576."[41] Newspaper resorts continued to be created for the remainder of the decade with a fair degree of success.

Other mid-decade colonies were begun in Ohio and New Jersey. Fairfield Beach, a promotion tied to the *Columbus Dispatch*, is on the south shore of Buckeye Lake, thirty-three miles east of Columbus, Ohio. The headline of the advertorial announcing Fairfield Beach, "Dispatch Offers Summer Home Sites for $69.50," dominated the entire width of the front page and included a prominent illustration and map centered just below.[42]

The partnership with the *Philadelphia Record* in 1925 that produced Penn Beach was repeated with another resort in southern New Jersey located fifty miles straight south from Philadelphia. When ads for the colony began appearing in May of 1927 the disagreeably named Buckshutem Pond had been enlarged by a dam, and, together with the land surrounding it, was renamed Laurel Lake after the bushes that thrived in the area.

A newshead article promoting Laurel Lake described a remarkable transformation of the pond and the surrounding woods by surveyors, landscape artists, builders, and road crews. Planned features included a wide road all around the lake with a bridge over the stream, park areas cleared of shrubbery and planted with cedar and shade trees, and a lagoon with four continuously operating fountains. Nearing completion was a large clubhouse, fashioned in Old English architectural style, with a main room consisting of an imposing two storied hall, adorned with balconies at both ends and a large fireplace on one side. Brick terraces led to a pier and boat moorings. An attractive island out in the lake was reserved as a park for the lot owners.[43]

Just as the advertisements and the newsheads could exaggerate, and at times even misstate the facts, so could legitimate news articles about the resorts. The cost of the considerable construction work at Laurel Lake was reported as $400,000, a figure probably provided by the developers seeking to call attention to the project and highlighted by the paper as good news for the local economy.[44] The Smadbecks had by this time established a two-year structure for colony development and exactly two years after Laurel Lake was begun, the local newspaper reported that construction work had been abandoned, an action that had a significant effect on local jobs. A failure to sell sufficient lots was cited as the cause[45] but this account was inaccurate.

There was an aggressive push for sales of lots at Laurel Lake for the first ten days of May in 1929 with the final ads warning that the promotion would soon close and urging buyers to take advantage of the last chance to buy lots.[46] The construction work at the colony was then suspended but not because of lack of sales—the Smadbecks had sold all but 900 of the initial 3,660 lots.[47] The reason for the abandonment of Laurel Lake was the imminent announcement of an adjoining venture.

Smadbeck and the *Philadelphia Record* had created a second, smaller lake by building a dam across Buckshutem Creek at the western point of Laurel Lake and, on May 12, 1929, began the newspaper promotion for Beach Club Lake.[48] Enough profits had been extracted from Laurel Lake and a new summer resort at a new lake with a fresh promotion was more likely to sell lots, and so the ongoing work at Laurel Lake was transferred to Beach Club Lake which now had the better chance of producing returns on the investment. The two adjoining colonies appeared to have both been successful, at least initially, and the Laurel Lake and Beach Club Lake Property Owners Association was formed in November of 1929.[49]

* * *

Constraints on prospective buyers deciding whether or not to invest in a colony were reassuredly and affirmatively addressed in the ads with information designed to dispel any such reticence. A clear deed was promised and sometimes a certificate of title insurance. The reputation of the newspaper was promoted as an additional guaranty.

A significant holdback for a buyer was the daunting thought of erecting a cottage. Ads headed off this resistance in several ways. They encouraged construction, arguing that it would spur more lot sales and increase land values, and they also provided assistance with the building process. Patchogue Lakes offered free home plans with each lot,[50] and at Lake Erie

6. The Later Colonies and the Display Ads 83

Beach ads proclaimed that "builders are on the ground prepared to furnish reasonable estimates for either homes or commercial buildings."[51]

There were other tie-ins between the developers and contractors. Summer Bungalow Corporation specialized in building cottages and followed the Smadbecks from resort to resort. In 1927 Summer Bungalow employed a force of men to do construction work in Mastic.[52] In July that same year, in a small ad in the *Minneapolis Daily Star*, Summer Bungalow described itself as "a national institution" which had decided to extend its operations to erecting summer homes at Carver Beach. A handsome cottage cost as little as $495 built on the owner's lot. Interested parties were invited to the *Minneapolis Daily Star* building where the contractor had agents most likely sharing a room with Smadbecks' lot sellers.[53] At Laurel Lake, the builder placed a good-sized display ad in the *Philadelphia Inquirer* offering free bus tickets for travel to the resort where potential customers could view a fully equipped bungalow purchasable for $890 including two lots.[54] Again, Summer Bungalow could be contacted at the offices of the newspaper. Another contractor established an office in the clubhouse at Lake Erie Beach and offered a variety of models, including a three-bedroom bungalow designed for a single 20' wide lot.[55]

* * *

The interaction between the display ads and the pseudo news stories was further buttressed by a third marketing tactic—contact with a lot salesman. At Lake Erie Beach the *Buffalo Enquirer* reported that the marketing staff consisted of eight secretaries, two bookkeepers, two cashiers, and thirty-one salesmen: five at the newspaper office, six at the site, and another twenty answering calls for information.[56] These jobs could be lucrative, especially for aggressive selling agents. Working on commission, salesmen could earn between $75 and $100 a week, or perhaps as much as $300 a week for go-getters as professed in a classified ad seeking sellers for Pell Lake lots. This was enough money to make it worthwhile for the peddlers to follow the newspaper resort trail.[57]

Readers were offered a variety of ways to obtain more information, all of which led to a face-to-face encounter with a pitchman. The ads contained clip-off, mail-in coupons that fed contact information to the eager sales force. At one colony it was claimed that every mail delivery brought a deluge of coupons and that hundreds of people besieged the sales office, leaving the large force "especially trained to take care of the crowds" almost inadequate to handle the many orders.[58]

Potential customers were also urged to call or visit the solicitation office at the newspaper's headquarters, where purchasers selected lots from a map. At Laurel Lake, prospects were lured to the office through a

This map was used by lot salesmen at the *Post*'s Chicago office to enable buyers to select their Pell Lake lots sight unseen. The wavy lines indicate shore line, nearly all of which shown here is actually swamp, a fact that the salesmen probably did not make known to the buyers.

cooperative deal with a local business. Potential buyers were invited to enjoy daily concerts played on the wonderful Orthophonic Victrola provided through the courtesy of Hopkins Piano.[59] The sales offices remained open as late as ten o'clock to allow people to come after work hours.

Another opportunity to learn more about the wonderful subscription offer was to visit the site itself where prospective buyers were met with a swarm of salesmen.[60] Weekend visits were particularly encouraged and people were invited to bring a picnic lunch. At Coon Lake it was reported that a thousand cars were at the resort on a Sunday. Some came on Saturday and camped on the grounds overnight while others arrived at dawn. The rush for choice lots continued far into the night with applications filled out by moonlight and automobile headlights.[61]

* * *

Pricing all the lots the same, one of Bertram Mayo's innovative ideas, was extremely effective in generating speedy purchases. Advertisements stressed that there were no favorites, lots were sold on a first-come-first-served basis, no lots were reserved, and the best lots went to those who bought early. The push to act in haste was reinforced with articles, such as one for Lake Erie Beach, bragging that records were broken when 3,200 lots were sold in the first ten days of the promotion.[62] Here too, resistance was cleverly deflected with the assurance that desirable locations were still available as "many of the choicest locations were overlooked in the rush."[63]

As a general rule the lot price was set at the start of the sales campaign and remained constant throughout. But there was occasional straying from the established pattern of advertising and several rules were broken at Knightstown Lake. During its debut year of 1923, ads for the colony ran continuously from May through early December. After a brief winter break, advertising resumed in February of 1924 with the announcement that lot prices would be raised to $68.50, a $10 increase, beginning May 1. The newspaper justified this change by pointing out that the colony now boasted a swimming pool for children, a golf and country club, a larger clubhouse, and an additional lake.[64] Announcing the price rise several months in advance motived purchasers to take advantage of the offer before the price went up. When the lot price increased in May, ads for the resort shrunk in size and frequency.

In April of 1925, two years after the start of the promotion, another rare promotional step was taken at Knightstown Lake. In an effort to be rid of the remaining lots the *Star* printed an ad announcing a "most attractive cottage" contest. The builder of the best-looking cottage between then and June would be awarded five free lots to be selected by the winner from the remaining unsold lots.[65] The announcement for the contest was the last ad for lots at Knightstown Lake. The *Star* never reported on the results of the cottage building competition. Except for one or two articles about the organization of the POA and its social activities, the paper's involvement with Knightstown Lake was over.

* * *

An expansion to the western part of the country was spearheaded by Arthur Smadbeck in 1927 and 1928. The formula was stretched from the east coast to the west coast with the establishment of Bolinas Beach in Marin County, California, in cooperation with the *San Francisco Bulletin*.

In February of 1927 he acquired a 300-acre dairy farm on a mesa with steep bluffs descending thirty-five feet down to the ocean.[66] The acreage was platted into 5,336 lots in the typical Smadbeck pattern, with the dense lot layout in geometric rows earning it the name "gridded mesa."

Development of Bolinas Beach was handicapped by its difficult to reach location at the southwestern tip of a teardrop shaped peninsula. While only thirteen miles northwest of San Francisco as the crow flies, reaching Bolinas Beach by car in 1927 was complicated. The only practical access from San Francisco was by ferry from the foot of Hyde Street to Sausalito followed by over an hour's drive on mountainous roads. Traveling from Oakland doubled the length of the ferry ride and the driving distance.

Nevertheless, Smadbeck promoted means of access combined with investment profit, claiming that lot purchasers would get a "real estate boost on account of the contemplated bridge across the Golden Gate."[67] Although the Golden Gate Bridge and Highway District Act was passed by the California legislature in 1923, construction on the bridge did not begin for another ten years and the bridge was not open until 1937. A railroad which would have connected Bolinas to the populated areas to the east and to San Francisco was never built.[68]

Bolinas Beach had other troubles including a scarcity of water. Residents of the already established adjacent community of Bolinas considered the newcomers on the gridded mesa as inferior but agreed to share their water source at a price. However, animosity flared up when Smadbeck's manager of the project, a man named Lowenthal, got into an argument with the butcher in Bolinas and threw hamburger in the butcher's face.[69] That ended the water arrangement and began a long saga of water procurement for Bolinas Beach that led to a 1971 moratorium on new water connections, a restriction that persists to this day.

Estacada Lake was a foray into the northwest in cooperation with the *Portland Telegram*. In early 1928 the Smadbecks paid cash for 200 acres fronting both sides of the Clackamas River thirty miles southeast of Portland. Now absorbed by the city of Estacada, the original colony is identifiable by the street names: Lakeshore Drive, Laurel, Juniper, Hawthorn, Dogwood, Larch, Poplar, Fuchsia, Endive, and Dandelion.

* * *

With Skyland near Ruidoso, New Mexico, Arthur Smadbeck created a mountain resort town. Here there was no ocean and no lake, only the Ruidoso River, a slim stream of water at the bottom of a canyon. But swimming and boating could be replaced by gazing at stunningly beautiful mountain views and, with an altitude of 7,000 feet, Skyland offered a cool retreat from the desert heat.

6. The Later Colonies and the Display Ads

In 1928 it took five hours to drive from El Paso through the rugged Sierra Blanca Mountains to Skyland. Alternatively, travelers could get within a mile and a half of the colony by taking a bus called the Pickwick Stage. The lots, available with a subscription to either the *El Paso Herald* or the *El Paso Times*, were described in an advertisement and an accompanying promotional piece in the *Herald* on April 4, 1928.[70]

Rental income and an increase in the value of the lots were not the only means of profiting from the purchase of land. The ads often emphasized that some parcels were set aside for businesses such as grocery and drug stores, confectionaries, refreshments, and other mom-and-pop operations. At Skyland lots were purchased for a tearoom, a lumberyard, an auto service station, and a barbecue sandwich place.[71] A dance hall and skating rink and a shooting gallery were also planned.[72]

From available accounts, Skyland prospered as a colony, partly because, as the ads touted, "cabins can be built on level ground" and also because the land could be purchased outright avoiding the local practice of rental on a ninety-nine-year lease. Another western resort developed by Arthur Smadbeck was Clear Lake Shores in Texas, roughly midway between Houston and Galveston. The island city was platted in March of 1927 and the 2,400 lots were marketed with a subscription to the *Houston Post Dispatch*.

Like Bolinas Beach and Skyland, Clear Lake Shores also encountered access problems, at least temporarily. Weekend visitors from Houston were sometimes made to wait as long as two hours for the ferry ride across Clear Creek. While the transfer took a mere five minutes, the ferryboat could handle only four to six cars at a time. In addition, the approaches to the ferry were in poor condition. Many resorters delayed building cabins waiting for a bridge over Clear Creek to be built.[73] In spite of these initial problems Clear Lake Shores turned out to be one of the most enduring of the newspaper resorts.

* * *

Warren, two years older than Arthur, was the dominant partner of the two-person family real estate business, at least initially. Arthur would come into his own in future years, but while the brothers were in middle age, Warren was the main operator. It was his name that appeared on land transfers and records for the colonies up to and including the creation of Pell Lake. By then the scheme had reached its maturity and, for the most part, the older brother passed the development of newspaper colonies on to his younger sibling.

After Pell Lake was completed Warren was tempted by new challenges, Cuba among them. The Smadbeck family had long had a fascination with Cuba perhaps due to roots in the tobacco business. Louis Smadbeck's father, Jacob, grew tobacco in Connecticut, probably the type that made good wrappers for Cuban cigars,[74] while Henrietta's brother, Joseph Freudenthal, produced Havana cigars at his factory in Sag Harbor, Long Island.[75] Louis traveled to Havana with his wife and daughter in the last year of his life, and Warren Smadbeck vacationed on the island in 1921.[76] Beginning in 1925 Warren was working to construct the Hotel Presidente in Havana, an impressive ten-story steel, stone, and brick structure that opened December 28, 1928.

He also took the newspaper deal in another direction, north to Canada. His first Canadian venture was Plage Laval, near Montreal, Quebec, on the banks of the Mille-Îles River. Here he used the same advertising copy and terms of the deal as at the Smadbeck colonies in the United States. Lots could be secured with a six-month subscription to *La Patrie* and all lots were the same size and the same price. The promised amenities included a waterfront park for residents, dressing rooms for bathers, playgrounds for children, wharves for boats, and a pavilion for dancers as well as tennis courts and a clubhouse.[77]

Plage Laval was followed with another Canadian beach development, Sandy Hook. Eighty kilometers north of Winnipeg on the western shore of the lake with the same name, it was a small development by Smadbeck standards with only 500 lots stretched along a mile of lakefront.

Ads for Sandy Hook began appearing at the beginning of August 1927 and required a one-year subscription to the *Winnipeg Evening Tribune*. The advertisements and the newshead articles applauding the development continued almost daily for a month, ending in early September. Ads resumed in the abbreviated Canadian summer seasons of 1928 and 1929.

There were some differences in the terms of the promotion for Sandy Hook. Lots had an average size of 50' × 150', with, according to the ads, many lots being larger. Presumably many were also smaller. Still, all lots were the same price without regard to location or size. The streets were not named for flowers but a clubhouse was built on the shore of the lake. A maximum of four lots could be purchased but there was no minimum. If anyone bought a lot before visiting the property there was a one-week window to obtain a refund.[78]

Warren Smadbeck had received early coaching on the promotion value to be gained by associating a business development with a benefit for underprivileged children, a lesson he employed at Sandy Hook. In 1893 at age eight, he and his younger siblings were credited with the idea of holding a fair and raising money for the Sick Babies' Fund. The surnames of the other children who participated matched those of Louis Smadbeck's real estate associates and the event was held at the Tecumseh Hotel, one of

6. The Later Colonies and the Display Ads 89

Louis' projects. The name of the hotel and its Sherman Park location were highlighted in the news report, no doubt stemming from a letter submitted to the paper by Louis, with the intent of promoting the sale of lots.[79]

Contemporaneous with the debut of Sandy Hook, Warren Smadbeck scheduled a charity event intended to bring tears to the eyes, buyers to the resort, and money to the pocket. A circus performance for orphaned and poor children of Winnipeg was arranged for Saturday, August 6, just days after the appearance of the first ad for the resort. The *Winnipeg Evening Tribune* printed an article in advance of the affair telling how the New York multimillionaire would be playing summer Santa to the children by hosting the circus spectacle. The impressive event was featured in a follow-up article that dwelled on the delight of the children, giving Sandy Hook a double dose of publicity and exhibiting a rare departure from Smadbeck invisibility.[80]

* * *

The summer of 1928 introduced yet another colony, this one in Sussex County, New Jersey.[81] Sparta Lake sits at an elevation of 1,260 feet in a wild section of the state, surrounded by craggy hills. The resort developer Arthur D. Crane considered the location for resort development in 1926 but rejected the site as too remote and instead opted for the much larger Lake Mohawk. This preserved Sparta Lake for the Smadbecks to create a newspaper colony two years later with the *Paterson Press Guardian*.

The Sparta Lake colony is most notable for the ambitious activity schedule of its Property Owners Association. For five years following the formation of the POA in January of 1929, it carried on a continuum of social events including annual masked balls, plays, card parties, Saturday night socials, Halloween dances, men's' nights, organization of a Rod and Gun Club, dancing parties, water carnivals with performers and entertainers, and boat, sack, and pig races. These nonstop events funded road improvements, construction of a new pavilion, the hiring of a caretaker, installation of a new beach, and other community improvements.

As the decade was coming to a close the *Chicago Evening Post* sponsored a third resort in the Lake Geneva area. This colony was Interlaken, pronounced, as the ads instructed, "INTER-LOCK-EN, meaning 'Between Lakes.'"[82] Smallest of the Walworth County newspaper resorts it was bordered by Silver Lake to the south and Lake Wandawega on the north. Lacking an established name this second lake was known, at various times, as Kinne Lake, Otter Lake, and then Russell Lake after one of the farmers who inhabited the area in the late 1800s.[83] It obtained the name Wandawega in 1925 when developers, subdividing acreage on the northern lake shore, decided that an Indian sounding name had more cachet.

Among the first structures to go up in this large, early development was the Wandawega Hotel which, by the time Interlaken was conceived in 1929, had become a popular place to find jazzy music, illicit alcohol, and a ready supply of girls.[84] In addition to this attraction on the other side of the lake, Interlaken, on the southern shore, offered a handsome colonial-style clubhouse with a drive-up entrance arcade constructed on a promontory between Lake Wandawega and Silver Lake. But with two different bodies of water drawing the cottagers in opposite directions and the land bisected by a county highway, Interlaken failed to achieve a cohesive community atmosphere. Sales of lots were no doubt also affected by the beginning of the Depression five months after Interlaken's opening.

Great Lakes Beach,[85] eighty miles northeast of Detroit on Lake Huron, was also developed at the end of the decade. A 1930 ad proclaimed that the new summer resort was created by the *Detroit Daily* for its readers but there was no talk of purchasing a subscription. The advertising copy, stating, "All you have to do to avail yourself of this offer is to be a reader of The Detroit Daily,"[86] hints that the newspaper collaboration was weakening.

There is one final newspaper colony to be acknowledged here. Woodland Beach, in Anne Arundel County, Maryland, was only four miles from Annapolis and thirty-two miles from Baltimore. Located along a stretch of waterfront on the South River, an arm of Chesapeake Bay, it was sponsored by the *Washington Post*. When promotion began in May of 1931, the initial advertisements specified that lot buyers must "subscribe for a limited period" to the newspaper with no specific subscription terms declared. Even this requirement was omitted in follow-up ads.

This seeming retreat from the requirement to purchase a six-month subscription gives warning of things to come. The Great Depression had begun at the end of 1929 and the developers and the newspapers were adapting their business practices to the changing economic climate. With the closing of the 1920s the ideal conditions for the newspaper deal were dissolving.

7

The Economic Aftermath

The growing financial despair in rural agricultural lands throughout the 1920s, while fueling the Smadbecks' ability to purchase farmland, nevertheless pointed toward the devaluing of real estate in general. The 1926 banking collapse and end of the land bubble in Florida were further indications.[1]

Still, it took some time for the economy to decompose. Even after Black Tuesday, October 29, 1929, economic contraction was not instantaneous—unemployment did not reach its high point until 1933. While the fad for newspaper resorts had been declining and the Smadbecks had already begun retreating from the scheme, there was still one very large last gasp—colonies created in partnership the New York *Daily Mirror* between 1928 and 1932.

Before the alliance with the *Daily Mirror*, the longest, and possibly the most successful, of the newspaper relationships was that with the *Chicago Evening Post* and its consortium of publications. The *Post* papers initiated seven colonies beginning with Mayo's Lakewood resort in 1912, then Lake Michigan Beach, Knightstown Lake, Pell Lake, Lake Louisvilla, and Lake Como Beach, before ending with Interlaken in 1929. In spite of declining economic conditions, the *Mirror* was able to match the *Post* record for number of resorts by becoming a real estate developer itself.

The beginning *Daily Mirror* colonies were on Long Island in Suffolk County. North Shore Beach was placed on Rocky Point where Radio Corporation of America had been using land for a radio transmitting facility before selling 950 acres to Warren and Arthur Smadbeck in April of 1927.[2] The following year the promotion was repeated with Sound Beach located immediately west of North Shore Beach. The association with the newspaper was a happy arrangement and additional resorts followed in short order.

In the late 1920s the Smadbeck brothers had begun buying land in Putnam County, just north of Westchester County where their father had created Sherman Park. The majority of the lakes in this area served as reservoirs to supply water for New York City and the Smadbecks remedied the shortage of lakes by creating new ones. Lake Carmel in the center of the county, was formed by building a dam in swampland along the middle branch of the Croton River. The *Daily Mirror* began offering lots at Lake Carmel in 1930.[3]

Throughout the 1920s the sponsoring newspapers had continued to assert that they were not in the real estate business. This statement was included in ads as late as 1930[4] and was made by the *Daily Mirror* in an ad for North Shore Beach.[5] But that claim was negated when the newspaper formed a spin-off corporation and formally entered into the real estate business. The Mirror Holding Corporation was registered on May 27, 1931, for the purpose of operating a real estate brokerage, developing real estate, and generally carrying on all types of real estate activities,[6] and so the Mayo/Smadbeck subscription premium scheme culminated in a complete merger of real estate and journalism.

It may be viewed as ironic that the alliance achieved its maximum potential just as the ideal conditions for the scheme were fading away. On the other hand, perhaps it was because of the worsening depression that the melding took place. With diminishing advertising earnings, the *Mirror* may have looked to broadening its scope of business operations to increase income.

Four more resort communities were spawned by Mirror Holding in collaboration with the Smadbecks. These included Putnam Lake, along the Connecticut border, created by damming Morlock Brook.[7] The partnership turned west to New Jersey in 1932 and created two lakes and two resorts—Lake Parsippany in Morris County and Upper Greenwood Lake in Passaic County. Yet another Mirror Holding development on eastern Long Island was Montauk Beach, begun in 1931 or 1932. The *Daily Mirror* colonies were founded using the established newspaper resort template with one notable departure—the practice of naming the roads after plants was largely abandoned with some hints of egotism creeping in. There is a Smadbeck Avenue in Lake Carmel and Warren Drives in both Lake Parsippany and Putnam Lake.[8]

Like Great Lakes Beach and Woodland Beach, developed in this same time frame, the *Mirror* colonies backpedaled on the subscription requirement. An ad for Putnam Lake used the indefinite language that buyers must agree to subscribe to the *Daily Mirror*[9] while a Montauk Beach mailer declared that lots could be purchased by assenting to become a reader.[10]

* * *

By 1932 it was apparent that the decline in the economy was forcing an end to the newspaper deal. As laborers earned less money or lost their jobs entirely, summer cottages and newspaper subscriptions were luxuries they could no longer afford. Those most affected by the depressed economy, the working classes, were the very reader base that the newspapers relied on for

7. The Economic Aftermath 93

the real estate sales arrangement. As the papers lost both subscribers and advertisers they began to dissolve, a situation that was not helped by the increasing popularity of radio as a source of news.

The newspaper publishing business has never been reliably sustainable and several of the journals sponsoring resort developments failed even before the Depression began. These included the two earliest papers involved in the promotion: the *Boston Evening Record* ceased publication in 1921 and the *Jewish Daily News* in 1928. The *Buffalo Enquirer* and the *Buffalo Courier* dissolved in 1925 and 1926, respectively. The *San Francisco Bulletin* only operated for a few years, from 1926 to 1929. Not even the Bolinas Beach promotion could save it.

Other newspapers ceased publishing in the early 1930s. The *Chicago Evening Post* fell victim to the Depression in October 1932 and was absorbed by the *Chicago Daily News*. The *Commercial Tribune* of Cincinnati disappeared in 1930, the two El Paso papers in 1931, and the *Houston Post Dispatch* in 1932. The year after the formation of Lake Louisvilla, its two sponsoring papers, the *Louisville Herald* and the *Louisville Post*, were merged into the *Herald-Post*. That paper went into bankruptcy in 1930 and again in 1936 when it closed down. Some newspapers held on. The *Daily Mirror* rode out the Depression and lasted for several more decades causing speculation that perhaps its foray into the world of real estate helped it get through the Depression years.

* * *

Two parties to the equation, the lot customers and the sponsoring papers, were no longer economically capable of sustaining their part in the deal. In contrast, the third element, the developers, chiefly the Smadbecks, capably weathered the financial difficulties.

The brothers were circumspect in both their business dealings and their personal lives. Warren married Madeline Lachenbruch in March of 1911.[11] By 1918 he sported a diamond and platinum solitaire ring[12] and in 1930 the couple had a butler, cook, and houseman.[13] With as many servants as children, their wealth was obvious.

During the 1920s Dr. Smadbeck was a frequent buyer at auctions, investing in sixteenth and seventeenth-century art and furniture. The antique purchasing continued throughout the decade; however, in 1936, Warren began disposing of the vintage Italian and French paintings, manuscripts, furniture, and carpets. The sale of these items was not spurred by the Depression or a need for money but rather by personal circumstances. Warren's wife Madeline died on December 28, 1934.[14] A year later he married Devereaux Fay[15] who had a background as an interior decorator. Within weeks of the marriage the heavy carved and gilded furnishings were auctioned off.[16] The marriage lasted about as long as the furniture had. Devereaux obtained a Reno divorce in July of 1943[17] and Warren went on to marry a third wife, one with Cuban heritage, Violeta Rodriguez.

Except for the succession of spouses, Arthur lived a parallel existence. He married Ruth Shear in 1919[18] and displayed his riches with a seven-passenger Sterns limousine[19] and his boating prowess by winning yacht club regattas.[20] In 1930 he and his wife maintained two children and four servants—a governess, a chambermaid, a butler, and a cook.[21] A cigar smoking, yet impeccable dresser, he was portrayed as donning a fresh shirt with nearly every cigar.[22]

Arthur was a braggart, but not always a factual one. During a 1957 interview[23] he asserted that he headed twenty-two corporations and was involved with a variety of businesses including citrus, cattle, oil, real estate, and hotels. The claim of citrus farming and cattle ranching was based on recent purchases of land in Florida that had been used for those purposes but was already in the process of subdivision.[24]

The interview also credits Arthur with this unbelievable statement about his father: "He lost everything during the depression years and my brother ... and I started from scratch." If Arthur was referring to the 1930s, he was extending Louis Smadbeck's life by twenty years. It would also be inaccurate to assert that his father lost everything in the Panic of 1893. Records show that, throughout the 1890s, Louis continued buying land and selling lots at Sherman Park. At his death in 1911 Louis Smadbeck had a net worth of more than $48,000,[25] well over a million dollars in current money. But Arthur's version better glorified his own accomplishments.

The brothers were active in civic affairs and philanthropy. Governor Alfred E. Smith appointed Warren to the state's first child welfare committee. Arthur served as president of the New York Coliseum beginning with its opening in 1956, and he and his wife Ruth were instrumental in the operations of the Heckscher Foundation for Children.

Both men traveled, with Cuba as a favorite destination for business as well as for pleasure. In addition to the Hotel Presidente they owned additional hotel properties, an apartment, bank accounts, cash, and other funds in Cuba—all of which were seized by the Castro regime in October of 1960. The Smadbecks valued their Cuban losses at $275,000.[26]

In addition to their suburban resort developments, they had dealings in real estate in New York City where they resided throughout their lives, and both men also had summer homes in the Lake Carmel area. Perhaps it was their management acumen that resulted in long lives. Warren lived to age eighty[27] and Arthur topped him by ten years, living to ninety.[28]

* * *

7. The Economic Aftermath

Like their father, Warren and Arthur Smadbeck were inventive and entrepreneurial. That they were also good money managers was evident from the manner in which the finances of the resorts were handled.

When the newspaper resort phenomenon began in earnest at the beginning of the 1920s, the lots were priced at about $50 each with some variances among colonies, probably due to location. Through the decade, prices increased an average of $4.50 per year, reaching $90 at the end of the 1920s and a high of $100 by the time Montauk Beach was developed in the early 1930s.

An easy payment plan was a feature of every promotion. Initial deposits were a modest $8.50 to $12.40 with monthly payments hovering around $3.00. As lot prices increased, the length of time to pay off the purchase price stretched out to as much as 26 months. This installment plan was a popular option as there were no interest charges.

The terms of the subscription and lot purchase were contained in a simple agreement identifying the lot numbers and spelling out the terms of payment. A deed would not be issued until the last payment was made and, if there was any default in payments, the seller could opt to cancel the contract.[29]

The two years or so it took buyers to pay for the plots coincided with the time it took the Smadbecks to buy the land, create the resort, sell most of the lots, help establish the POA, and then exit the scene. At most of the colonies, once the majority of the platted lots had found customers, the leftovers were sold in bulk at a discount or otherwise transferred out of the Smadbeck name, using a variety of methods.

At Bolinas Beach, less than two years after purchasing the land in February of 1927, Arthur Smadbeck sold the remaining lots to San Francisco real estate operator Joseph Jacoby who then advertised them for sale without the newspaper connection.[30] King Lake was slower to wrap up. With about a third of the land still unsold four years after the project was begun, the remaining lots were purchased by Frank Norton, a local abstractor who had been serving as trustee.[31]

Madeline Burdett was sales and managing agent for Skyland, operating out of an adobe house at the resort in the summer and an office at the newspaper's headquarters in El Paso during the winter. When the Skyland lot boom was over, she was asked to sell the surplus plots for whatever she could get. Burdett objected, fearing that lower prices would lessen the value of the lots already sold, to the detriment of those who had paid full price. She teamed up with Stella Campbell and together they bought the lots from Arthur Smadbeck and continued selling them on their own.[32] Pell Lake demonstrates yet another approach—the 1,300 or so lots that remained unsold in 1927 were deeded to Smadbeck employee Matthew Jonap, thus keeping the land within the corporate family but removing it from direct ownership by Warren Smadbeck.

* * *

The information available for Pell Lake demonstrates that the profit realized from a resort development can only be estimated. In 1924 farmland in Walworth County, Wisconsin, was valued at about $100 per acre but a buyer would need to pay more to convince the farmers to sell. Revenue stamps establish that $86,000 was paid to farmers by Ludwig Freudenthal but it is uncertain if this represents all of the land purchased.[33] Assuming that 700 acres were purchased for $86,000, the farmers were paid an average of $122 per acre.

If all of the platted lots were sold at the advertised price of $67.50, gross receipts in excess of $660,000 would have been realized. However, many lots were sold for less. Some lots were not full size and deals were likely made on these small, triangular slices. A few lots, such as those where the clubhouse sat, were given to the POA at no cost and the leftover lots deeded to Jonap were surely disposed of at a discount.

In addition to the cost of acquiring the acreage, there was the considerable expense of improvements: dredging the lake, constructing the dam, and building the clubhouse, dance pavilion, and beach structures. At Times Beach $200,000 was claimed to be invested[34] while an ad for Mastic Park states that $250,000 was being spent on improvements.[35]

There were also professional fees paid to surveyors, engineers, and attorneys, and of course, a hefty amount went toward advertising and sales commissions. Travel expenses, employee salaries, and overhead at the New York office might also be factored in. A return on investment in the range of $200,000 to $250,000 per resort is a reasonable guess. With five newspaper colonies developed in 1924, the Smadbecks likely had profits in excess of a million dollars for that year from newspaper resort development activity alone.

* * *

Selling off the remaining lots, even at a reduced price, proved to be a prudent move when the Depression deepened and land prices dropped precipitously. Baker's Department Store in Buffalo, having secured all the unsold lots at Lake Erie Beach, advertised them for $14.95 in 1932[36] compared with their 1922 price of $57.50. Arthur Smadbeck set the price for lots at Bolinas Beach at $69.50, an amount that real estate promoter Jacoby immediately raised to $79.50 when he took over.[37] By 1933 they were being sold by the insurance commissioner of California for $25 cash "at forced sale by order of the courts."[38] That same year an advertisement for Lake

7. The Economic Aftermath

Sam-O-Set lots, originally costing $77, were offered at "A Great Sacrifice!" for $18.75.[39]

Initially, lots in the Pell Lake Addition were priced at $67.50, the same as the Smadbeck Pell Lake lots, and included free membership in the Pell Lake Golf Club, a promise that went unrealized. The area designated for the golf course still remains a woody gulch. Neither was the Pell Lake Hotel built. By the mid-1930s the price for lots in the Addition was halved.

A poster from the mid-1930s advertises lots in the Pell Lake Addition: three for $100—half their original cost (courtesy Art Oster).

But at one of the Smadbeck colonies the lot price increased during the Depression in an unusual offer. Lots at Mastic Beach on Long Island sold for $89 in 1926. Ten years later ads appeared offering a free bungalow to anyone who subscribed to the *Brooklyn Citizen* for three months and purchased four lots at a cost of $96.50 each.[40] The available lots were most likely those farthest from the shore and the cottage pictured in the ads is quite modest. Still, it was a tempting offer for anyone who still had $400 to spend on a summer home.

Industrious workers who had jobs and some disposable income took advantage of these bargains. They bought lots at the discounted prices and other lots were obtained by contacting the original buyers, many of whom had never visited their still vacant property, and, in hard times, could easily be talked into selling the land for a few dollars.

Tax sales were still another source of summer resort lots at greatly reduced prices. In 1935 forty parcels at Lake Sam-O-Set were the subject of a tax forfeiture.[41] A few months later four of these lots were sold by the local taxing authority for $8.75 each, approximately 10 percent of the original asking price.[42]

Although property taxes were less than a dollar a lot, owners with little income could not afford to pay the tax bill and even lots with cottages on them were abandoned. Initially counties were slow to seek recovery of back taxes at the newspaper resorts because the dollars owed on the tiny lots were insignificant compared with the work involved in pursuing collection. But counties were also in need of cash during the Depression and long lists of delinquent properties began to be published in the 1930s.

The Smadbeck name appears repeatedly in these listings.[43] In some cases buyers failed to make all of the installment payments on the lots and deeds were never issued to them. Other buyers had not bothered to record their deeds, leaving the lots in the developer's name on the tax rolls. In these situations the Smadbecks had been paid for the lots, or had been paid enough, making it more cost efficient to just ignore the tax bill and allow the county to take ownership.

Even when buyers completed the payments and recorded their deeds, they did not always know about the pending tax foreclosure proceedings. The required legal notices were published in small newspapers in the county seat where the resort was located, papers that the owners living in the big city never read. Some developers overextended themselves and, when the Depression hit, were unable to sell the lots at a good price. If they could not afford to keep up with the taxes on the unsold lots, they too, lost the land to the county. At Pell Lake Highlands nearly a quarter of the lots were forfeited to Walworth County for back taxes in 1933.[44]

Many of the Pell Lake lots that the county obtained through tax

7. The Economic Aftermath

foreclosure, as well as some of the lots transferred into Matthew Jonap's name, eventually ended up in the hands of Charles H. Wendell, an Illinois real estate agent. Wendell set up shop in a house on Thistle Drive and began selling lots in July of 1933. A map he published in 1947 has over 1,000 lots marked with Xs, presumably representing those that could be purchased from or through him. These included lots in all of the Smadbeck sections as well as in the Addition, the Highlands, and the Sitterlee subdivisions. Charles Wendell and his wife Adele monopolized the real estate market in Pell Lake for decades.

* * *

The Smadbecks became involved with back taxes at Pell Lake in a different context. In November of 1930 a newspaper reported that thousands of lots in Walworth County were in default. It noted that the assessor particularly singled out the developments sponsored by the *Chicago Evening Post* and denounced the Smadbeck brothers for making enormous profits but refusing to pay state income tax.[45] Walworth County District Attorney Arthur Thorson, running for reelection against an impressive opponent, boasted in a campaign ad that he was "pressing a claim against the Smadbecks and Chicago Evening Post for $50,000 delinquent income taxes" for the benefit of taxpayers.[46]

The action was apparently aimed at recovering Wisconsin income taxes assessed on the profits made in developing Pell Lake, but the unavailability of the court documents leaves the details and outcome unknown. What is obtainable are court records in ancillary proceedings. There Thorson obtained writs of attachment preventing the Smadbecks from disposing of any property they owned in the county to ensure that assets would be available to satisfy a potential judgment for the taxes allegedly owed.[47]

But the New Yorkers were cleverer than the local district attorney. The Smadbecks were adept at land-laundering, that is, transferring ownership of realty from one entity to another, a practice that insulated their assets from just this type of exposure. The tactic was activated in the Pell Lake tax case when Matthew Jonap intervened to assert that he was the owner of the land affected by the attachments. When he produced the deed to the lots given to him by Warren Smadbeck in 1927[48] the writs of attachment were promptly dismissed leaving the tax collector with no means of enforcing a judgment.[49]

In the paperwork Jonap filed with the court, he had no reason to provide information on his employment and he made no effort to do so. His World War II draft registration form listed his employer as Warren and Arthur Smadbeck.[50] In 1937 Jonap transferred the still unsold lots to Gustave Schulze.[51] A New York resident, Schulze is identified as a bookkeeper for a real estate firm in both the 1930 and 1940 censuses.[52] Chances are good that he too was employed by the Smadbecks. In this way the brothers were able to keep land in the business family while still protecting it from satisfying judgments.

* * *

Lakeside resorts for the middle classes had a resurgence of popularity after World War II, again fueled by post war prosperity, but the concept of creating resorts through newspaper subscription offers had been exhausted. Knowing that their real estate endeavors would be more successful if they had a front to disguise the profit motive, the Smadbecks looked for another way to work the deal and tried a tie-in with magazine subscriptions. Lots at Saint Augustine South in Florida were marketed with a subscription to *Florida Speaks*, which billed itself as the national magazine of Florida living,[53] and were later offered to the readers of *Sunrise Magazine of Southern Living*.[54]

But the Smadbecks found an even better instrument of camouflage for their developments when they began pairing with local chambers of commerce, a good choice given the non-profit status of most such groups and their interest in advocating community development. This approach was used in 1952 to develop South Venice on 3,000 acres of land in Sarasota County, Florida. Employing their standard Smadbeck blueprint, the South Venice promotion was aimed at a nationwide audience with ads and reinforcing articles appearing in dozens of upper Midwest city papers. As with the newspaper resorts, many of the lots were purchased sight unseen with all 19,587 lots reportedly sold in two years.[55]

This new version of the deal did not go unchallenged. Noting that the lots were selling like hotcakes and recalling memories of the Florida realty boom days, the Sarasota County Commission conducted a hearing to investigate the arrangement. The commissioners questioned whether the Venice Area Chamber of Commerce was illegally using advertising funds allocated to it by the county or was violating its charter by competing with private businesses. The president of the chamber denied the accusations of wrongdoing and assured the commission that no chamber money was being used in the promotion, that no profits were earned by the chamber, and that the organization only benefited by gaining new residents.[56]

This contractual arrangement with chambers of commerce reconstituted the newspaper alliance of thirty years earlier. A chamber would lend its name and endorsement to the project, news articles would stress that the organization made no profit from lot sales, and, for the most part, the Smadbeck name was kept out of the press. The community was improved by the enhancements that the developer provided—engineering and construction of streets, parks, ponds, and drainage systems. The Smadbecks

7. The Economic Aftermath

guaranteed to spend a minimum amount in advertising the development and the community. Another significant incentive for the chambers of commerce was obtaining, free of cost, a headquarters building when the Smadbecks agreed to buy or build a sales office and deed it to the chamber at the end of the contract period.[57] As with the newspaper deal everyone benefited from the scheme.

While nothing could quite match the uniqueness of the newspaper deal, the brothers had found another inventive way to market real estate. Alliances with chambers of commerce were employed in other Florida developments including Palmetto Point[58] and Avon Park Lakes[59] and, after some fits and starts, Chesapeake Landing[60] with the Chestertown, Maryland, chamber. Other similar alignments were Waynesburg Lakes[61] in Greene County, Pennsylvania, and, amazingly, Knightstown Lake in Indiana.

Begun in 1923 Knightstown Lake quickly ran into trouble. Already by 1927 many lots were on the delinquent tax list.[62] By mid-century, Indiana's Henry County owned more than 1,000 lots acquired through tax forfeitures. The difficult topography of the area had resulted in postage size, irregular lots, some measuring only 20' × 20',[63] a situation that created a costly paperwork nightmare for the county tax collecting agency. Attempts were made to market the lots, and the county even considered replatting them, but by 1961 less than a quarter had been sold. Appraised at $9 per lot, the county decided to auction off the remaining 775 lots for not less than two-thirds the appraised value.

At the auction on July 12, 1961, the only bid was placed by plucky Warren Smadbeck who purchased all the available land for $4,700, the lowest acceptable amount. Without bothering to replat, he proceeded to resell the very same lots he had sold forty years earlier.[64] Then the lots were priced at $58.50, and now, having repurchased them for $6 apiece, Smadbeck sold them for $150 each, marketing them in groups of five.[65]

Although this time around Warren Smadbeck's name appeared in some news reports, the ads proclaimed that the Knightstown Chamber of Commerce was involved in the real estate offer to further community development and bring to the area more people, more industry, and greater prosperity. A press account noted that a new chamber of commerce building had been erected at Knightstown Lake and, while the lot offer was ongoing, the building would also be used as the sales office.[66] Much of the area had reverted back to wilderness but Smadbeck installed new roads and developed a ravine into a recreational area. In less than a year, most of the lots were sold.[67]

Knightstown Lake thus achieved the distinction of being the only development to be profitably marketed by Warren Smadbeck both as a newspaper colony and as a chamber of commerce resort.

8

Hybrids and Clones

While the terms "colony" and "resort" are, for the most part, used interchangeably in this book, "resort" was the prevailing term used in the advertisements. Presumably "resort" came closer to evoking an image of a settlement offering water activities. Regardless, not all newspaper real estate developments fit neatly into the definition of a newspaper colony. Some developments did not have all the necessary characteristics, some were not conditioned on the purchase of a newspaper subscription, some fell outside the relevant time frame, and others, while technically qualifying, were attempted clones of the Smadbeck projects.

Two Massachusetts colonies, Long Lake Beach in Littleton and Lake Sam-O-Set in Leominster, represent hybrids or, perhaps, half-siblings to the Smadbeck newspaper resorts. Neither body of water is very large: Long Pond is less than a square mile in area and Lake Sam-O-Set is a loop of water around a narrow peninsula. Both are located northwest of Boston no more than fifty miles distant.

In 1925 Warren Smadbeck tried purchasing all the land around Long Pond, but was able to acquire only four parcels along the northeasterly shore. He renamed the body of water Long Lake, "Lake" sounding more substantial than "Pond," and built a handsome clubhouse with a columned wrap-around porch supported by a high foundation made of New England stones.

The Lake Sam-O-Set property has an unusual background for a Smadbeck development. It is true that peaches grew here but they were more a conceit by the wealthy landowner than a cash crop. The land was owned by a Leominster insurance man until Francis A. Whitney purchased it in 1894. Whitney owned many patents and a shirt making company as well as other businesses, but his most lucrative occupation was as owner of the F.A. Whitney Carriage Company, a manufacturer of beautiful, and expensive, baby carriages made with elaborate wicker designs and charming umbrellas to shade infant faces.

The 150-acre site Francis Whitney acquired suited his love of nature. There was a large brook running through the land and several springs

8. Hybrids and Clones

providing a perfect place to build a dam and create a lake. Whitney had the financial resources to see that the dam was solidly built of mud and rocks and fortified with granite boulders. He stocked the lake with fish and introduced wildlife to the area. Bathhouses were built in addition to a nine-room weekend home and a cow and horse barn, all set on grounds maintained by two caretakers.[1]

Following Whitney's death in 1922 the tract passed through several hands until it was acquired by Warren Smadbeck in October of 1925. With a sturdy dam forming a manmade lake surrounded by undeveloped but nicely tended rural property, Smadbeck acquired a landscape far lovelier than the swamp surrounded Pells Lake. Ownership of Lake Sam-O-Set itself permitted Smadbeck to promote the site with exclusive access to the lake for fishing, swimming, and boating, as well as private use of the surrounding parkland.

The developments at Long Lake Beach and Lake Sam-O-Set had all the usual features: clubhouse, bathhouses, docks, a beach, parkland, a surrounding road named Lake Shore Drive, and flower and plant names for the side roads. Lot ownership included free lifetime membership in the clubhouse and exclusive rights to use the beach. Both colonies had all the elements of the newspaper deal except for the prerequisite of purchasing a subscription.

The *Boston Post* carried ads for the colonies but images of those ads are not obtainable except for a reconstruction of part of the text from an advertisement for Long Lake Beach printed in a history of the area. There the language used is "The Opportunity of a Lifetime Presented exclusively to readers of The Boston Post."[2]

Ads for Lake Sam-O-Set appeared in the *Fitchburg Sentinel* beginning in July of 1926. For the most part these were characteristically wordy Smadbeck advertisements, offering an installment payment plan, a clip-off coupon, and photos of the lovely forested lake captioned "For many years Lake Sam-O-Set was the private estate of a millionaire, and the public never even saw its beauties."[3] Headlines promoted Lake Sam-O-Set as the greatest summer resort development ever offered to the people of Fitchburg and linked it to Long Lake Beach with a testimonial from the Publicity Director of the *Boston Post* saying that Sam-O-Set was expected to repeat the success of Long Lake.[4]

Neither the paraphrased ad for Long Lake, nor the *Fitchburg Sentinel* ads for Lake Sam-O-Set make mention of the need to subscribe to the *Boston Post* or any other newspaper as a prerequisite to purchasing a lot. Apparently these two colonies lacked a sponsoring newspaper and are thereby seemingly eliminated from the definition of a newspaper colony.

* * *

While Long Lake Beach and Sam-O-Set were resorts without a newspaper affiliation, Lakewood had newspaper affiliations without being a resort. This Lakewood was quite different from the Lakewood developed by Bertram Mayo in the wilderness surrounding Fox Lake in Michigan. Here, the land was part of the already established municipality of Lakewood Township, Ocean County, New Jersey.

The Smadbecks promoted their Lakewood lots with both that name and the name Lakewood Pines, varying it for the readers of no less than three different newspapers. Ads first appeared with an overture to the Jewish community. Having successfully promoted Asbury Park Estates with the *Jewish Daily News*, the Smadbecks again teamed up with that newspaper to sell Lakewood lots in February of 1919 with advertisements in both Yiddish and English.[5] Two years later Jews in Philadelphia were presented with the lot offer through the *Philadelphia Jewish Morning Journal*,[6] a second newspaper used to sell Lakewood lots.

Subscriptions to *The Chief* offered the opportunity to buy lots at Lakewood Pines to a different group of readers. *The Chief* was, and still is, a long established, privately owned newspaper focused on civil service and government employees. Beginning in 1921 it promoted lots at Lakewood Pines to employees of Jersey City and Hudson County[7] and to government workers living in Brooklyn.[8]

The ads do not list the precise location of either Smadbecks' Lakewood or Lakewood Pines. Hints are contained in ads for Lakewood—a six-minute walk from Lake Carasaljo in the Cedar Bridge Avenue section of Lakewood, and for Lakewood Pines—facing River Avenue. This was likely one tract of land marketed over a period of years with subscriptions to several publications.

Lakewood Township encompassed a string of three lakes, Lake Carasaljo, Lake Manetta, and Lake Shenandoah, all created by damming up the Metedeconk River in the eighteenth and nineteenth centuries. But the Smadbecks could not offer either immediate or private access to these bodies of water. So the ads for Lakewood stressed a locality with prominent business streets, stores, schools, synagogues, a public library, motion picture theaters, and a large hotel. Here was an opportunity for investors, home builders, storekeepers, and boardinghouse operators. The word "resort" was avoided, instead deeming it a "vacation colony" with free membership in a clubhouse and emphasis on companionship, a brotherly hand, and good fellowship.[9]

Variances in the name of the colony and in the audience targeted were matched with an inconsistency of price and terms. Most of the ads listed all lots at the same price—$47.50. Other ads indicated that some lots at the Pines were $50. A few advertised that a subscription must be purchased while others said that the price included a subscription to *The Chief*.

8. Hybrids and Clones

Without private or immediate access to a waterfront these Lakewood communities fall short of full qualification as newspaper resorts in spite of being sold in conjunction with a subscription to a newspaper.

* * *

When the economy began declining at the end of 1929, the brothers owned considerable parcels of still undeveloped real estate. In spite of the economic times, they went ahead and turned some of this land into resorts, similar to what they did in Putnam County with the *Mirror* colonies, the last of the Smadbeck newspaper resorts. Nevertheless, the brothers continued developing waterfront property throughout the 1940s and 1950s— they just did it without the newspaper subscription tie-in. All of the resorts known to have been created by the Smadbecks after 1932 lacked alliance with a newspaper. Iron Mountain Lake is a prime example.

The area around Iron Mountain in the Ozarks had been a significant mining center in the mid-nineteenth century. The lake was created to serve as part of a hydraulic pumping system used in the early mining of iron ore from Iron Mountain, and the Iron Mountain Railway, built to transport the ore, served the area. After World War I iron mining became unprofitable and the land passed from owner to owner until Warren Smadbeck purchased it in 1926 or 1927.[10]

Located only eighty miles from Saint Louis and served by a rail line, the 1,200 acres, encompassing a private man-made lake, had all the features of an ideal spot for a newspaper colony. As promising as the location was, Iron Mountain Lake was a victim of bad timing. Either the Smadbecks had too many other projects demanding their attention in the late 1920s or they were unable to align with an appropriate newspaper.

Having missed the opportunity to develop the site as a newspaper resort, the land sat idle until 1939 when Warren Smadbeck finally set to work on it. The project had most of the earmarks of the earlier ones with the same small lots all priced at $89 and the roads and parkland destined to be deeded to a POA for use by the residents. Absent only were newspaper sponsorship and the promise of a clubhouse.[11]

But Iron Mountain Lake never really got its footing and the outbreak of World War II did not help. By 1943 the lots were being sold as "little estates," a quarter-acre (five lots) for $150, the equivalent of $30 a lot.[12] The POA was not formed until 1954[13] and was administratively dissolved in 1989. About that time, Iron Mountain Lake incorporated as a city only to file for bankruptcy protection in 2003 in an effort to reorganize its debts.[14]

Fire Island Pines was another delayed project. Fire Island, the outer bank off the southern edge of Long Island, is a narrow strip of dunes about thirty miles long. Home Guardian purchased 200 acres there, pretty much in the center of the barrier island, in 1924. This piece of land, between Great South Bay and the Atlantic Ocean, was a little more than one mile long and about a quarter of a mile wide.

There was no rail service, the sandy topography prevented roadways and automobiles, and the site was not within convenient reach by ferry. Because these conditions made the parcel more challenging to develop as a newspaper colony compared with other locations, the investment languished throughout the Depression years and World War II. One source claims that during this time Home Guardian sold the property and then regained it in a mortgage foreclosure. Squatters, unconcerned about modesty in their dress, arrived in the 1940s and lived on the beach in tents and makeshift huts. Nudists, gays, and lesbians followed.

Finally in 1949 Warren Smadbeck persuaded the ferry company in Sayville to run ferry service from that point on Long Island to what was to become Fire Island Pines. The ferry was essential to transport the equipment and supplies so that Smadbeck could dredge out a harbor basin to accommodate more than 70 berths for boats, construct a real estate office, attract business enterprises, and build boardwalks for easier navigation across the sand.[15] It was also vital for potential customers to reach the Pines. The lots were fewer and larger than at the newspaper resorts—they numbered only 122 and measured a generous 60' × 100' with a minimum purchase of three lots.[16] Fire Island Pines was promoted as a getaway for the family, a place loved by children. But attempts to outlaw bikinis and exhibitionism eventually gave way to acceptance of varied lifestyles.[17]

The Smadbecks continued to have connections with Fire Island Pines. In 1960 Home Guardian planned a 100-unit cooperative apartment project,[18] Warren Smadbeck's son-in-law, Theodore Taussig, sold real estate there in 1959,[19] and his daughter was still living at the Pines in 1993.[20]

Iron Mountain Lake and Fire Island Pines were both potential newspaper resorts but neither met the time frame standard. The Iron Mountain site was suitable for the task but was handicapped by delay. Fire Island was never compatible with the newspaper colony concept and, by being shelved for nearly 30 years, was more appropriately developed into an exclusive enclave.

* * *

There were also newspaper resorts that were blatant clones—resort colonies marketing lots as newspaper subscription premiums and resembling the Smadbeck developments in many ways, but organized by someone else. Lots were laid out in the same standard grid and the ads were similar in appearance and content to those of the Smadbecks. The marketing approach also mimicked the Smadbeck pattern of large, frequent ads with corresponding feature articles. But the Smadbeck formula was so rigid that variations in marketing strategy employed by these clones set them apart. Two such projects were initiated in 1927 in New Jersey and Indiana.

Sea Isle Estates offered a six-month subscription to Wilmington, Delaware's *Sunday Star* and a summer homesite for $58.80. This price was considerably lower than the Smadbeck lots at the time, but then Sea Isle offered no clubhouse and had no beach of its own. Rather, it was promoted as being in the heart of the beach region of Cape May County, New Jersey. Ads displayed photos of happy swimmers at Ocean Beach, twelve miles distant.[21]

It was a clever clone, one that copied much from the Smadbeck ads. The initial advertisement was a two-page spread with the banner headline "greatest subscription offer ever made." It stressed that the paper was not in the real estate business, made no profit, and only sought to serve its readers by providing them with this extraordinary opportunity. There was an installment payment plan and the ostensible limit of four lots was imposed. The ads did not indicate that all lots were the same price but did say that no partiality would be shown or reservations accepted—first come, first served.

Sea Isle differed from the usual Smadbeck formula in its pricing terms. The purchase price bought both a lot and a subscription to the paper, heirs would receive a free deed if the buyer died before final payment was made, and, after a summer full of ads, came a warning to buy now because the price is about to increase by $10.[22] The free deed assurance was never used by the Smadbecks, Lakewood Pines is the rare example of a Smadbeck resort that coupled the cost of the newspaper with the cost of the lot, and Knightstown Lake is one of the few Smadbeck promotions that used the threat of a price rise to stimulate rapid sale of the remaining plots.

As the Sea Isle Estates promotion progressed, the advertising formula strayed more and more from the Smadbeck template. The size of the lots, 20' × 100', appeared in some ads and the price was framed as a daily cost of 16⅓ cents. The promotional material described Carroll W. Griffith as one of Wilmington's foremost realtors and head of the committee that chose the site. In reality Griffith was the owner of the land and developer of the resort. He had developed other housing projects before attempting the Sea Isle arrangement but his newspaper resort career ended in September of 1931 when he took his own life.[23] A collateral sale was held in March of 1932 to satisfy outstanding mortgages on Sea Isle Estates.[24]

At the same time that Griffith was promoting his newspaper resort on the east coast, resorts were being developed on the northeast shore of Hudson Lake in the northern Indiana county of LaPorte. The lots were marketed under two different names, Sentinel Beach and Hudson Lake Beach, with subscriptions to two different Chicago newspapers, *The Sentinel* and the *Southtown Economist*.

Sentinel Beach came first when sales were inaugurated on May 13, 1927. *The Sentinel* was an English language paper that billed itself as the leading American Jewish weekly and largely appealed to immigrant Jews. Its publisher, Louis S. Berlin, announced in early May that he had purchased 500 acres on Hudson Lake and had plans to subdivide the property into summer homesites and to dedicate free use of a clubhouse to the property owners.[25] The beginning advertisement consumed a showy two pages and was accompanied by a lengthy article in the same issue.[26]

Ads and articles promoting Sentinel Beach continued in nearly every issue of the paper but the promotion was short-lived—less than two months. The ads quickly became equivocal on the need to subscribe to the paper and then advertising terminated all together just before the promotion for Hudson Lake Beach began on July 8, 1927. On that date the *Southtown Economist*, a weekly south side Chicago community paper, began marketing lots at the resort. The clubhouse depicted in the ads was the same one shown for Sentinel Beach. The two colonies also shared the lake front with its beaches, piers, and bathhouses. George Illges, manager of the *Economist*'s subscription department, led in promoting the Hudson Lake venture and perhaps Sentinel Beach as well since the plat for the entire area, including both beaches, bears his name as owner of the tract.[27]

The Smadbacks did something similar when they promoted one colony, Laurel Lake, and then abruptly abandoned it to begin anew with its ill-fated neighbor Beach Club Lake. The Sentinel Beach and Hudson Lake Beach arrangement was also somewhat akin to how the Smadbecks handled Lakewood and Lakewood Pines, selling lots in the same tract through two different publications. But the Lakewood and Lakewood Pines promotions were several years apart while Illges was selling his land back-to-back with two separate newspapers.

In addition to providing a clubhouse and exclusive use of the beach facilities, Hudson Lake Beach and Sentinel Beach mimicked the Smadbeck developments in other ways. The lots were the same size, some streets had botanical names, there were highway arrows pointing the way, and POAs were formed to take over ownership of community property. But again, there were stark differences in promotional methods.

The Smadbecks were charging $69.50 for lots at Bolinas Beach in California, Clear Lake Shores in Texas, and Carver Beach in Minnesota, all developed in 1927. While the lots at Griffith's Sea Isle Estates, at $58.50, were cheaper than those at the Smadbeck resorts, Illges priced his lots considerably higher. The lots at Hudson Lake Beach were $88.00 although

8. Hybrids and Clones

purchasers would have saved 50 cents if they had bought lots at Sentinel Beach for $87.50.

A second deviation was the advertising emphasis on "free" offers such as one headlined "Free Lots! at Hudson Lake Beach." The word "Free" stood out with exaggerated size type in white lettering on a black background. The fine print under the heading "Here is our Whole Proposition" explained that the free lot required, in addition to subscribing to the paper, the purchase of two other lots at $88.00 each, resulting in an average cost of $58.66 per lot and almost exactly matching the cost of lots at Sea Isle Estates. The offer was limited to twelve days, and the free lots were those farthest from the lake.[28] "Free" also headlined another ad saying that the paper was handing over to lot buyers on a platter a free, magnificent clubhouse. There were also free waterfront rights, free beaches, free piers, free bathhouses, free graded roads, and free auto road maps.[29]

The use of newsheads was modified by presenting them in a concentrated manner. The *Southtown Economist* spotlighted Hudson Lake Beach by printing a splash of advertorials, seven on one page, with a banner headline proclaiming "SUCCESS OF SUBSCRIPTION OFFER SENSATIONAL!" Each article emphasized a different aspect of the promotion. Phrased to encapsulate content in the headlines, the articles were titled "10,000 South Siders Visit Hudson Lake This Past Month," "Hudson Lake Noted for Good Fishing," "Hudson Lake Lot Buyers Are Enthusiastic," "South Shore Makes Resort in 1 3-4 Hours" (referring to a trip on the South Shore electric rail line to the resort in one hour and forty-five minutes), and "Southsiders Flock to Hudson Lake Beach; Unusual Summer Colony." The article headed "Famous Casino a Delight to Dance Lovers" called attention to the preexisting casino located at the far eastern end of the lake with a dance palace capable of accommodating one thousand persons dancing to teasing, toe-tapping rhythms played by famous New York and Chicago orchestras. While close to Hudson Lake Beach, the casino was not so close as to infringe on relaxation and quiet. Yet another article, "Historical Background Filled with Romance," told of Pottawatomie Indian villages, a post established by the Great Western Stage Coach line, land grants signed by President Andrew Jackson, and how the original settlers persistently and flatly refused to sell their land to shrewd real estate men trying to purchase this extremely valuable lakeshore frontage and capitulated only when the *Southtown Economist* arranged this offer for its readers. Pictures were titled "Nature's Own Garden Spot" and "Scenes at the Site of the Hudson Lake Summer Colony."[30] All this was in addition to a full-page ad on the succeeding page and a front-page article proclaiming that the demand for lots made it necessary to open yet another section.

The copious use of endorsements was another distinction. Warren

Smadbeck confined outside recommendations to the Lake Sam-O-Set ad providing congratulations from the *Boston Post* publicity director, while the promoters of Sentinel Beach and Hudson Lake Beach made liberal use of testimonials from purported lot buyers.

A full-page ad in the May 27 issue of *The Sentinel* was preceded by an overly large reproduction of a letter on the letterhead of the Chicago City Collector's Office praising Sentinel Beach and signed by Morris Eller, City Collector.[31] In four sentences, filled with grammatical and typographical errors, Eller praised the property and the ten Sentinel Beach lots that he purchased.

Morris Eller had a colorful background as a Prohibition era political boss of questionable repute. He began working in real estate but soon shifted to politics and became "one of the reigning political bosses of the impetuous prohibition era in Chicago." A year before writing the laudatory letter used in the Sentinel Beach advertising campaign, there was a bombing at Eller's home attributed to political strife and he was accused of ordering jailers to show every courtesy to incarcerated beer barons because they were election vote getters. In 1928 he was acquitted of criminal charges ranging from the protection of gambling and prostitution to conspiracy to commit murder.[32] During his lifetime *The Sentinel* printed flattering articles about him and supported his political campaigns. But when *The Sentinel* published a history of Jews in Chicago five years after Eller's death, only one sentence was devoted to him: "During the roaring twenties, another East-European Jew, Morris Eller, was high in the councils of the Republican party, because he could deliver the votes, and never mind how."[33] Whether promises were made or property transferred to Eller in return for his endorsement of Sentinel Beach can only be speculated on.

Advertisements and articles in the *Southtown Economist* for Hudson Lake Beach were also rife with quotes from buyers attesting to the value of the lots. The advertorial titled "Hudson Lake Lot Buyers are Enthusiastic" bears the subhead "Testimonial Stories" and quotes three men. John Paurch said he owned three lots and hoped to buy more, Fred Belfuss was on his way to the office to buy lots, and James Besset said he bought lots that morning. All three praised the value of the land and found the lot offer to be a great buy for the money. Belfuss was glad the newspaper got hold of this property instead of a bunch of real estate men. However, the claims of these three endorsers raise questions. None of their names appear in the deed index at the LaPorte County Recorder's Office.

Claims of gains made on the resale of lots also deserve scrutinizing. An August 30, 1927, ad in the *Economist* quoted three buyers telling the stories of their experiences with amazing resale profits. Records at the LaPorte County Recorder's Office provide deed dates indicating when

8. Hybrids and Clones   111

ownership was transferred but do not reveal the purchase price. A review of these records indicates that none of the statements made in the ad were entirely accurate and that some were blatantly false.

Morris Williams commented that Hudson Lake Beach lots were a wonderful value, claiming to have purchased eleven lots at $88 and to selling them a month later at $300 each. Williams did buy eleven lots but they were not deeded to him until November 13, 1927, and January 19, 1928, most likely the dates when he finished paying for them. Thus, he could not, and in fact did not, sell the lots prior to August 30, 1927. They were sold a few at a time between November 1928 and August 1929.

George Brinkman's story was also probably untrue. He said that his lots were bought from someone who had purchased them at the original price. He claimed to have paid $300 per lot but felt that he still only paid a small portion of their actual value. Deeds for six lots were issued to Brinkman on November 30, 1927, not by an individual owner but rather by the bank acting as the trustee for the newspaper.[34] Brinkman obtained the lots during the promotion and the deed was issued by the trustee, strongly suggesting that he purchased the lots from the newspaper at the $88 offered price and not at an inflated figure.

In a third testimonial Catherine Gustavus claimed a profit of $458 in one week by reselling her lots for $200 each. No record of the purchase or sale of any lots at Hudson Lake Beach by Gustavus appears in the deed index at the LaPorte County Recorder's Office. Curiously her name shows up in the county index as the person who filed a subdivision declaration for Southtown Beach on Fish Lake, another newspaper resort marketed through the *Southtown Economist* a decade later.[35]

Located fifteen miles south of Hudson Lake, and likewise in LaPorte County, Fish Lake, is actually two lakes—Upper Fish Lake and Lower Fish Lake. In the 1880s Swift & Co., the big Chicago meatpacking concern, obtained the land surrounding both lakes and constructed three ice houses and a boardinghouse for workers. During the winter months Swift would transport several hundred men from Chicago to Fish Lake to cut the ice into blocks and store it until it was needed in the summer months at their meatpacking facility.[36] By 1899 Swift was shipping 18 carloads of ice from Fish Lake to Chicago every day.[37]

When the supply of ice diminished Swift began to collect swamp muck and send it by the train load to Chicago for the manufacture of fertilizer.[38] Eventually refrigeration became available and the ice, and apparently also the muck, was no longer needed. Swift continued to use the Fish Lake site as a summer recreational camp for its female employees,[39] initiating a reimagined use for the land around the lake—a seasonal resort area for Chicagoans. In 1938 a portion of the northwestern shore of the lower lake became Southtown Beach, a second newspaper colony for the *Southtown Economist*.[40] It could be argued that Southtown Beach was the final newspaper colony, and, as with the last of the Smadbeck developments, only lip service was paid to the subscription purchase requirement. Lots continued to be marketed through the *Economist* until the beginning of World War II with the last of the lots auctioned off in 1947.[41]

* * *

A 1928 promotion in the *Paterson Evening News* in Paterson, New Jersey, reveals yet another Smadbeck clone, this one selling lots around two lakes, Walton Lake and Round Island Lake, with a subscription to the paper. These two rather small lakes with only a few hundred yards between them at their closest points are actually across the state line in New York, but only thirty-three miles from the center of Paterson, where the development was marketed. The offer featured a banner headline above the front-page title of the *Evening News*: "The Greatest Offer Ever Made by Any Paterson Newspaper to Its Readers Appears on Pages 4 and 5 of Tonight's Issue—Read it—Then Act," referring to the two-page advertisement inside the paper. There was also an article about the colony on the front page.[42]

Aside from the price of $99.50 per lot, the ads for Walton Lake and Round Island Lake strongly resembled those for the Smadbeck colonies, except for one very glaring difference. The ads prominently identified the developer to be Lake Region Home Sites Company and its principals, president Philip C. Wadsworth and real estate expert Frank Stead. Some of the ads even listed the figure of $120,000 as the amount of invested capital. No attempt was made to pretend that the newspaper was promoting sale of the lots on its own, that there were no developers involved, or that no profit was being made.

Wadsworth was a local lawyer and his legal thinking resulted in the insertion of an interesting condition in the contractual relationship. He promised that, along with a deed, the seller would issue a lease to the buyer with a yearly rental rate of $1 for use of the lakeshore in common with the other purchasers. Wadsworth thus insured a source of future funding to maintain the shared property. The failure of the Smadbecks to bother with such a concern was a major flaw in the newspaper deal, one that continues to haunt many of the newspaper colonies.

But Wadsworth allowed his legal background to get in the way of promoting real estate when he listed, in the body of advertisements, restrictions affecting the lots. These covenants, such as what type of building could be erected, the minimum it must cost, and the necessary distance it must be set back from the lot line, would have been more suitably raised after a decision to purchase had been made. Nor did it help to refer to the

8. Hybrids and Clones 113

seller in the ad as the "the party of the first part" and to the buyer as "the party of the second part."[43] Wadsworth did not seem to appreciate that cluttering the advertisement with such legal specifics detracted from selling the dream of owning a cottage at a lake. Perhaps he would have been a better real estate promoter if he had been a dentist rather than an attorney.

The subscription promotion for Walton Lake and Round Island Lake began on August 30, 1928, rather late in the season to begin selling summer lots especially since the Smadbeck colony of Sparta Lake had debuted with a different Paterson newspaper earlier that summer. Wadsworth continued the promotion the following year by opening a new section of lots with the higher price of $130 per lot, a cost that included a subscription to the *Paterson Evening News*.[44] Either the location of these lots was more desirable or the earlier lots had sold well enough to justify the substantially higher price.

In spite of the seeming saturation of the area, both Smadbecks' Sparta Lake and Wadsworth's Walton Lake and Round Island Lake appeared to have met with success. This part of the state was ripe for resorts of this type and the Smadbecks would go on to develop Lake Parsippany and Upper Greenwood Lake in the same region of northern New Jersey in coming years.

* * *

Some less effective clones offered a watered-down version of the newspaper deal. Lakewood Gardens and Cedarwood Park, both in Brick Township, Ocean County, New Jersey, provide examples. The two communities are less than four miles apart on opposite sides of the Metedeconk River and their location is significant with respect to other newspaper resorts. About five miles to the west is Lakewood where the Smadbecks marketed lots as both Lakewood and Lakewood Pines, and eight miles south on the Garden State Parkway is the exit for Mayo's Beachwood. This confluence of developments indicates that this was another fertile area of New Jersey for land speculation in the early decades of the century.

A display ad from November of 1924 describes Lakewood Gardens as "The Beautiful Suburb of 'Lakewood, The Fastest Growing Resort in the World'" and offers "a bungalow or camp lot 25x100 feet, more or less" for $49.80, only ten cents per day, with a three-month subscription to the *Hudson Dispatch*, a Union City, Hudson County, newspaper. Bathing in the Atlantic Ocean was available at Point Pleasant, a fifteen-minute bus ride away and it was noted that Lakewood Gardens was only a short distance from the estate of John D. Rockefeller.[45] The *Hudson Dispatch* advertised Cedarwood Park two years later with a lot price of $59.80 (twelve cents per day). Ads for Cedarwood promoted healthy, happy surroundings in an environment of balsam pines away from the noise and turmoil of the city.[46]

These earlier ads for Lakewood Gardens and Cedarwood Park contained no mention of a clubhouse, beaches, or parklands. Some historical accounts assert that only the first lot could be purchased for the advertised price while the cost of a second lot made the total outlay for a buildable plot comparable to other developments in the area,[47] a tactic that was more akin to the promotion for Orienta Park than to that of the newspaper resorts.

However, the advertisements are not clear in this regard. Initially the ads did not explicitly state that all lots were the same price but did specify that several lots could be purchased with the equivalent number of subscriptions, implying that additional lots could be had under the same terms. Later ads, speaking in terms of "a" lot or "this" lot, were more ambiguous but promised equal rights to the riverfront beach and free life membership in the clubhouse.[48] The *Hudson Dispatch* was still selling lots at Cedarwood Park in 1930, with no mention of either a subscription or a price.[49]

There does not appear to have been any organized effort to create owner associations at Lakewood Gardens or Cedarwood Park for management of shared property, and especially not for the roads, such as they were. In 1931 a group of Cedarwood Park residents petitioned the township to open roads and lay sidewalks and curbs. The petition was denied since the area was a private development and it was felt that streets should be created in the same manner.[50] A delegation of property owners tried again a year later telling the township council that they were given the impression by the owners of the development that roads would be built.[51] On a third try in 1933 the township finally agreed to adopt the streets in Cedarwood Park.[52]

No evidence could be found to link the Smadbecks to either Lakewood or Cedarwood Park. The *Hudson Dispatch* was the only developer identified in the ads which proclaimed that the newspaper was not in the real estate business and merely wanted to add a host of new subscribers to its list of readers.

* * *

Hybrid and clone colonies highlight a dilemma. Their existence demonstrates the difficulty of defining "newspaper colonies of the 1920s." An attempt is made in the introduction of this book to delineate a newspaper colony as a real estate development that imposed the purchase of a newspaper subscription as a prerequisite to buying a lot. But what seems like a necessary element, the purchase of a newspaper subscription, may not have been essential.

It seems unfair to exclude such places as Smadbecks' Long Lake Beach and Sam-O-Set in Massachusetts which were newspaper colonies in every way except for an affiliation with a newspaper. And what of the later colonies where the requirement to buy a subscription was softened or abandoned all together? Was Woodland Beach a newspaper colony when a lot purchase was conditioned on subscribing only to lose its standing when the subscription obligation was no longer being enforced? Access to a body of water should not be an unequivocal requirement either. Most of the colonies were immediately adjacent to the ocean, a lake, or a river but to exclude those a few miles distant imposes an arbitrary distinction.

Specifying a particular decade in the definition of a newspaper colony appears to be a reasonable qualifier since the scheme was at its height during the 1920s. But this specification is also liquid. Mayo's colonies of Lakewood and Beachwood are prime examples of the newspaper resort—the forebears of all the others—and they came into being in the years preceding the 1920s. There are also resorts, notably several of the *Mirror* developments, that were created in the early 1930s. These are the ultimate newspaper colonies representing the melding of journalism and real estate. For purposes of trying to settle on a clear definition, the designation "the 1920s" is more aptly applied to the circumstances and style of a resort's creation than to the exact date of its establishment.

There is a temptation to confine the newspaper colonies of the 1920s to those created by the Warren and Arthur Smadbeck who clearly dominated the market. But exclusion of clone colonies developed by others having all of the primary features is unwarranted. Sentinel Beach and Hudson Lake Beach were newspaper colonies of the 1920s just as much as those created by the Smadbecks. Perhaps a defining element should be the premise that a resort was created by a newspaper with no mention of the developer. Here too, nothing is black and white. Crystal Lakes began with sponsoring newspapers, but evolved into a project advertised with Arthur Smadbeck as the promoter.

There are many other factors that are common to nearly all of the colonies—convenient access to major metropolitan area, lots sized at 20' × 100', all lots the same price, payment available on an installment plan, and a zealous advertising campaign—none of which are exclusive to the newspaper communities. Free use of a community clubhouse, shared parkland, and property owner associations, while less common, were not unknown.

Ultimately the phrase "newspaper colonies of the 1920s" remains elastic, stretching here and there to include this colony or that.

9

William Randolph Hearst

There is one remaining clone, or almost clone, that requires discussion. Herald Harbor stands out among the field of newspaper resort imitators for a number of reasons. It was one of the earliest of the Smadbeck clones—Southtown Beach was developed in 1938, Walton Lake and Round Island Lake in 1928, Sea Isle Estates, Hudson Lake Beach and Sentinel Beach in 1927, Cedarwood Park in 1926, and Lakewood Gardens in 1924. The birth of Herald Harbor was announced on May 25, 1924, just as Pell Lake was about to be created and right at the peak of the Smadbecks' success with the newspaper colony scheme.

Herald Harbor also had the shortest life as a newspaper colony. The plan to sell the lots as a newspaper subscription premium was renounced on June 12, 1924, just eighteen days after its premiere. The person responsible for changing the course of Herald Harbor was the invincible William Randolph Hearst.

* * *

The presence of William Randolph Hearst cannot be overlooked in any consideration of journalism at the beginning of the twentieth century. His political aspirations and his journalistic practices made him a well-known figure of the time, someone who was both admired and despised. Given his broad ownership of newspapers and his prominence in news publishing, it was inevitable that Hearst would come into contact with the newspaper deal, and he did so, but in an unexpected manner.

The way in which Hearst conducted his business operations was entirely consistent with the newspaper colony idea beginning with the targeted customers. The gossipy Hearst newspapers focused on sensationalism in a deliberate attempt to appeal to the middle and lower classes,[1] the same readers most likely to buy into the subscription offer.

The core element of the promotion, offering the purchase of a lot as a premium for buying a subscription, was effective in increasing circulation and Hearst was tenacious in the use of all manner of circulation-building mechanisms. In addition to an unceasing use of premiums,[2] he also used prizes, puzzles,[3] and voting contests. Competitions that awarded votes for signing up new subscribers became so popular that companies specialized in organizing these contests for newspapers. In the spring of 1915, just as the investigation of the *New York Tribune*'s Beachwood promotion was getting underway on behalf of Hearst's *American*, a different Hearst newspaper, the *Los Angeles Examiner*, engaged the services of the Myers Circulation Company to conduct a contest with 143 various prizes valued at $56,000, including automobiles, pianos, gold watches, and notably, building lots.[4]

Hearst's aggression in seeking to increase circulation was so extreme that his newspapers were involved in the bloodiest confrontations of the circulation wars. These battles involved sabotaged delivery routes, commandeered newsstands, and murdered carriers with Hearst circulators often named as the instigators.[5] Hearst placed few limits on what he was willing to do to increase sales of his newspapers.

Will Irwin recognized the journalistic force of William Randolph Hearst, describing him, in 1911, as the "one American journalist of our period whom the historian of the year 2000 can not ignore."[6] Half of Irwin's string of articles in "The American Newspaper" series discussed Hearst. The third article traced the early journalistic careers of Pulitzer and Hearst and their progression into yellow journalism—sensationalized news, exaggerated headlines, crusades against social injustice, and cartoon features.[7] A subsequent installment focused solely on Hearst, recognition not afforded by Irwin to any other publisher. Titled "The Unhealthy Alliance," that article appeared in the June 3, 1911, issue of *Collier's* which bore a caricature of Hearst on a bright yellow cover and highlighted his use of advertorials, also a practice central to the newspaper scheme. Here again Hearst flirted with questionable ethics.

Irwin's "Unhealthy Alliance" referred to a gentleman's agreement between Hearst newspapers and theatrical management where a thousand dollars bought a full-page advertisement and a favorable editorial. Five hundred dollars paid for a half-page ad and a lesser promotion. Although there were no signed contracts it was common knowledge in the New York theatrical world that this was how things worked at Hearst publications.[8] Irwin portrayed Hearst as being in the business of selling advertorials and judged his refusal to print anything at all, or only negative news about a theatrical performance in the absence of paid advertising, to be the lowest degree of newspaper business standards.[9]

Hearst's career was far broader than the newspaper business. Politics consumed much of his time during the first ten years of the century. He was practiced in using journalism as a governing tool and emerged as a political activist while supporting William Jennings Bryan for president in 1900.

He began to aspire to elected office and twice was chosen to represent a midtown Manhattan congressional district. Hearst campaigned with showmanship, extravaganzas, and fireworks but was unable to achieve elected office again. He lost bids to become a presidential candidate in 1904, two races for mayor of New York, in 1905 and 1909, and, in 1906, the campaign for governor of New York. His commercial activities expanded into other fields and by 1914, he had turned over editorship of the *American* to his long-standing friend and employee Arthur Brisbane, added magazines to his newspaper conglomerate, delved into book publishing, and begun dabbling in motion pictures.

He was also engaged in real estate, having formed Hearst-Brisbane Properties with Arthur Brisbane.[10] Although Hearst's realty involvement was geared toward investment rather than development, he easily could have hired someone to handle that aspect of the newspaper deal for him. Doing so would have enabled him to work both sides of the alliance, functioning as the developer as well as the newspaper publisher. While he would not have had income from ads for the promotion, he conversely would not have had to pay for advertising the real estate deals. In addition, he surely would have increased circulation allowing him to raise rates for other advertisers. The profits from the sale of the lots would have gone into his pocket rather than that of an outside developer.

But William Randolph Hearst was a strange, complex personality. Will Irwin was critical of Hearst's ethics and wrote that his "task was to cheapen the product until it sold at the coin of the gutter and the streets." Nevertheless Irwin defended the journalist, finding that his cold exterior disguised a sympathy for the cause of the downtrodden and that his actions should be viewed in a generous light while maintaining a sense of proportion.[11]

* * *

When the *Tribune* mailed out the extra edition in November of 1914 offering lots at Mayo's Beachwood with a subscription to the paper, Hearst most certainly recognized the scheme as a profitable stroke of genius which would seem to fit ideally into his operations. Yet, instead of embracing the newspaper deal, the complicated Mr. Hearst found more satisfaction in using it as a vehicle to embarrass and denigrate a rival publication while portraying himself as a defender of the lower classes. His implement of vilification in this effort was Victor Watson.

For most of his journalistic career Watson was a loyal Hearst sidekick, implementing Hearst's policies and often seen at his side.[12] Watson's personality and business ethics qualified him to work for Hearst as a reporter, drama editor, associate publisher, troubleshooter, troublemaker, and all-around attack dog.

Victor Watson has been accused of forging documents aimed at provoking an American invasion of Mexico,[13] conjuring up grievances and creating feuds,[14] and laying the trap that brought down James Gordon Bennett, owner of the competing *New York Herald*.[15] Watson's methods were far from reticent. He brazenly attended court trials, at times interrupting the proceedings, questioning witnesses, and otherwise acting like a prosecutor.[16] At congressional hearings and grand jury inquiries he was a willing witness, sometimes a little too willing.[17] And if Watson did not find enough evidence to support his boss' position, he invented it himself.

Many of Watson's efforts for Hearst operated to the detriment of his enemies, and Hearst had many of them including nearly every other New York newspaper and its publisher. In one speech in 1906 Hearst reviled against a handful of opponents including the *Herald*, Pulitzer's *World*, Oswald Villard's *Post*, William Laffan of the *Sun*, and Adolph Ochs of the *Times*.[18] The *New York Tribune* was another notable Hearst adversary. The *Tribune* and Hearst's *New York American* were journalistic adversaries in two significant respects—politics and circulation. The publishers of the *Tribune*, Whitelaw Reid, and after his death in 1912, his son Ogden Reid, were Republicans and favored America's participation in World War I. Hearst, at the other end of the political spectrum, was a noninterventionist. The *Tribune* routinely attacked Hearst on his politics and was notably vicious toward him in his 1905 campaign to become governor of New York.[19]

The two papers were also at opposing ends of the circulation ratings. Among the competing New York papers, the *Tribune* scraped the bottom while the *American* was in the top position. When Ogden Reid took over the *Tribune* in 1913, its circulation was one-twentieth that of Hearst's New York newspaper holdings.[20] The *Tribune*'s poor circulation rankings made it an ideal customer for Mayo's scheme and was likely the reason Mayo approached that paper with his plan.

So here was a Hearst enemy, working a very Hearstian ploy. Being one-upped by his inferior and political rival must have rankled the prominent newspaperman and infused him with considerable incentive to expose the Beachwood venture as a fraud and engage in a journalistic war with the *Tribune*. A snarling Victor Watson sunk his teeth into the hostilities and began delving into the promotion shortly after it was initiated in November of 1914.[21]

Watson planted spies in the *Tribune* office[22] to go about "swindling the public" right alongside Mayo's men[23] and collected correspondence from disgruntled lot buyers. Some of these letters bear the imprint of fabrication, such as one from a purchaser who wrote, "I wish that Mr. Hearst could hear of this: I am sure that he would do something to those scoundrels," and another where the writer wanted "to give the story to the New York

American and have them let the people know what kind of swindle scheme the Tribune is running."[24]

Toward the end of May 1915 editors at the *Tribune* became aware that the *American* was looking into the Beachwood campaign and promptly retained counsel. They were astute in choosing Henry A. Wise, a former U.S. attorney for the Southern District of New York and well known to his successor in that position, H. Snowden Marshall. A short time later the *Tribune* agreed to issue a refund to an unhappy lot purchaser and Mayo ceded control of the railway at Lakewood to the Lot Owners Association, actions likely taken on the recommendation of Attorney Wise. The *Tribune* also enlisted support from its truth in advertising expert Samuel Hopkins Adams who centered an Ad-Visor column on dispelling suspicions of swampland, tidewater, or flawed deeds at Beachwood and firmly defended the virtues of the newspaper's real estate circulation enterprise.[25]

* * *

Watson presented his evidence to U.S. District Attorney Marshall and managed to convince the two postal inspectors assigned to the Beachwood inquiry that the scheme was dishonest. But the inspectors passed their findings on to the U.S. attorney without making any recommendations. An assistant to Marshall also agreed with Watson that the *Tribune* had engaged in deceptive practices,[26] but in spite of his tenacity, Watson was unable to convert Marshall to his cause.

Hearst was not yet willing to concede defeat. He failed in his effort to persuade the District Attorney to prosecute the *Tribune* for employing the newspaper deal but he found a new opportunity to expose the fraud allegations. He had considerable political sway and apparently enough to convince a member of the House of Representatives to take up Hearst's cause, along with his own, by prosecuting the prosecutor for failing to prosecute their enemies. This resulted in impeachment hearings against H. Snowden Marshall.

The hearings had a complicated background. President Wilson appointed H. Snowden Marshall U.S. district attorney for the Southern District of New York in 1913. His prosecutorial actions were largely focused on convicting German spies, plotters, and agents for violations of the federal neutrality statutes. As part of this pursuit he convened a grand jury in 1915 to investigate Frank Buchanan, an Illinois congressman who was employed as an iron worker, rose to president of the International Association of Bridge and Structural Iron Workers' union, and then entered politics.

Marshall accused Buchanan of conspiring with the Germans to foment labor strikes designed to interfere with the production of American munitions factories supplying the World War I allies. Along with several others, Buchanan was indicted in late December of 1915.[27] While Buchanan was being investigated and charged by the grand jury, he instituted impeachment charges against Marshall in the House of Representatives. These accusations included the claim that Marshall indicted Buchanan in retaliation for the speech he made on the floor of the House asking for Marshall's impeachment, thus hopelessly ensnarling the indictment of Buchanan with the impeachment of Marshall.[28]

Among the many claimed instances of dereliction of duty alleged against Marshall was his failure to investigate the *Tribune* for fraud in connection with the Beachwood promotion. This charge was unrelated to any of the other claims listed in the impeachment papers and minor in importance by comparison. But Hearst, in both politics and publishing, was a strong supporter of organized labor and, most probably, Buchanan included the allegation as a reciprocal act. As a result Hearst's and Watson's complaints against Marshall were entered into the tangle.

The Judiciary Committee of the House of Representatives commenced hearings on the impeachment issues in January of 1916. By April 24, when witnesses began testifying about Marshall's failure to pursue the fraud claims against the *Tribune,* most of the lots at Beachwood had been sold, the building structures completed, and the roads were in better shape. But these developments did not prevent Watson from slanting his testimony to support his baseline allegations. Rather than viewing the completion of the work as an ameliorating action, Watson found it to constitute proof of the *Tribune*'s guilt. He urged the hearing examiners to look at the situation as it existed in 1915 when the lots were being actively marketed, and he offered into evidence the year-old photographs and letters of complaint. Watson argued that the *Tribune* never intended to complete the work and did so only because of his legwork and the threat of a grand jury probe.[29] He characterized the completion of the work as a cover-up, attributed it to the retention of Attorney Wise, and discredited Marshall's inaction by blaming it on his chumminess with Henry Wise.[30]

Throughout, Watson made frequent use of the words "swindle" and "fraud" and generally painted an unflattering picture of Beachwood even suggesting the presence of quicksand.[31] To add credibility to his testimony he introduced news articles praising his integrity[32] and cited successful investigations he had conducted in the past. He denied that his efforts were an attempt to "get something" on a rival publication and claimed that he resisted the urgings of the postal inspectors and one of Marshall's assistants to publicize the Beachwood fraud in the *American.* Instead, Watson insisted, the accusation of misrepresentation was pursued with U.S. Attorney Marshall because the newspaper had received complaints from readers and only a grand jury could issue subpoenas and obtain the sworn testimony necessary to prove mail fraud.[33]

While the *American* refrained from writing about the claimed Beachwood fraud, it did not exercise the same restraint in reporting on the hearings. The day following Watson's first appearance before the Committee, two companion articles, extensively quoting his testimony, appeared in the paper headlined "Says Marshall Shields Tribune; Agent of American Attempts to Prove Beachwood a Swindle" and "Attack on Marshall Baseless, Says Wise."[34]

When the Marshall impeachment hearings ended, some members of the Committee praised Watson's testimony and concluded that mail fraud was proven. Predictably Frank Buchanan was the most outspoken on this issue.[35] But the committee did not impeach Marshall and when the allegations against him eventually petered out,[36] so did the mail fraud claims against the *Tribune*.

The hearings were finally concluded in the summer of 1916 but resolution of the underlying controversy lingered. Marshall had written a letter in March rebuking the House Committee "in language which was certainly unparliamentary and manifestly ill-tempered and which was well calculated to arouse the indignation not only of the members of the subcommittee but of those of the House."[37] The Committee, finding the letter to be defamatory and insulting, reacted by holding Marshall in contempt and issuing a warrant for his arrest. Marshall sought dismissal of the contempt charge by means of a petition for habeas corpus but the writ was denied by the federal district court.[38]

In November of 1916 Buchanan was defeated in his bid for a fourth term as Illinois representative, in spite of strong labor union support.[39] Meanwhile Marshall had appealed to the U.S. Supreme Court for reversal of the denial of habeas corpus. The Supreme Court heard oral arguments in December of 1916 and on April 23, 1917, ruled in Marshall's favor finding that the language in his letter did not prevent the subcommittee from performing its legislative duties. During this time the criminal charges against Buchanan went to trial. In May of 1917 three of his codefendants were found guilty of conspiracy. The jury deadlocked on the other four defendants—reportedly the jurors were evenly split on Buchanan's guilt.[40] Marshall was not impeached nor was he found to be in contempt of Congress and Buchanan was not convicted. Each man failed in his attempt to punish the other.

By May of 1917 Marshall had left his position as U.S. district attorney,[41] but his wartime political sentiments remained strong and he offered his services as a prosecutor when conspiracy charges were brought against others.[42] An attempt was made to retry Buchanan on the criminal charges but it eventually fell by the wayside. By early 1918 he had returned to his earlier trade as a structural ironworker,[43] but was unsuccessful in avoiding trouble. Dating to his years as a congressman, Buchanan had an involvement with his secretary. He was separated from his wife when, in August of 1918, the wife encountered Buchanan and the secretary on a Chicago street and, becoming enraged, snatched an umbrella from her husband and used it to attack both him and the girlfriend.[44]

Buchanan remained active in union affairs and in 1924 was elected business agent of the Bridge and Structural Iron Workers' union. At a labor meeting called to install him in office, a shooting erupted seriously injuring the man he defeated in the election and killing another.[45] Buchanan died in April of 1930[46] and was mentioned in the obituary for Marshall who died the following May.[47]

The newspaper deal not only managed to survive this imbroglio but flourished in spite of it—and perhaps because of it. If indeed the allegations against the *Tribune* and its hiring of Attorney Henry Wise furthered the work at Beachwood as Watson claimed in his testimony, the result was a better community than Mayo originally intended and one that matured more quickly than anticipated. The POA was certified by the end of August 1916[48] and Beachwood was incorporated as a borough the following March, a month before the United States Supreme Court absolved Marshall of the contempt allegation and two months before the jury deadlocked on Buchanan's guilt.[49] By then Beachwood was being described as "a wonderful little place" and cited as a model for Mayo's upcoming colony at Browns Mills.[50] The Smadbecks had already begun advertising Asbury Park Estates with *Jewish Daily News* and when Buchanan was being hit over the head with an umbrella by his wife, the Smadbecks were gearing up for the promotions of Lakewood and Patchogue Lakes.

Hearst's attack on the *Tribune*, rather than hurting the newspaper deal, served to strengthen it, presenting the newspaper czar with a frustrating loss.

* * *

The *New York Tribune* had worked hard to promote itself as the standard bearer of truth in advertising and, accordingly, its reputation was at stake in Hearst's campaign to expose the Beachwood promotion as fraudulent. When it became clear in May of 1916 that Watson, and thereby Hearst, had been defeated, the *Tribune* lost no time in rubbing salt into Hearst's wounds.

The retaliation began in the May 12, 1916, issue of the *Tribune* with a printed announcement adorned with a photo of an attractive home built at Beachwood, pointing out the defeat of the Hearst newspapers, and inviting readers to watch for a photographic display in the Graphic Picture Section the following Sunday.[51] There, a full page of photos depicts the Yacht Club, Dining Room, Clubhouse, bungalows built in the forest, and a "Bathers' Paradise," while the text reiterates praise for Samuel Hopkins Adams' exposure of the advertising practices of the Hearst newspapers.[52] The gloating continues in a news story titled "Hunting for Trouble and Finding Truth: Attack on the Toms River Community Centre Fails Completely." This article, relegated to page fourteen by war news, disavows many of Watson's factual claims and points out the futility of his investigation and testimony at the Marshall inquiry. It asserts that the *American* did not publicize the alleged fraud because the allegations were unsupported and the accusing newspaper feared a libel action.

This did not end the *Tribune*'s shaming of Hearst. His campaign against America's participation in World War I provided plenty of fodder for Hearst's adversaries and, after the United States joined the action, the *Tribune* painted him as a German ally and propagandist. A pointed siege against Hearst was announced by the paper in September of 1917 with a promise of three powerful articles by Samuel Hopkins Adams headlined "Who's Who Against America: William Randolph Hearst."[53] In these editorials Adams reshapes Hearst's pre-war noninterventionism into a wartime pacifist campaign for peace but on Germany's terms. Adams asserts that Hearst's outward appearance as a flag-flying zealot of Americanism was a subterfuge used to disguise the voice of the Hearstian dove that spoke with a Prussian accent. This message was reinforced in the first of the articles with a satirical cartoon of Hearst adorned with white feathers and thinly veiled in the American flag while clasping hands with Kaiser Wilhelm II.[54]

Adams argues that Hearst glorified Germany's virtues while inciting fear of the nation's allies and created obstacles to war measures proposed by the U.S. He also characterizes war reporting in Hearst papers as bluff and camouflage, intended only to aid circulation and promote the publisher as a patriot. In the second and third of Adam's columns, also printed on the front page of the Sunday *New York Tribune*,[55] Hearst is further Germanized with the title "Herr" inserted before his name and a drawing of his head adorned with a spiked German helmet and a Prussian black pattée Iron Cross. Throughout this period *Tribune* cartoons lampooning Hearst are unrelenting and unforgiving.

The *Tribune*'s disparagement of Hearst was renewed the following spring with a series of op-ed pieces, authored by Kenneth Macgowan, that consumed the entirety of the front pages of Sunday editorial sections and spilled over to the inside. The promotion for this assemblage of essays had the Hearst name fashioned into a hissing snake "Coiled in the Flag."[56]

Macgowan then moved on to Brisbane, who had recently acquired the *Washington Times,* continuing use of the graphic hissing reptile and titling the stories "Coiled in the Capital—Bris-s-s-bane—What Hears-s-s-t's Editor Did with the Washington Newspaper German-American Brewers Bought for Him."[57] Feature stories in the *Tribune* belittling Hearst and Brisbane finally ended shortly before the Armistice, but the sniping persisted for years.

* * *

While the competing *Tribune* no doubt would have portrayed Hearst as pro–German regardless, his campaign against the *Tribune*'s newspaper subscription promotion intensified the enmity. Hearst had misplayed his hand in the game over Beachwood and was beaten. He must have been annoyed, yet having suffered this defeat, he could not backtrack. A person with his mien was compelled to continue to uphold his position even in the face of lost opportunity, and so Hearst again railed against the newspaper scheme in 1924, this time in a situation where the alliance would have benefited him directly.

Hearst continued acquiring existing newspapers to add to his growing collection of holdings. He added yet a different newspaper to his publishing empire when he purchased the *Washington Herald* in late 1922.[58] Rhey Snodgrass, a man with a solid background in advertising when he first joined the staff at Hearst's *Cosmopolitan* magazine in the spring of 1923,[59] quickly advanced to publisher of the *Herald.* Like other publications when acquired by Hearst, the *Herald* was struggling with poor circulation figures causing Snodgrass and William Shelton, the circulation manager, to explore ways to increase the subscription base.

Anne Arundel County, Maryland, roughly thirty miles east of Washington, D.C., has a mid-county finger pointing into Chesapeake Bay. This strip of land is bordered on one side by the South River and, on the other, by the Severn River. In the 1800s the area upriver from the Naval Academy, the point at which the Severn empties into the Chesapeake, was known as the Marsh plantation. Complete with slave quarters, it was conveyed to Henry Hall in 1886. In the early 1900s it consisted of farmland and orchards. Barges and boats transported the peaches, apples, and other produce north to Baltimore.[60] This agricultural land, adjacent to water, presented a good prospect for a newspaper colony but was somehow overlooked by the Smadbecks. They would not establish a newspaper colony in Anne Arundel County until the founding of Woodland Beach, ten miles away on the South River, in 1931.

Recognizing the potential of the orchard on the Severn, Rhey Snodgrass, William Shelton, and C.S. Eddy, a third member of the *Herald*'s management team, purchased 460 acres from the descendants of Henry Hall on May 17, 1924. The three men, all principals at the *Herald*, immediately implemented their plan. Imitating the Mayo/Smadbeck template they partitioned the land into 25' × 100' lots and platted them as though the land was flat. Some lots were under water, some were on a steep grade, property lines were ambiguous, and the plats were studded with paper roads—streets that existed only on paper.

Barely a week after acquiring the property, their newspaper subscription promotion was announced. On Sunday, May 25, the *Herald* printed an article on the front page headlined "Herald Harbor Plans Announced." A lot at this new summer beach colony, named for Hearst's newspaper, could be purchased with a weekday subscription to the paper, a second lot could be procured by also buying a subscription to the Sunday paper, and a third and fourth by enticing a friend to subscribe to the daily and Sunday editions. There were other differences from the Smadbeck formula: each of the principals, Snodgrass, Shelton, and Eddy, had a road named for him, the lots varied in price from $25 to $200 depending on location, and, while aimed at the working classes, the resort was overtly restricted to white people.[61]

Here was a further chance for Hearst to participate in the newspaper colony scheme and profit both from selling newspapers and selling real estate. But Hearst was still feeling the sting from being thwarted by the *Tribune* in the Beachwood fraud allegation fiasco. So when Hearst learned of the project initiated by Snodgrass, Shelton, and Eddy, an article appeared in the *Herald* on June 12, 1924, prominently proclaiming that "Herald Harbor Company Is Not a Hearst Newspaper Project." Two of the newspaper men, Snodgrass and Shelton, lost their jobs at the *Herald*, unwitting victims of Hearst's antipathy toward the scheme, and Eddy was no doubt fired as well.

On July 1, 1924, the land was conveyed to an independent corporation, Herald Harbor, Inc., with Rhey Snodgrass, the former publisher of the *Herald*, as president, William Shelton, the former circulation manager as secretary-treasurer, and C.S. Eddy as vice president.[62] Snodgrass took a job as advertising manager for *Pioneer Press Dispatch*,[63] a newspaper in Saint Paul, Minnesota. Soon after, William Shelton, as principal stockholder of Herald Harbor, Inc., took over as president of the corporation. Herald Harbor retained the paper's title in its name and the lots were capably marketed but not as newspaper subscription premiums.[64]

* * *

Hearst had one other involvement, or rather noninvolvement, with the newspaper deal. In addition to acquiring existing newspapers, he also created new ones and the New York *Daily Mirror* was a 1924 invention. Just as he was distancing himself from the Herald Harbor promotion, he debuted the *Daily Mirror* on June 24, 1924. He sold the newspaper in 1928 and then bought it back in 1932. The seven newspaper resorts created by the *Mirror* in collaboration with the Smadbecks were all developed within those four years, the exact time frame when Hearst did not have ownership of the paper. This could be coincidence but more likely it is additional evidence of Hearst's aversion to newspaper real estate ventures.

* * *

William Randolph Hearst had three close encounters with newspaper colonies. In 1914 when he could see what was happening with the *Tribune*'s Beachwood, he could have taken advantage of the scheme either by teaming up with Bertram Mayo or by stealing the idea. While Mayo could copyright the ad text, he could not prevent others from imitating the basic framework of the newspaper arrangement. But Hearst's ego got in the way. Influenced by politics and swayed by emotion, either his hatred for the competing *Tribune* or his compassion for the rights of the little guy, Hearst chose to attack the scheme rather than embrace it.

This was an irreversible decision. If Watson had been successful in convincing Marshall to prosecute the *Tribune* and the paper had been found guilty of mail fraud, neither Hearst nor any other publisher could use the scheme, at least not in the same form, without threat of prosecution. Having failed to accomplish the desired goal of criminalizing his competitor, Hearst still could not pursue the newspaper deal. To do so would expose him to agonizing ridicule and self-derision.

In 1924 a newspaper colony opportunity in the form of Herald Harbor was handed to him by his new management team at the *Washington Herald*. The groundwork had already been laid and the promotion was in progress. But Hearst's decision of ten years earlier made it necessary for him to denounce the project and fire his staff, even though doing so did not prevent them from pursuing the resort development for their own benefit. By the time Hearst repurchased the *Mirror* in 1932, the colony fad was winding down and the possibilities for the promotion scheme were evaporating. As a result the Hearst name is aligned with the *Mirror* newspaper but not with the *Mirror* colonies.

Perhaps if William Randolph Hearst had not been William Randolph Hearst there would have been many more newspaper colonies created in the 1920s.

10

Environmental Factors

Pell Lake played an early, and significant, role in the interplay between the newspaper colonies and the environment. With environmental consciousness still decades in the future, ecological concerns in the beginning years of the twentieth century were focused primarily on industrial pollution. Newspaper resort advertisements used this to advantage by promoting the developments as healthy places where families could breathe fresh air.

Even sanitary conditions were not a big concern. Outhouses were often the first structures built, but a hole in the ground with some canvas screening around it would also do. Zoning was in its infancy in the 1920s and largely confined to urban areas. In rural Wisconsin in 1924, there simply were no zoning regulations or building permit requirements for Warren Smadbeck to worry about.

A revision in the marketing terms midway through the decade implies that the Smadbecks had encountered a bump in the road. Ads for the newspaper colonies specified five lots as the most that could be purchased by any one buyer. No minimum number of lots was imposed at Pell Lake or the resorts that came before it. But after Pell Lake this changed and the reason is explained by a series of news articles.

In July of 1925 Wisconsin real estate broker licenses were denied to Ivan Bell Realty and Pell Lake Development, the respective creators of Lake Ivanhoe and Pell Lake Addition. The news item providing this information did not report the reason for the rejection.[1]

An article on the May 17, 1926, front page of the *Wisconsin State Journal* revealed that the state health department was investigating the Pell Lake subdivision regarding sanitary conditions. When this investigation began or how it came about is not specified, but apparently, local real estate agents, chafing at commissions going to out-of-state salesmen, were behind it and probably behind the license denials of the previous year. The *State Journal* article, titled "State Arrests 6 on Real Estate Count," reported the arrest of R.B. Hussey and five others, all solicitors from the circulation department of the *Chicago Evening Post*. Their arrest was based on a warrant sworn out by an attorney for the Wisconsin Real Estate Brokers Board. The six men were charged with selling Wisconsin land without licenses. When arrested, they were peddling lots at Lake Como Beach and the news article claimed that licenses were never issued by the real estate board for the sale of Pell Lake lots.

The same day that the report of the arrests appeared in the press, the just-formed Walworth County Real Estate Board adopted, as its first order of business, a resolution denouncing the platting and selling of lots on any lakeshore property in the county with less than 40' frontage.[2] The board members disapproved of the narrow lots as creating unwarranted congestion and unhealthy and unsanitary conditions. In response, the state halted the sale of 20' lots pending the outcome of the charges against the real estate salesmen.[3] This action effectively suspended the sale of all Smadbeck lots in Walworth County.

Then, several things occurred on May 26, 1926. Following his arrest, R.B. Hussey, his father Frank Hussey, and Carroll Shaffer, general manager of the *Chicago Evening Post*, applied for a license to sell lots at Lake Como Beach. A hearing was conducted by the state real estate board to inquire into the plans for marketing and sanitary conditions at the Lake Como project. The board issued a license to R.B. Hussey with the stipulation that no less than two lots be sold to a purchaser and that sanitary conditions and the water supply meet state requirements.[4] That same day ads for Lake Como Beach debuted in the *Post* specifying a minimum purchase of two lots.

The Wisconsin realty agents, in an effort to punish the out-of-state encroachers on their territory, actually did them a favor. The developers and their sales team now had a legitimate reason to require that buyers purchase at least two lots and two newspaper subscriptions. Newspaper colonies continued to be platted with 20' wide lots but subsequent ads for most of the resorts specified the two-lot minimum.

A resulting change also took place in deed language. Pell Lake deeds required outhouses to be suitably screened while deeds for Lake Como Beach and Interlaken prohibited the erection of outdoor privies, requiring chemical toilets instead. This left Pell Lake as the only newspaper resort in Walworth County with outhouses.

The attack on the narrow lots was prompted more by rivalries among real estate salesmen than by concerns over sanitation. Still, it effectively ended outhouses in Walworth County and made money for the sellers of chemical toilets. It did not, however, prevent sewerage from seeping or being channeled into the lakes. Today, the few outhouses that still exist in the backyards of some cottages at Pell Lake have been deactivated by filling the pits with sand or dirt and the structures repurposed for garden storage or preserved as oddities.

* * *

The modern-day movement toward environmentalism in the 1960s and 1970s was spurred on by a few prominent ecological disasters, one of which involved a Smadbeck resort. The environmental flap that consumed Times Beach had little to do with Warren Smadbeck unless he is to be blamed for not paving the roads. Through the years the development struggled economically and, even though it became a city in 1957, most of its roads remained unpaved.

In an effort to quell the dust stirred up by traffic, the community hired a local waste hauler to spray the roads with used motor oil. Unfortunately, the hauler blended the oil with chemical manufacturing waste containing dioxin, a highly toxic industrial byproduct. The Environmental Protection Agency began taking soil samples at Times Beach in 1979 and, finding high levels of dioxin, ordered the town evacuated in 1982. Bulldozers leveled Times Beach, heaping everything into one huge pile which was then incinerated and covered with soil. That grassy mound is now part of the Route 66 State Park, opened in 1999 on the site of the former colony.

Times Beach garnered much attention in the press as the first town entirely bought out by federal Superfund dollars. As such, it became the only newspaper colony to have completely disappeared. Environmentalists continue to debate the need for the extreme remedial actions imposed at Times Beach.

* * *

At some resorts the Smadbecks purposefully altered the environment by damming up rivers to create artificial lakes. Knightstown Lake and Lake Louisvilla were among the first locations where this was done. The Smadbecks exhibited either inexperience or unwillingness to pay for sound engineering when the dam at Knightstown failed almost immediately and had to be rebuilt.

Knightstown Lake property owners lost the parkland along the stream bed when it was the subject of a condemnation action brought by a conservancy district created in 1965 to monitor the Big Blue River watershed. The property owners objected to the condemnation complaint, filed in March of 1974, and the matter languished in the courts for eight years. During the course of the proceedings the court determined that the POA was dissolved as of August 19, 1976, and may have been inactive as early as 1932. The case was finally resolved in July of 1982 with an appraisal value of $5,374.22 assigned to the parkland. This amount was allocated among the lot owners with each receiving only a few dollars for his interest in the parkland.[5]

With a declining economy, the abandonment of many cottages, and wooded areas to provide cover, both Knightstown Lake and Lake Louisvilla came to be used as disposal sites for old tires, worn-out appliances, and other refuse. Knightstown Lake residents feared that the lake would be drained due to the debris,[6] while residents at Lake Louisvilla took a different approach, purposefully causing the lake to be drained in 1969 in an effort to clean it up. When several feet of mud on the lake bottom made it impossible to bring in bulldozers, Lake Louisvilla was refilled with water, leaving most of the rubbish intact.[7]

* * *

It was the condition of the dams, rather than the debris, that would prompt conservationists to bring an end to Knightstown Lake and Lake Lousvilla. Both dams were found to be in disrepair by state agencies created to oversee environmental issues. In Indiana it was the Department of Natural Resources (DNR) and in Kentucky the Natural Resources and Environmental Protection Cabinet (NREPC). At both Knightstown and Louisvilla, roads had been constructed on the berms of the dams contributing to their deterioration and involving highway departments in the litigation that was to follow.

Lake Louisvilla was the first of the two lakes to come under attack when, in 1984, the NREPC found the dam in need of repair and classified it as "high hazard." The state did not want to pay the cost of repairing the dam and planned to drain the lake. Residents, fearing a decrease in property values, joined together under the banner "Save Lake Louisvilla" and challenged the state's right to empty the lake.

The lake had been conveyed to the Lake Louisvilla POA in 1925, an entity that ceased to exist when Lake Louisvilla became a city in the 1950s. The municipality was disincorporated in 1972 giving rise to issues of ownership of the lake and responsibility for the dam. Legal notices were placed in the newspaper but no one stepped forward to claim title to a dam in need of repair.

The dispute between the state and the residents took nearly five years to progress up the legal ladder from the circuit court to the state supreme court and back down again. It was finally concluded that the lake had been abandoned and thereby belonged to the state, clearing the way for it to do as it wished. Lake Louisvilla was drained for the second and last time in October 1989 and the backhoes again got stuck in the mud.[8]

Since the property owners had denied ownership of the lake, the action of the state did not constitute a compensable taking of property. At least the property owners could take solace in the fact that the state was unsuccessful in its attempt to sell the muddy lake bed to recoup the expense of draining.[9]

* * *

At Knightstown Lake the property owners lost the parkland in 1982 but they still had use of the lake. Then in 1994 the Indiana DNR claimed that water, trickling through cracks and crevices in the embankment, was causing a supporting arch to cave in, rendering the dam unsafe. The DNR ordered the water level lowered to five feet and the county commissioners closed the portion of Star Boulevard that spanned the berm of the dam.

Further attempts to drain the lake or repair the dam were delayed while ownership issues were sorted out, a process that would take ten years. The Conservancy District took the position that while the lake was within its watershed, it had no ownership or control of the dam itself. The Knightstown Lake POA may have owned the dam initially but that entity had long been defunct. The county claimed that the property owners nevertheless obtained ownership of the dam when they bought their lots, and the lot owners argued that the county assumed control of the dam when it constructed the road across the berm. Both the lot owners and the county wanted the dam repaired but neither had the money, or the desire, to pay for it.[10]

Matters were further complicated when residents formed a Save Knightstown Lake committee, the county filed a court action against 300 lot owners to determine ownership of the property, and a resident bought the property for delinquent taxes but could not claim ownership pending payment of tax liens by the undetermined owner.[11] By the turn of the century nothing had been resolved and ownership of the dam was still in limbo.[12] In 2004, ten years after first being declared unsafe, the DNR finally determined that the dam had been orphaned and was owned by no one. The dam was decommissioned and the lake drained to silt level.

Satellite views of Knightstown Lake and Lake Louisvilla now depict mudholes where the lakes were. These two lakes were not the only Smadbeck developments where dams had a limited life span but lacked a legal structure to ensure the availability of funds for repair.

* * *

Beach Club Lake came into existence in May of 1929 when the Smadbecks, having created a dam to enlarge Buckshutem Pond into Laurel Lake, installed another dam to create Beach Club Lake next door. This second dam failed shortly after construction,[13] and with the onset of the Depression, the Beach Club Lake resort, lake, and dam were all abandoned. This presents the unusual situation of a newspaper resort having a vastly truncated life largely due to its dam.

At the adjoining resort of Laurel Lake, the city of Millville, New Jersey, took over the unsold lots by tax forfeiture in the 1940s; these lots, primarily those on the south shore of the lake and probably other property in the area as well, were purchased by Laurel Lake Development.[14] In 1956 the Laurel Lake dam also failed and, through the joint efforts of the Laurel Lake and Beach Club Lake POA and the Development Company, both dams were reconstructed.[15] What had been Beach Club Lake for a few short months in 1929, ultimately became Beaver Lake.

* * *

In the mid–1920s in Wisconsin, the jurisdiction over dams was assigned to the Railroad Commission. The Water Power Law of 1917 was developed to ensure that dams were safely built, operated, and maintained, and that water level and flow were properly controlled. It might be expected that this type of legislation would aid in resolving conflicts between landowners such as the long simmering feud between two of Ira Pell's neighbors.

Since about 1870 Arthur Olden, seeking to drain water from his marshland north of the lake, would open up the southern outlet of the lake to allow lake water to flow out and be replaced with drainage from his land. This operation caused the outflow of water to flood the farmland of Marvin Acker. Acker reacted by shoveling dirt to rebuild the bank and keep the overflow off of his property. The two men argued over this situation, the conflict escalated, and in 1885 Olden and Acker resorted to a fist fight. Acker was arrested and made to pay a fine of $26.07.[16] The newspaper that reported this incident suggested that the matter might be satisfactorily settled if the parties got together and shared the cost of a ditch to carry off the marsh water.

An analogous situation arose when the outlet of Pell Lake at its southern end was completely closed off by Warren Smadbeck in the spring and summer of 1924. He also blocked the inlets at the northern end in an effort to raise the level of the lake a desired thirty inches. Charles Gleason, Hattie Hibbard, and George Sitterle, all owners of marshland north of the lake, objected to Smadbeck's operations which had effectively prevented their swamp land from draining into the lake and eventually into Nippersink Creek. Rather than engaging in a physical altercation, the land owners, joining with the Town of Bloomfield, lodged a Water Power complaint with the Railroad Commission. Smadbeck responded by petitioning for a permit to build a dam at the outlet sufficient to raise the lake level about three feet,[17] an action which, in fact, he had already taken.

Since Smadbeck had constructed the dam without permission and was in the midst of actively selling lots, it was crucial that he obtain approval from the commission. To accomplish this, he acceded to the petitioners' demands that he install a pipeline channeling the swamp water around the eastern shore of the lake to link up with the natural outlet into the creek—basically what had been suggested in 1885. Smadbeck purchased twelve carloads of tile and work on the conduit was in progress even before the two related cases were heard by the commission on October 20, 1924.[18] Thus, Warren Smadbeck was able to demonstrate his good faith and have the matters postponed while he worked out the details of a settlement with the land owners. This was accomplished in the spring of 1925 and embodied in a stipulation that appears very one-sided, suggesting that Smadbeck acquiesced to every demand made by the landowners, their engineer, and their lawyer.[19]

The commission established a benchmark to measure the water level and the petitioners withdrew their objections. An order was issued on June 11, 1925, approving the agreement of the parties and finding that the proposed dam at Pell Lake would not materially obstruct existing navigation or violate other public rights, and would not endanger life, health or property.[20]

In the order granting Smadbeck's application for the dam, the commission added a gratuitous comment,

> the Commission is only performing its duty under the statutes and is not in any way passing upon the advisability of the project. It would seem that the purposes for which the dam is to be maintained can be effected only temporarily and that the permanent success of the dam in securing those ends is doubtful.

This proved to be a sage observation.

Just three years later William Kaufman, a civil engineer in Smadbeck employ,[21] appeared at Pell Lake to supervise repair of the pipeline.[22] These remedies were also short-lived and by the spring of 1931, the president of the Pell Lake POA, William McManus, began several years of correspondence with the Public Service Commission (PSC), the successor body to the Railroad Commission.[23]

McManus was concerned about the low water level in the lake and initially wanted to conduct more dredging. PSC inspections revealed that the joints in the pipeline had not been properly sealed and the piping had again settled out of position. In addition, a pump used to help drain the north marshes broke down, was disassembled, and eventually went out of commission altogether. The POA sought closure of the pipeline so the lake level would rise while the marsh owners wanted it to remain open to drain the swamps. The PSC would not allow the closure unless the tile drain was made water tight or the pump was restored to operating condition.[24]

When the Smadbeck agreement to maintain the pipeline proved ineffective, the two sides resorted to self-help. In August of 1933, and again in March of 1937, the PSC noted that the outlet had been filled with sand and gravel when the road was widened.[25] In April of 1962 the commission reported that persons wanting a higher lake level had placed rocks and stones in the culvert while others took them out to lower the water, and that "there were several rocks inside the culvert about fifteen feet from the upstream end. They blocked about half of the culvert."[26] And so, fifty years after Acker and Olden argued over the drainage, and after a ditch had been constructed to resolve the argument, the successor owners of their marsh and riparian land were doing basically what Acker and Olden had done.

Seven water level measurements taken off the established benchmark between May of 1925 and August of 1969 indicate that the water level of the lake averaged halfway between its original level and the three-foot rise sought by Smadbeck. The remedial actions taken by the two opposing sides in the dispute resulted in a near exact compromise—the culvert was half-blocked and the water level increase was reduced by half. All in all, this was a saner resolution than resorting to petitions, lawyers, engineers, and formal hearings or a fighting bout.

While these actions impaired the function of the conduit, Warren Smadbeck's dam endured and still exists at the southern end of Pell Lake. Nearby is another embankment. This low earthen structure, roughly the same level as the roads at either end, extends from the western terminus of Lake Road across the slough, meeting up with West Lakeshore Drive near Holly Road. It may have been created as a means of moving ice harvested from the lake onto an adjoining railroad spur. Today this berm serves as a frequent muskrat crossing and bears only occasional foot traffic. The locals have an affectionate name for it—the rubber bridge—perhaps an accidental pun for a retaining structure at a development created by a dentist.

11

Legal Aspects

The newspaper colony offer was an unusual proposal, one that readers had no experience with and nothing to compare it to. Purchasers of lots had only a dim understanding of what they were buying. The ads proclaiming that they were entitled to equal ownership and exclusive use of the waterfront parkland and "free life membership in the clubhouse" made it all sound like such a good deal, at least at first. While there was nothing dishonest about the promises made—most were kept—the list of fringe benefits ignored the responsibilities that accompanied them.

The promised rights were conveyed through the Property Owners Association.[1] Once the majority of the lots had been sold, a POA would be formed with the assistance of the newspaper trustee. The Smadbecks would then deed the clubhouse and parkland to the trustee who would, in turn, deed ownership to the POA. Things ran smoothly as long as the developer was still around to oversee the properties. But once the Smadbecks and the newspaper pocketed their money and walked away, the POA was required to take over management and maintenance responsibilities of the shared properties and the disadvantages of the system began to surface.

The Lake Como Beach POA incorporated on December 4, 1926,[2] a mere seven months after the lots first went on sale. Soon the colony was dealing with a range of infrastructure problems. Governed by five officers and another six-member board of directors, all Chicago residents, sixteen committees were formed, a few dealing with finance and administration and a few more with entertainment and sports. The majority of the committees were burdened with responsibility for the community property. The lake weeds cut down during development had reappeared and property owners had been bolstering the dam with rock and cement bags. The new president of the POA in 1929 indicated an immediate need for a main road in good condition running the full length of the colony so that everyone could have access to his cottage in wet weather. He also called for extension of electrical service to assure eventual access to electricity for all cottagers. The POA president proposed dredging the lake of mud, filling in the low land, raising

11. Legal Aspects

the water level, and building a road across the lake at the east end.[3] It took a year to determine that a new concrete spillway was needed and another three years and court proceedings to secure the necessary easements. Card and bunco parties, carnivals, tag sales, and even a Miss Popularity contest were organized to raise the money to pay for the repairs.[4]

Similarly, at a Knightstown Lake POA meeting on July 10, 1927, two years after the group was organized,[5] members met to discuss the need to excavate one of the lakes. Then the men spent the day scraping and grading the roads while the women prepared lunch.[6] The fun the lot buyers bought into for a few dollars quickly turned into work, responsibility, and expense.

* * *

The legal structure used to convey rights to the communal property was problematic. An arrangement where buyers own their individual lots and have use of shared property, falls generally into the category of a common interest community. While common interest communities were not a new concept in the Smadbecks' time, they were still largely unregulated and unstandardized.

Deeds to the lots differed in wording from colony to colony. Some made an attempt at defining rights to exclusive use of the mutually owned areas, but the greater share of the deeds used a thicket of legal terminology, the most apt phrase being that the land purchased came "together with all ... appurtenances" without specifying what the appurtenances were. This left the entitlements of the lot owners to the shared grounds to be dictated by the deeds given to the POAs by the trustees. Here again, the deed language lacked uniformity.

The trustee deed sometimes obligated the POA to maintain the clubhouse for the benefit of the lot owners and sometimes for the benefit of the POA members. If roads were included in the deed, their use was usually, but not always, allotted to both lot owners and the general public. Use of the parkland might accrue to the lot owners, the POA members, and/or the general public.

Adding confusion, phraseology varied among deeds even if the beneficiaries were the same. Whatever the language of the provisions, there was ample opportunity for uncertainty and litigation.

* * *

Lake Erie Beach has a protracted history of disagreements arising from these documents. In February of 1924, Home Guardian deeded all of the roads, streets, and parkland to newspaperman Eugene Murphy as trustee to "be held to the use and enjoyment of the various owners and inhabitants of the [Lake Erie Beach lots] ... as well as the general public."[7]

A few days later Murphy deeded the property to the Lake Erie Beach POA under the same conditions.[8]

In 1932 Warren Smadbeck signed a deed correcting the language to reflect the intent that the beach and parkland be held for the use and enjoyment of the lot owners and residents of Lake Erie Beach to the exclusion of the general public. The public would, however, continue to have free access to the streets and roads. The precipitating event for the issuance of this deed is not apparent.[9]

By 1987 the POA found responsibility for the premises to be increasingly difficult and expensive. In order to obtain park renovation funds from a waterfront commission, it was decided to transfer the land to the Town of Evans "for public use and maintenance." An agreement was entered into between Home Guardian,[10] the Lake Erie Beach POA, and the Town, waiving the prior conditions and allowing unrestricted use and enjoyment of the beaches and parks, but requiring that the Town maintain the land for park purposes. In accordance with this agreement, the POA deeded the parkland and roads to the Town of Evans.[11]

While giving the parks to the Town solved the financial troubles, legal complications arose both with regard to the streets and the parkland. Some roads on the Smadbeck plat maps were termed "paper streets," reminiscent of the early wildcat paper subdivisions in California. These roadways were never created, existed only on the maps, and arguably included some of the parkland or access to it. After acquiring ownership, the Town sold portions of these paper streets to individuals, much to the chagrin of former officers of the POA who claimed violation of the deeds and agreements. The matter went before the courts, both lower and appellate, with the Town prevailing.[12]

The bickering continued with a former president of the Lake Erie Beach POA claiming that a homeowner was allowed to build a deck extending over park property. This allegedly led to a threat with pruning shears and a punch in the mouth,[13] similar to the altercation between the Smadbeck agent and the butcher in Bolinas. Dissatisfaction with the Town's handling of the parkland is ongoing.[14]

* * *

Apparently anticipating that the newspaper resorts would develop into more permanent settlements, the Smadbecks stipulated in the trust deeds that, if and when a municipal corporation was formed, the common lands and clubhouse would be deeded to the municipality which would assume operation and maintenance. Incorporating as a village or city appeared to be a solution to a major defect in the POA arrangement, namely the lack of taxing authority and a resulting deficiency of funds. But incorporation could be problematical and its very process presented hurdles.

11. Legal Aspects

In 1938 Lake Michigan Beach, concerned about traffic control, policing, fire protection, availability of utilities, and clubhouse and park maintenance, sought to incorporate as a village. Most of the cottage owners lived in Illinois and, as non-residents of Michigan, were unable sign the petition calling for a special election, the first step in the process. The attempt fell short of supporters,[15] and Lake Michigan Beach has remained unincorporated.

Once achieved, city status can have its own array of disadvantages. In general, towns and villages can rely on volunteer fire companies and perhaps on state police, but a municipality may be required to provide a paid police force and fire department which can be quite costly.

Lot owners at Mastic Beach on Long Island were bothered by boarded-up houses and absentee landlords who did not maintain their property. There was a feeling among the residents that the township ignored the situation out of lack of interest in the beach community. Expecting incorporation to be tax neutral—tax dollars that went into the general township fund would instead specifically benefit Mastic Beach—the community incorporated as a village in 2010. The idea looked good on paper but the new village forfeited economy of scale. Proponents of the move had estimated an annual operating budget of $600,000 but the first budget exceeded $3 million. There were 486,000 residents in the town while the village had only 13,000—too few to pay for legally required services. The new village of Mastic Beach was effective in cracking down on the unkempt properties, but in the end it was just too small to function independently. In 2016 the community unincorporated and returned to being part of the Town of Brookhaven.[16]

Lake Louisvilla was another newspaper resort that incorporated and unincorporated. After becoming a city in the late 1950s, the residents found their tax base small and their needs great. Feeling that they were not getting any services for their tax dollars, some residents just stopped paying and the city voted to dissolve in 1970.[17] The POA was never revived.

Rather than becoming municipalities on their own, a few newspaper colonies were absorbed by existing cities in close proximity, thus avoiding both the problems of the incorporation procedure and the burdens of trying to stay afloat as an independent governmental entity. Examples of these community marriages include Estacada Lake, now part of Estacada, Oregon; Skyland, consumed by Ruidoso, New Mexico; Marshfield Estates, consolidated with Marshfield, Massachusetts; and the Lake Louisvilla area, merged with Louisville, Kentucky. Ruidoso still recognizes Skyland as a district of the town, but as for the others, the names are too similar and the borders too blurred to keep the memory of the newspaper resort alive. For them the consequence of survival as part of a larger city resulted in a surrender of identity.

Still, becoming an independent city was an effective answer for some of the colonies. Lake Saint Croix Beach incorporated as a village in 1952 and became a city in 1974. Bertram Mayo's Michigan resort of Lakewood developed into the village of Lakewood Club in 1967 and Clear Lake Shores converted to city status in 1962. Nevertheless, most newspaper resorts remain unincorporated areas of townships.

* * *

Some, if not all, of the trust deeds included a little used but powerful stipulation. It provided that if the conditions specified for the use of the parkland were violated, the grantor, that is the Smadbecks, could reclaim title.

In the 1950s this clause was employed at Bolinas Beach when no municipality had been formed and the POA was presumably dissolved for failure to pay property taxes. Ownership of the parkland reverted to Arthur Smadbeck, and then his descendants, who proceeded to pay property taxes on the land.[18] The 47½ acres of parkland and bluffs were sold by Smadbeck heirs in 2004. The buyer, Jeremy Kidson, paid a purchase price of $250,000, a sum that probably exceeded the profits Arthur Smadbeck made on the original development in the 1920s.

Kidson wanted to build a three-story barn house, but his plans were quashed when the county found that the 1927 plat map designating the acreage as parkland was still operational. The buyer did manage to recoup the purchase price from the title insurance company after it either neglected to discover the parkland covenant or failed to disclose it to him.

Jeremy Kidson later attempted to market the land for $3.9 million according to one report[19] or $4.5 million according to another.[20] There were no takers. In November of 2011 he offered to donate the land to the Bolinas Community Public Utility District (the closest thing to a governmental body in Bolinas Beach) but the offer was refused. The Marin County assessor's office still lists the owner as Bolinas Beach Preservation,[21] the ecologically friendly name given to the holding entity created by Kidson.

* * *

The POAs were amorphous. While they could limit membership to lot buyers, there was no advantage in doing so. More members meant more dues collected and more volunteers. Owners of lots in Pell Lake Highlands, Pell Lake Addition, Sitterlee's Subdivision, and Pell Farm Annex were all welcome to join the Pell Lake POA even though they had not purchased a newspaper subscription. Correspondingly, membership in the POA was voluntary. Lot owners were not required to join. It might be necessary to belong to the POA to have use of the clubhouse, but, whether a member

11. Legal Aspects

of the POA or not, lot owners were able to use the roads, beaches, and parkland.

This created a tricky situation for the POAs. Trust deeds prohibited the sale of the common properties saddling them with perpetual ownership and maintenance. The POAs were unable to levy taxes, could not compel membership, nor were they able to force collection of delinquent dues. In addition, dues needed to be kept to a minimum to attract members.

The POAs operated effectively when the resorts were new and there was still an excess of enthusiasm. Everyone wanted to be part of the POA since membership was the entry to the dances, dinners, and parties. Belonging was inexpensive and provided neighborly interaction and entertainment.

But as the eagerness and the economy declined, so did membership and dues income. This occurred just as the clubhouses and beach structures were aging, driving up maintenance costs. As more years passed and the character of the resorts changed, residents made less use of the facilities and incentive to belong to the POA diminished. A 1960 newspaper report on the finances of the Pell Lake POA demonstrates the situation. For the previous fiscal year, the POA had expenses of $4,939 for beach maintenance, insurance, and other clubhouse costs. Income consisted of $2,544 mostly from memberships and fundraisers. The deficit was paid from cash on hand but there clearly would not be enough resources to make up a similar deficit the following year.[22]

Aside from dues, fundraisers, and contributions, the POAs had no source of income. New, more inventive ways had to be found to bring in the needed dollars. In recent times some of the associations have bolstered revenue with clubhouse rental, structured membership fees, and special assessments.

Newspaper colonies that could be segregated or somehow sectioned off from public beaches began charging fairly hefty membership fees for the use of facilities. Since not all residents were interested in the beaches, sports, and other entertainments, why not charge fees for those who are? And, by the way, why not also sell memberships to those willing to pay to use the facilities even if they are not lot owners?

This approach invites the question of whether nonresident members can vote on management issues. Laurel Lake handled this situation by creating two classes of membership, Property and Social. Yearly fees are the same for both and can run close to $700 a year depending on factors such as volunteer hours, size and type of boat, and use of a pier. But only property members can vote on administrative matters. To qualify for property membership, a resident must present a deed showing that his or her land is within the original Laurel Lake POA tract or an approved expansion.

Laurel Lake is a private lake and access is easier to control than a strip of beach land on the shore of Long Island Sound. The lots at North Shore Beach are on the top of high cliffs with steep stairways leading down to the water. Access to the beach is controlled by locked gates at the top of the stairs, twenty-four-hour security guards, and video cameras. Only paid members of the North Shore Beach POA are entitled to parking permits, keys to the locks, and beach usage tags. Membership fees pay for lifeguards, beach cleanup, maintenance of the stairs, prevention of cliff erosion, and portable toilets.

The POA members contend that the beach is private under the terms of their deeds and they have the right to restrict access. This position has provoked bitter complaints from taxpayers who argue that the Public Trust Doctrine allows public usage of waterfront property, at least below the high tide level, and it is unfair and selfish, and maybe even illegal, to obstruct access with fences and locks.

At Lake Parsippany, another private lake, the POA found the membership fees of $450 insufficient to combat drainage issues and, in late 2016, decided to impose a mandatory assessment on lot owners. Less than 5 percent of approximately 2,000 lot owners belonged to the POA which voted, 101 to 16, to impose a $115 annual assessment on all lot owners.[23]

Within days a group of residents filed a legal action to prevent implementation of the assessment,[24] arguing that the POA abandoned its status as a common interest community and breached the deed covenants by ceding trash collection and road repair to the township, selling the tennis court land to a residential developer and the clubhouse site to a local fire department, and opening membership to nonresidents.[25]

The facts were not in dispute, enabling the court to determine, as a matter of law, that Lake Parsippany was a common interest community. The court held that the POA had an obligation to do all that is reasonably necessary to manage the shared property and, accordingly, had the implicit authority to compel lot owners to contribute to the maintenance of that property either through dues or assessments.[26]

While the Lake Parsippany POA won this battle, the judgment of the court does not necessarily end the war. State legislatures on occasion, with admirable intentions, enact or attempt to enact laws imposing penalty-laden requirements on developers of modern-day common interest communities that inadvertently and unduly affect colonies created decades ago. Active POAs, such as the one at Lake Parsippany, keep busy tracking these laws and urging their members to oppose or support the legal changes.

* * *

11. Legal Aspects

If the Smadbecks anticipated that the newspaper resorts would grow into little cities which would take over control of the clubhouse and park grounds, their expectations fell short. Only a small percentage of the developments, those that effectively incorporated or were absorbed by existing municipalities, achieved this objective. The rest, including Pell Lake, were left to flounder.

A push toward making Pell Lake a municipality began in November of 1997. With 44 percent of the town's assessed valuation and 70 percent of the town's residents within the proposed borders, it had a reasonable chance of survival as a city. But its potential for success remained untested when the voters soundly defeated the idea at the polls in early 2001.[27]

The concept was revived several times[28] and was eventually accomplished in a roundabout way. In November of 2011, voters overwhelmingly approved the creation of the Village of Bloomfield, a twelve-square-mile area encompassing all of Pell Lake and considerable land around it.[29] The POA continues to exist and maintain ownership of the clubhouse and parkland. With the creation of the village, only the POA, a highway exit sign for Pell Lake Road, and the lake itself continue to formally bear the Pell Lake name.

12

Racial Issues

In addition to Prohibition, the years between the War and the mid–1920s were memorable for racial tension and violence. Neither the resort developers nor the lot purchasers were immune from the effects of these animosities.

The United States entry into World War I in April of 1917 caused young men to be drafted into military service and removed from the labor force just as more workers were needed to produce required war goods. At the same time an active union movement was demanding increased wages and improved working conditions, putting further strain on employment. As a consequence, southern Negroes were motivated to move farther north in a quest for better jobs and better pay, favoring manufacturing centers as their destinations. East Saint Louis, on the banks of the Mississippi River in Southern Illinois, with its many railroad trunk lines and heavy industry, attracted workers both colored and white.

In the spring of 1917 workers at an ore plant in East Saint Louis initiated a strike in an attempt to gain union recognition and to stem the influx of colored workers. The employer defeated the walkout and destroyed the union by stockpiling weapons, securing the presence of state militia, exerting political influence, and hiring scab workers.

The Negro migrants became the convenient scapegoats for the union defeat as well as other ills that threatened the white population. In the ensuing months a series of racial confrontations took place finally erupting into a full-fledged race riot on July 2, 1917, that resulted in the killing of nine whites and about thirty-nine Negroes.[1]

These tragic events inspired Warren Smadbeck to write to the editor of the *New York Evening Journal*. In his letter he denounced the actions of the instigators and participants in the riots as "disgraceful" and championed equal rights for Negroes. Stating, "It is high time that our Government recognize the inequalities which have been meted out to the Negro," Smadbeck argued that, given the same power as the white man, the Negro would prove equally capable and energetic and should not be denied opportunities by an accident of birth resulting in a black skin instead of a white skin. His ardent message was reprinted in *New York Age*, a prominent Negro newspaper, on July 12, 1917.[2]

Warren's letter made clear his sentiments toward the colored race, sentiments that were ostensibly shared by his brother Arthur and Arthur's wife Ruth. For example, as head of the Heckscher Foundation for Children, Ruth Smadbeck arranged a donation of playground equipment for a Negro recreation center near Fort Myers, Florida, in 1954.[3] On the other hand, Ruth Smadbeck exhibited a different attitude when the issue of race was closer to home. In 1921 she placed a help wanted ad seeking a "white" houseworker.[4]

* * *

Chicago was another northern city that attracted colored workers during the wartime years with employment in the meatpacking houses and steel mills. Negroes faced discrimination not only in employment but also in housing, transportation, and access to recreational facilities. Their presence was unofficially outlawed and violently discouraged at Chicago parks, beaches, and swimming pools.

Racial troubles in Chicago arose in July of 1919 when a Negro teenager swam too close to a white beach and was struck in the head with a rock, allegedly thrown by a white man, causing the boy to drown. An inadequate response from the police sparked protests and erupted into rioting that spread well beyond the beach and lasted for nearly a week. Dozens were killed and hundreds wounded.[5]

Escape from the city, with its unwelcoming pools and beaches, to a summer cottage in Wisconsin presented other hurdles. During the time frame of the newspaper resorts, policies that promoted racial segregation in housing were common and accepted, at least by whites. Some communities enacted municipal ordinances that prevented African Americans from buying or moving into neighborhoods occupied by a white majority. (Notably, such restrictions did not prevent colored servants from living in white households in white neighborhoods.)

The United States Supreme Court considered just such a provision in 1917 and ruled that the ordinance violated the due process clause of the Fourteenth Amendment of the Constitution.[6] But the court came to a different conclusion when presented with neighborhood association provisions. In that situation racial segregation was not perpetrated by a municipally enacted statute but rather through contractual restrictions agreed to between individuals. Since the Fourteenth Amendment prohibits only the enacting or enforcing of governmental laws which inhibit property rights, it was found not to apply to contracts between private parties.[7] With no constitutional provision at issue, the restrictive covenants were allowed to stand and, in the aftermath of the decision, to proliferate.

A sampling of deeds displays inconsistency in the use of restrictive covenants at the newspaper resorts. At some colonies nonwhites were outright prohibited from owning land while at others their exclusion was only latent. A deed for Pell Lake Highlands included this wording:

> The title to the property conveyed by this deed or any part thereof shall never vest in a person or persons of African descent nor in any colored person or persons, and this property, or any part thereof, or any building erected on it, or any part thereof shall never be rented or leased to or occupied by any person or persons of African descent nor to any colored person or persons.[8]

In comparison, there was no such restriction in a deed for lots in Pell Lake Addition.[9]

Neither the Highlands nor the Addition were Smadbeck projects, but the same disparity is found in their newspaper colonies. There were no racial restrictions in deeds for the Smadbeck lots at Pell Lake or Lake Como Beach.[10] But a deed for the Smadbeck resort of Interlaken provided that "said premises shall not be sold, leased to or occupied by any persons other than of the Caucasian Race."[11] Similarly, deeds for Bolinas Beach and Skyland prohibited ownership by non-Caucasians.[12]

Apparently, the Smadbecks' purported support of equal rights for Negroes did not necessarily extend to the fine print. The presence of racial restrictions in deeds however is not necessarily indicative of purposeful prejudice on the part of the developers. The language may have just been happenstance, due to reliance on standard form deeds rather than to any overt bias.

Still, even where there was no express exclusion of nonwhites, there were a few instances of assurances that lots would only be sold to the right kind of people. Although the deed for Smadbeck Pell Lake lots did not contain a race clause, a promotional article for the development incorporated this caveat:

> This paper reserves the right to refuse to sell these lots to applicants who, on investigation, appear to be undesirable.... A careful investigation will be made of every applicant, and Post readers may be assured of having agreeable neighbors.[13]

No criteria for what made a person "undesirable" were specified.

* * *

Negroes were further stymied in buying undeveloped land. Some owners simply refused to sell to them, a situation that was aggravated by the presence of the Ku Klux Klan (KKK). Organized in Wisconsin in 1920, indications of a Lake Geneva chapter of the Klan, the Knights of the

Nightshirts, was hinted at in May of 1923[14] and an initiation took place near Genoa Junction a few months later.[15] Jews, Catholics, immigrants, and Negroes were all among the Klan's targeted groups. While the KKK was already in decline by 1926 and had mostly disappeared from Wisconsin by 1928, it was at its most robust earlier in the decade.[16]

Laws requiring that secret organizations publicize their membership rosters and making it a crime to wear a hood to disguise identity were introduced in several states, including Wisconsin.[17] Although the governor vetoed an anti-masking bill passed by both houses of the Wisconsin legislature in the spring of 1923,[18] the timing of this attempted legislation indicates the height of KKK concern.

The existence of Klan chapters in Elkhorn, Lake Geneva, and Delevan, in addition to a general feeling of animosity toward colored people, made it uncomfortable and problematic for them to purchase land in Walworth County.[19] In early May 1925, a group of Negroes from Chicago attempted to buy lakefront property at Russell Lake, later to be renamed Lake Wandawega where Interlaken came to be established. An offer of $150,000 was made to a broker representing an owner of 106 acres. The real estate agent, perhaps suspicious of the lavish offer, investigated the proposal and discovered that the land was scheduled to pass through five hands and eventually become the property of the Chicago Negroes. The offer was turned down.[20]

The identity of the Chicagoans who failed in this attempted land purchase is unknown, but likely did not include Jeremiah Brumfield or Bradford Watson. Neither of these Negro men was moneyed enough to make such a generous offer. They and their families did, however, vacation in the area, renting rooms from a colored dairy farmer who lived at nearby Lake Delevan.[21]

Brumfield, originally from Kentucky, worked as a night janitor during college before graduating as class valedictorian at age nineteen.[22] He moved to Chicago, obtained a law degree in 1912, and became an assistant city attorney.[23] Bradford Watson had been a railroad porter but by 1918 was employed as an "oiler" for the city of Chicago.[24] Brumfield and Watson had much in common. Their children attended the same school, both men were employed at City Hall, and they shared an avid interest in politics.

The two became acquainted with another colored Chicagoan, Frank Anglin who came from Jamaica as a teenager. Initially he was engaged in seafaring but apprenticed as a machinist and eventually migrated toward automobile mechanics. He worked as a truck inspector for Swift & Co.,[25] managed a truck rental service, and became an automotive engineer.[26] Anglin owned land at Idlewild, a summer resort in northern Michigan where Negroes could enjoy big band entertainment and outdoor recreation.

While welcoming, the resort's distance from Chicago rendered it unavailable as a weekend destination.[27]

These Chicago community leaders, Brumfield, Watson, and Anglin, sought to remedy the vacation dilemma by creating a summer colony for affluent African Americans. In 1924 they targeted Lake Ryan, five miles north of Pell Lake and six miles east of Lake Geneva. Lake Ryan was a mere twenty miles distant from Russell Lake where the unknown group from Chicago had sought to acquire waterfront acreage. Both groups attempted their purchases in May of 1925 but only Brumfield and his friends were able to complete the deal. They were successful with an offer of $60,000 for 600 acres[28] ($100 per acre was the going rate for farmland at the time), while the Negroes willing to pay nearly three times as much money for a fraction of the acreage were turned away. The difference in outcome was due to the willingness of James Reeves, owner of a realty company in Waukegan, Illinois,[29] to negotiate with Negroes. Recognizing its potential for resale, Reeves had acquired the Lake Ryan acreage a few years earlier. It can perhaps be imputed that he lacked racial prejudice or maybe he was just not concerned about the race of his customers because he was not a local owner.

The sale to Brumfield, Watson, and Anglin was conditioned on their ability to raise the needed $60,000 purchase price. They were directed toward Ivan Bell, a white real estate agent with a spotty reputation in gambling and speculation. Bell was advised against the investment but a relative nevertheless backed him financially in the hope that the project would keep him out of trouble. The men were so pleased with the financial support secured for them by Ivan Bell that they named the colony Lake Ivanhoe.[30]

They proceeded to plat out an initial 83 acres mimicking the lot pattern Smadbeck used at Pell Lake, but instead of flowers, the streets were named for famous Negro people and schools.[31] The centerpiece of the resort was a hillside pavilion. Built at a cost of $40,000, its generously sized inlaid dance floor was surrounded by a veranda that overlooked the lake. A wide stairway with a series of landings led down to the beach and a pier. Beginning with Lake Ivanhoe's grand opening in the spring of 1927 the pavilion was a locus for entertainment that included dance bands, prize fights, and gambling. Together with swimming, boating, fishing, tennis, and horseback riding, the resort attracted eager elite Negro Chicagoans, enough to cause Frank Anglin to quit his job to manage the sale of lots.[32]

While some white developments excluded Negroes, this Negro development did not exclude whites. Deeds to the lots contained no racial restrictions,[33] but Lake Ivanhoe nevertheless practiced its own form of discrimination. It was advertised as "The Preferred Summer Home of Discriminating Colored People" with sales aimed at "high-minded colored people ... church going people of education and refinement."[34] Today Lake Ivanhoe is an integrated community with a spread of black, white, and Latino residents.

Lake Ivanhoe, lacking a subscription purchase requirement, was not a newspaper colony, but it nevertheless replicated the Smadbeck projects in shape, size, accouterments, and success. Warren Smadbeck was validated in his assessment that, given the same opportunity as white men, Negroes would prove equally capable, although he probably did not envision that some would become developers, following in his footsteps.

* * *

Whether or not discriminatory covenants were embodied in deeds, the prevailing attitude at Pell Lake was not welcoming to those of color. This frame of mind was displayed on July 4, 1950, when four boys from Lake Ivanhoe hitched a ride to Pell Lake on a milk truck to swim with some white friends. The "beach deputy," a man named Dan Young, ordered them off the southern beach and told them not to return. Signs were then posted at both swimming places reading "Restricted. For Club Members Only. No Dogs Allowed."

When the incident came to the attention of the *Janesville Gazette* the editor assigned reporter Alice Hackett to investigate. Hackett and her husband took photographs of the signs, one of which was published in the *Gazette* on August 1, 1950. The accompanying article reported that several bathers understood that the signs were meant to keep Negroes off the beaches. Dan Young stated that he posted the warnings on his own authority and vowed that they would remain as long as he was in charge of the lake. The president of the Pell Lake POA, Paul Wilkes, denied that he or the POA authorized Young's actions. Wilkes declared that he knew of "no legal backing to prejudice," and that, if necessary, he would tear down the signs himself.[35]

An opinion piece also appeared in the paper decrying bigotry and commending Wilkes for his insistence that the signs be removed. The *Gazette* expressed the hope that the Pell Lake POA would fully support Wilkes and eliminate the illegal signs at the beaches.[36] A short time later the *Wisconsin State Journal* printed a letter to the editor from Alice Hackett which repeated much of the content of the *Gazette* article and added an update on her recent conversation with Wilkes to find out if he had torn down the signs. Indicating some backtracking, Wilkes said that he was only one board member of nine, that he spoke with Dan Young who refused to remove the signs, that feelings were strong, and that he needed to research the powers of the POA.[37]

Wilkes asked the reporter to retract her statements quoting his criticism of the signs and his intent that they be torn down. He said he had been subjected to threats on his life and requested Hackett to attend an upcoming meeting of the Pell Lake POA where the matter was scheduled to be discussed. When interviewed about the meeting two decades later Alice recalled an atmosphere of hate and anger which she described as "suppressed violence."[38]

In response to the hostility directed toward Wilkes and its reporter at the emotionally charged meeting, the *Gazette* published a softened follow-up article, reporting that at the meeting Hackett explained to the property owners that Wilkes was not responsible for the initial article and editorial. She characterized his remarks as the sentiments of a Christian gentleman and noted the difficulty of balancing religious principles with social practices. Wilkes apologized for assuming that the beaches and lakefront were public property and told about his trip to the county courthouse where he discovered that the shoreline was owned by the POA and thus was private property. The group accordingly voted to remove the signs and replace them. The new signs clarified that the beach was restricted for the use of property owners and their guests rather than for club members. The replacement signs still contained the wording "No Dogs Allowed."[39]

The POA also voted to write a letter to the *Janesville Daily Gazette* criticizing its reporting of the incident and the editorial in praise of Wilkes. Then, in a paradoxical move, the property owners reelected Wilkes president of the POA for another year. Paul Wilkes nevertheless found it difficult to remain in Pell Lake and, as Samuel Gonzales reports in his history of Lake Ivanhoe, Wilkes soon sold his home and moved away.[40]

Gonzales met with resistance when he attempted to review records of the August 1950 meeting. He was first told that meeting minutes only went back as far as 1955, then that the clubhouse had been vandalized and the records for the year 1950 had been stolen and perhaps destroyed, and finally that it would not be possible for him to make a personal examination of the clubhouse files.[41]

Just how long the signs disallowing dogs remained at the beaches is uncertain. Perhaps as long as several decades before they were removed and stored in the attic of the clubhouse. In 2010 members of the Pell Lake POA raised concerns about the dangers presented by debris and pets, specifically dogs, at the beaches.

Upon learning that dogs were in fact prohibited by a town ordinance, the old signs, including the banner reading "No Dogs Allowed," were resurrected from the attic, refurbished, and once again erected at the beaches,[42] presumably in innocence of their history, because, after all, the records from 1950 had disappeared. The old signs remained at the Pell Lake beaches until they were replaced in 2019 with new ones reading, more appropriately, "No Pets Allowed on the Beach."

* * *

The resorts established by Bertram Mayo similarly exhibited racial prejudice and, in at least one instance, overtly demonstrated the manner of enforcement. The deed involved contained a clause similar to that in the deeds for some of the Smadbeck resorts limiting use of the land to those of the Caucasian race.[43] Butler attributed this language to Mayo and faulted him only for not also excluding howling dogs.[44]

A director of the National Association for the Advancement of Colored People purchased a subscription to the *New York Tribune* and a lot at Beachwood. His check for a recent payment was returned to him by the paper's promotion department with a letter explaining that the deeds for Beachwood contained a clause excluding ownership or occupancy by any non–Caucasian and that it had just been learned that the buyer was a member of the colored race and therefore was unable to hold title to Beachwood lots. The letter was reprinted in *The Crisis*, a civil rights journal published by the NAACP, prefaced with the observation that the *Tribune* had recently assumed a pose of high moral standards.[45]

It is notable that *The Crisis* printed the letter on the page following an editorial extolling the network of alliances, committees, federations, societies, and councils organized by Jews in an effort to promote publishing, education, and charity, and to prevent infraction of their rights. The opinion piece suggests that Negroes emulate the organized activity of the Jews recognizing that Jews, along with Negroes, can experience exclusion and segregation.

While the Beachwood Religious Association claimed to be nondenominational and welcoming to all,[46] the borough also described itself as having a reputation as a Christian community and being religiously unified,[47] although Beachwood deeds apparently did not contain a clause restricting sales to non–Christians. While discrimination against Jews in land acquisition certainly existed, Mayo nevertheless sold his idea to the Jewish Smadbeck brothers, certainly realizing they would market land to members of their own ethnicity. It is even possible that this was the reason Mayo was willing to involve the Smadbecks in the promotion. Consider that Mayo initiated the Browns Mills in the Pines promotion concurrently with that for Asbury Park Estates, the Smadbecks' first newspaper colony. Perhaps Mayo did not view the brothers as competitors, but instead as persons who would apply his promotional idea to a different audience.

* * *

Although subtle, the portrayal of a resort community as having been created especially for readers of the sponsoring newspaper was a significant aspect of the newspaper colony advertising campaign at many of the resorts. The assertion generated a feeling of exclusivity. All other lot owners would be readers of the same paper and, presumably, like-minded folk. The clear implication was that neighbors at the resort would be socially and culturally compatible, and, perhaps, also racially and religiously compatible.

This was particularly played up at the early colonies. Advertising for Asbury Park Estates was designed to attract Yiddish speaking New Yorkers through alignment with the *Jewish Daily News*. Lakewood Pines was aimed at government employees with ads placed in their association newsletter *The Chief*, and the *Brooklyn Citizen*, the sponsor of Patchogue Lakes and Mastic Park, was the vehicle for marketing lots to residents of German ancestry which largely made up the readership of that paper.

As the Smadbecks sought to expand the audience for their resorts, the ethnicity of the targeted populations became less specific. Pell Lake was not aimed at any particular audience and the deeds had no restrictions affecting race or religion. Still, the *Chicago Evening Post* was read by lower middle-class residents in the heavily Polish northwest side of the city and the lot owners were exclusively white and predominately Polish, Italian, German, and Bohemian. A few Scandinavians were also represented, and in later years Ukrainians moved in.

Warren and Arthur Smadbeck had at least one real estate development in mind for Negroes. In 1944 they placed a classified ad in the *Philadelphia Inquirer* seeking an estate manager for a "colored development" near Philadelphia.[48] But they apparently did not design any newspaper colonies specifically for Negroes. Nevertheless, one of their subscription premium ventures became a colored community quite unintentionally on their part.

Chagrin Falls Park had been destined for a very different demographic. With 156 acres of land purchased in Geauga County, Ohio, southeast of Cleveland, the colony was promoted with a subscription to Cleveland's *Jewish World* (*Yidishe Velt*). Apparently attempting to replicate the success of Asbury Park Estates, an agent of Home Guardian approached Samuel Rocker, publisher of the Yiddish paper, with a proposition akin to the arrangement worked out with *Jewish Daily News* two years earlier. By June of 1921 the acreage had been platted into 1,386 lots in the standard size and pattern, with one of the main streets named Rocker Avenue, and full-page advertisements began appearing in *Jewish World*.[49]

There are conflicting reports on what happened next. A smallish display ad in June of 1922 claims that "about 1,000 lots" were sold for $58 with the 450 remaining lots being sacrificed for $50. Inquiries were directed in care of *Jewish World*.[50] A month later the price had dropped to $30 per lot when parcels 40' × 100' were advertised for $60.⁵¹ If indeed approximately 70 percent of the lots had been sold in the first year it seems unlikely that the price would be cut nearly in half, a price reduction not seen at any other colony in such a brief period of time. This early and deep discounting of the cost of the lots suggests that there had been some difficulty in selling them.

In his book on African American suburbs, in a chapter devoted to Chagrin Falls Park, author Andrew Wiese reports that the lots marketed through *Jewish World* had sparse sales and speculated that the cause was the absence of sewers, water, electricity, and paved roads. As a result, the newspaper disposed of the lots in 1924 by selling them to Akron real estate agents Grover and Florence Brow.⁵²

Wiese further states that the price of Chagrin Falls Park lots fluctuated wildly during the 1920s and by the mid–1930s the Brows sold lots for $25 and at tax forfeiture sales some lots could be had for as little as $2.⁵³ Although the Brows were white,⁵⁴ they marketed the lots primarily to Negroes and Chagrin Falls Park became a predominately colored community rather than the Jewish summer colony that was intended.

Anderson Hitchcock, in a book of remembrances and musings on growing up in Chagrin Falls Park,⁵⁵ provides a very different explanation for the poor lot sales. He asserts that when Samuel Rocker marketed the lots to Jews, residents of adjacent Chagrin Falls, a tony suburb of Cleveland, burned a cross on the property scaring off buyers.⁵⁶

Hitchcock goes on to suggest that the Jewish newspaper editor hatched a scheme to retaliate against the people of Chagrin Falls for their hostile attitude toward Jews. He effectuated a cruel hoax by subdividing the property into 5' × 25' lots and selling them for $5 each with ads placed in the *Negro Digest*, making the land attractive to Negroes. Elsewhere in the book the author has Rocker placing the ads in the *Cleveland Spectator*, presumably a reference to a Negro publication.

The lack of utilities and paved roads did not inhibit the development of other newspaper premium resorts, so perhaps Hitchcock is accurate in his claim that the reason for the failure to sell lots was a hostile attitude toward Jews. However, the assertion that Rocker sold to African Americans in revenge is at odds with Wiese's more plausible and better documented explanation that Chagrin Falls Park evolved into a Negro enclave simply because the newspaper sold the lots to real estate agents who advertised them in a manner that appealed to the group. Hitchcock provides no source material and admits that some of the content of his book "comes from anecdotal information and lacks empirical facts." His explanation also contains blatant factual errors casting skepticism over his entire narrative.⁵⁷

Chagrin Falls Park was not the only Smadbeck newspaper resort targeted at Jews that ran into trouble. The Smadbecks again aimed at Jewish customers when, in 1928, they obtained land surrounding Madron Lake in Berrien County, Michigan. The land was purchased by Ludwig Freudenthal from three farmers and encompassed all of the lake shoreline except for a portion occupied by a Boy Scout camp.[58] The colony of Madron Lake was platted out in February of 1929[59] employing street names such as Fern, Dahlia, Acacia, Dandelion, and Clubhouse Circle Drive.[60] Lots were advertised as newspaper subscription premiums in alliance with the *Chicago Jewish Chronicle*.[61]

Records establish that some lots were transferred by Warren Smadbeck to purchasers[62] and that several hundred lots were offered for sale at auction in 1945. Since the auction was scheduled to be held at the Real Estate Exchange on Vesey Street in New York City it would appear that Smadbeck or an associate was the seller.[63]

Perhaps the alliance with the *Chronicle*, a weekly publication, could not provide enough exposure, perhaps the dawn of the Depression a few months after the lot promotion began dampened sales, perhaps the physical characteristics of the lake were not attractive, or perhaps all or some combination of these factors worked against the development of Madron Lake. However murky the reason, the roads and narrow lots platted by the Smadbecks for the planned summer community do not appear on current maps. If the newspaper colony of Madron Lake ever existed, no trace of it remains today.

* * *

Few distinct conclusions can be gleaned from the muddle of postures exhibited by the Smadbecks toward race and ethnicity. The brothers designed summer colonies for Jewish populations while also aligning with newspapers that appealed to Catholics and Protestants. Arthur and his wife supported the donation of equipment to a playground for African Americans, yet they would not welcome a nonwhite worker into their home. Warren wrote a public letter to a newspaper supporting equal opportunities for Negroes, but made no effort to attract them to the newspaper developments even though Lake Ivanhoe illustrated that there was an audience for such a venture. Then, in a contrary action, the brothers attempted a colored housing development in the 1940s. Deeds to lots in their colonies vacillated among excluding African Americans, excluding anyone who was not Caucasian, and an absence of any racial restrictions.

Still there is one conclusion about the characteristics of the intended Smadbeck audiences that emerges. None of the newspaper colonies were directed toward an elite, wealthy clientele. There was no attempt to sell large, expensive lots to a limited number of people. Instead Warren and Arthur Smadbeck set their sights on a different, more diffuse following.

12. Racial Issues

Their goal was to market small, inexpensive lots to masses of customers regardless of their nationality, ethnic background, or religion. The newspaper communities were clearly, and invariably, aimed at a middle- or working-class audience. Thus, economic status was the predominant element common to the populations targeted by the newspaper subscription promotions.

13

Social Considerations

The clubhouse was a defining feature of the newspaper resorts. A vital element of the formula established by Bertram Mayo, clubhouses were erected by Mayo at his Beverly Glen, Lakewood, Beachwood, and Browns Mills resorts and nearly every Smadbeck newspaper colony was equipped with a clubhouse as well.

The building served a variety of purposes. Most evident was as a lure to the lot buyers. Not only did they obtain a piece of land for a modest sum of money, but it came with free use of a clubhouse. On the surface this appeared to be a generous handout from the developers, but a second function of the clubhouse was solely to their benefit. A sales office on site was needed and the clubhouse provided the perfect location. The design often included sleeping rooms where the sales staff could bunk overnight, at least in the warm summer months, making it more convenient to accommodate buyers late into the evening. At some colonies the clubhouse also served as a lodging facility for lot buyers. Once it was deeded over to the POA, it provided a space for organizational meetings and communal entertainment.

Clubhouses were built in a prominent location, often inland rather than directly on the waterfront, and frequently mounted on a hill or promontory. At least one clubhouse, that at Crystal Lakes in Ohio, was built on an island in the lake.[1] Beginning in about 1926 many Smadbeck resorts had a road named Clubhouse Drive making it easier to now identify the original location of the building.

Most clubhouses were new construction, but in a few instances an existing building was adapted. Advertisements for Marshfield Estates proclaimed that "the famous old Peregrine White home is being remodeled into a clubhouse for the exclusive use of lot owners."[2] (Peregrine White was the first child born to the Mayflower pilgrims in America.) At Madron Lake, where a large farm formed the nucleus of the tract, a barn was remodeled for the clubhouse.[3]

Clubhouse structures were sometimes described as "rustic" which can be interpreted as simple or rough construction. Some were quite large and impressive looking even if not durably built. Designs varied and no two clubhouses appear to be identical.

Skyland's clubhouse had a spacious clubroom centered with sleeping rooms for gentlemen on one side and ladies on the other. A large fireplace with a cobblestone chimney could accommodate four-foot logs and, in a promotional article, the building was described as being equipped for "telephonic communications with the outside world." Running water was not mentioned, rather readers were told of a spring-well providing a source of unsurpassed "mountain fluid" in the rear of the lodge.[4]

Despite being dubbed the "white clubhouse," the facility at Clear Lake Shores has a colorful history. It began life as the sales center for the resort and then functioned as the community center fitted out, according to one resident's journal, with Persian rugs. Its location just off Galveston Bay and the Gulf of Mexico, subjected the building to hurricanes and tropical storms. At one time holes were drilled in the floor to let flood water drain out and keep it from floating away. In 1947 it was used as a temporary morgue and, on other occasions, as a storm shelter. When Clear Lake Shores incorporated as a city in November of 1962, the Smadbeck structure became the City Hall as well as a polling place. The oldest public building still in use in Galveston County, it was raised ten feet above its former elevation in 1990 and now perches on concrete blocks and steel beams.[5]

A number of clubhouses were left to decay and several, including the clubhouse at Nassau Lake Park, were destroyed by fire.[6] Among the surviving clubhouses, at least one—the structure at Interlaken, with its portico entrance still in place—has become a private residence. Others maintain themselves as rental halls for weddings and other functions such as the clubhouse at Lake Como Beach which was renovated in 1993 for this purpose.[7]

The North Shore Beach clubhouse, damaged in a fire and extensively restored in 1979, still hosts monthly civic association meetings in addition to being available for party rental. Lake Parsippany advertises its clubhouse for rent, however, the fire department bought the original clubhouse grounds on Club House Court in 1996, and the present clubhouse occupies a building on the lakefront.[8]

The clubhouse at Pell Lake was constructed on eleven lots at the corner of Jasmine and Florence Roads. An unpretentious two-story building, it had open air porches on the upper level supported by squared stone pillars. A photo dated September of 1991, now on display at the clubhouse, shows the second-floor porches removed and the roof reconfigured with the two stone posts standing awkwardly apart from the building, and from each other.

* * *

Club House, Pell Lake, Wis.   87806-nv

The clubhouse at Pell Lake was modest by comparison with those at other newspaper colonies. The far right side of this 1927 photograph of the clubhouse depicts a narrow dirt road typical of the roads throughout the resort.

Curiously, while the clubhouse was waved as a carrot to tantalize potential lot buyers, another structure provided by the developer at Pell Lake was not mentioned in the promotional verbiage. This building was likely an even stronger customer magnet yet Smadbeck called no attention to it, and while the clubhouse was specifically mentioned in the trust deed, this simple wooden building was left out. Built on the parkland along the lakeshore at the southern beach was a pavilion for dancing. A dance hall alongside a lake evokes romantic visions of music wafting over the water in the moonlight, but the pavilion may have served a shadier purpose.

Dance halls were common in the Prohibition era and were frequented by those looking for an opportunity to obtain illicit liquor. This was especially prevalent at country roadhouses that operated without regulation by city governments. Social welfare groups frowned upon rural dance halls and, in Wisconsin, Walworth County was at the forefront of efforts to stem the combination of moonshine and moonlit dancing.

Members of the County Ministerial Association met in early 1923 to shake fists at this social evil that imperiled the health and morals of young people.[9] In an attempt to remedy the situation, the clergymen drafted a resolution and forwarded it to their state senator, a local physician from Elkhorn. Given his Quaker upbringing, his identification as a "Dry," and his position as chairman of the senate committee on education and welfare,

Eldo T. Ridgway, was the ideal person to champion the ministers' cause in the state legislature.

Dance hall reform was one aspect of the national Progressive Movement that engulfed the country in the first few decades of the twentieth century. This trend toward social activism and reform motivated the enactment of laws regulating dance halls throughout the country which, in turn, enabled Ridgway to borrow preexisting language and ideas in formulating his proposed law.[10]

The resultant Ridgway Dance Hall bill received much attention in the press throughout the state. Its proponents employed alarmist rhetoric to urge passage of the bill describing country dance halls as places where young teenage girls became intoxicated and staggered home in the early morning hours. It was asserted that mothers no longer looked after their daughters, making it necessary for the state to extend a protecting hand to rein in the "dark picture of public dance halls running wild, moonshine parties and social diseases on the spread."[11] These claims were not without merit. Dance halls were reputed to be hangouts for gangsters and prostitutes. Naive, young working girls were lured to these roadhouses by the availability of liquor, sensuous new dances, and free or low-cost admission, often resulting in seduction.[12]

Supported by most of the socially progressive organizations in the state, the Ridgway bill wound its way through both houses of the state legislature, navigated many hearings and proposed amendments, and was signed into law by the governor in June of 1923. Basically, it was an enabling act, giving county boards the prerogative to license, inspect, and regulate carnivals, street fairs, and particularly, dance halls.[13]

Walworth County, as the birthplace of the law, enthusiastically embraced its new authority. On November 16, 1923, the Walworth County Board, backed by the Anti-Saloon League and the Woman's Christian Temperance Union, passed a dance hall ordinance.[14] Pursuant to the law a committee on dance hall supervision was formed, and it appointed a team of thirty supervisors of amusements who were issued badges, vested with the powers of deputy sheriffs, and charged with enforcing a set of rather drastic rules.

Intoxicants and intoxicated persons were, officially at least, prohibited. While the proprietor had the primary responsibility for complying with the rules, the amusement supervisors or inspectors were empowered to arrest anyone who became intoxicated or possessed liquor, and to seize the goods as evidence. Their authority extended to liquor provided by an automobile owner or driver outside the facility. Violations could result in license forfeitures and fines and jail terms for both the dance hall operators and any offending minors. The inspectors were duty bound to file a written report describing the circumstances of the dance party in order to collect their compensation.

Most of the seventy-two counties in Wisconsin passed similar ordinances and the lively, and sometimes contentious, county board discussions about dance hall regulations continued to be a favorite topic for the local newspapers. First came the arguments over whether the dance halls should be regulated at all. This was followed by squabbling over what provisions to include or exclude, how much to charge for license fees, during what hours and on which days of the week dance pavilions could be open, how the inspectors would be selected, and how much they would be paid.

A vigorously debated provision was whether to allow "pass out checks," slips of paper that allowed customers to leave the hall for a short period of time, and then re-enter without having to pay again. The desire to prevent dancers from leaving to obtain alcohol from a vendor in the parking lot, was so strong that some county ordinances prohibited the use of pass out checks—even though many country roadhouses had no indoor toilets.[15] Walworth County wisely chose to omit any reference to pass out checks in its regulations.

With each county fashioning its own ordinance, there was a myriad of differing rules, a situation that resulted in claims of discrimination, appeals to the state attorney general for interpretations of the ordinances, and lawsuits. These local rules were unpopular with many segments of the community. The dance attendees would not report violations[16] and jurors refused to return guilty verdicts against dance hall operators and dancers even in the face of conclusive evidence.[17]

Those operating the halls complained about being forced to pay for supervision of their events while many dances—those held at hotels, churches, and schools, or sponsored by farmers clubs—were exempt from the provisions.[18] A variety of strategies were employed in an attempt to evade the restrictions and the fees. The definition of a dance hall was challenged by assertions that it did not include a roadhouse[19] or an eating venue with a coin operated player piano.[20] A few claimed that a dance was not open to the pubic if the hall was rented to an individual who issued indiscriminate invitations[21] or if no admission fee was charged but the price of drinks was increased to compensate.[22] County boards were kept busy trying to close these loopholes and the press was kept busy reporting on their efforts.

The job of dance hall inspector was often viewed as a political plum. The pay was good, around $5 a dance, and free beer and food was usually offered. Some overindulged becoming intoxicated themselves[23] or used the promise of a favorable report to connive with the proprietor.[24]

The assignment also had its detractions. The supervisors were blamed

13. Social Considerations

if the ordinance was not accomplishing its purpose. The suspicions of one county board were raised when a group of inspectors wrote "none" on dance hall reports asking for the number of underage dancers, individuals denied admission, and intoxicated persons, but then appended requests for billy clubs to protect themselves.[25] Elsewhere a second layer of inspection was added with the appointment of a special dance hall committee of the county board to visit dances and determine whether or not the inspectors were doing their duty.[26] Some inspectors were criticized as being too lax in enforcing the regulations and others were chastised for being overly strict, as where inspectors stopped a quadrille because it was too noisy and expelled patrons for engaging in "fancy dancing."[27]

The inspectors had their own gripes, complaining that the dance hall proprietors and local law enforcement tried to tell them how to do their job, that girls and women bobbed their hair making it difficult to judge whether they met the age requirement, and that the contortions performed by dancers interfered with determining whether or not they were intoxicated.[28] The job could also be dangerous—more than one inspector was clobbered on the head with a beer bottle.[29]

Walworth County sought the help of the Ku Klux Klan in enforcing its ordinance. One hundred and fifty knights were deputized who, in one incident, swooped down on a dance hall and blocked the exits to prevent the drinking dancers from escaping. Twenty liquor flasks were strewn about the floor but, since it was impossible to determine ownership, no arrests were made.[30] Another time the Klan lit a cross on fire causing dance attendees to attempt to extinguish the blaze. The inspector was blamed, at least in part, for the fight that ensued.[31]

Although concerned with nonenforcement of the ordinance during the summer of 1924, the county remained determined to persevere in the campaign to "clean out the nest of bootleggers." To accomplish this objective the dance hall inspectors were summoned to a meeting in May of 1925 to be given a pep talk by the District Attorney, the county board members, and representatives of the civic-minded organizations that promoted the legislation.[32]

It was in this atmosphere that the Pell Lake pavilion held its first dance on Saturday, August 8, 1925.[33] Since the facility was not mentioned in the trust deed granting the POA ownership of the land where the pavilion was located, its use was not restricted to lot buyers. As such, the dance hall was open to the public bringing it within the purview of the Ridgway bill and the rigid provisions set out in the county ordinance.

A rather plain, rectangular building (pictured on this book's cover), the pavilion was built on stilts allowing it to extend out over the lake.[34] The interior space was a large open room with a concession area at the front end where snacks were sold. A series of posts separated the dance floor proper from a string of benches lining the side wall where windows looked out over the lake. As required by the ordinance, there were no private rooms and the hall was brightly lit. A live orchestra, including a violinist, provided music[35] until the mandatory midnight closing time.

The Pell Lake dance hall was presumably operated as a private enterprise charging an admission fee of twenty-five cents. Children under the age of sixteen were excluded unless accompanied by a parent or guardian. The proprietor paid the yearly $10 license fee plus a $5 per dance charge which covered the salary of the supervisor.

County boards continued to reevaluate whether the dance hall ordinances were a good idea after all, providing more fodder for the press as succinctly expressed in a news article headline: "Tramp, Tramp, Tramp: County Board Marks Time with Dance Ordinance and Renews Griefs of Yester Year."[36] Sauk County enacted its dance hall ordinance and then rescinded it at the next meeting.[37] Another handful of counties repealed their laws after a year or two.[38] In some cases a particular provision, or even the entire ordinance, was revoked only to be reinstated a short time later.[39]

A few months after the Pell Lake dance hall opened, the Walworth County Board met to assess the effectiveness of its ordinance. The county clerk felt it was a matter of personal opinion as to the success or failure of the enforcement provisions while E.T. Ridgway defended the legislation he had championed. He attributed its success to the hiring of competent inspectors while encouraging stricter enforcement and better inspection. During 1924, the only full year for which figures were available, a profit of $400 was realized on the 650 dances held in the county. This excess revenue, Ridgway argued, rendered the ordinance both morally and financially prudent, and he credited it with preventing venereal disease and illegitimate children which would incur costs for the taxpayers. None of the dance halls in the county had sustained any license revocations. This flawless record was cited as proof that the ordinance was a success while overlooking the possibility that the lack of license revocations could also be evidence of look-the-other-way enforcement. In the end, Walworth County was not among those willing to forgo dance hall control and the result of the review was to leave the ordinance in effect.[40]

It was clever of Warren Smadbeck to include the pavilion as an added attraction for customers while not calling attention to it or becoming involved with its operation. Clearly this was done because of the illegal drinking that took place in such venues.

Although not mentioned in the advertisements, the other Smadbeck colonies throughout the United States surely had dance pavilions. A news item described the construction of a dance pavilion on an island in Laurel

Lake.[41] A dance hall is also documented at Lake Louisvilla but only because it is mentioned in the caption of a 1932 aerial view of the resort.[42] It is noteworthy that the only advertisement for a newspaper subscription colony to mention a dance pavilion is one for the resort of Plage Laval in the Canadian province of Quebec,[43] an area unaffected by the prohibition of alcohol during the 1920s.

* * *

Initially the POAs were the social arbiters of the summer communities. Sometimes a distinct women's club was incorporated as well, but usually such groups were organized informally as subsets of the POA. These women's contingents enthusiastically arranged dances, dinners, card and bunco games, costume parties, and other functions. Some had boat races, swimming races, and beauty contests.

At Pell Lake bake sales, auctions, and bingo games were conducted as money raisers by the Women's Club while the Highlands Sunshine Club held weekly card parties to help pay for lake improvements.[44]

Other groups connected to the newspaper resorts were formed as well and a survey of these organizations in Walworth County shows that club activities parallel the progression of societal change. In the beginning years of the colonies, clubs were designed to extend the camaraderie into the winter months, meeting off-season in city neighborhoods. Pell Lake lot owners who lived in the Chicago Garfield neighborhood and those in the suburb of Oak Park held winter card parties to get together with their friends seen otherwise only at the lake. Pel-Lakens, a group for young people, was organized in 1928. It held meetings in Chicago during the fall and winter months and grew to over seventy members. The Pell Lake Baseball Association was yet another social group that arranged winter dances in the city to maintain interest in summertime sports activities[45] and the Women's Club even had a sub-contingent called the Women's Winter Club.[46]

The deterioration of the economy in the 1930s altered the character of the resorts when some city dwellers without prospects for work moved to their summer cottages to save money. At some colonies trailers were brought in for cheap housing. Abandoned cottages provided opportunities to squatters, while at a few of the colonies people lived outdoors in the woods. The organizations reacted by redirecting socialization to financial assistance for needy individuals, giving rise to a new round of club activity.

Two such groups were founded in Pell Lake in 1934, patterned after immigrant confraternities. The Pell Lake Social Club was incorporated in August and the Pell Lake Friendship Club in November. The reason for two clubs is not obvious as many of the same people appear as officers and directors of both associations. Additionally, both clubs had the same declared purpose of promoting sociability and giving financial aid to members: $1.50 in the event of sickness and $2.50 in the case of death. Any person could apply for membership but had to be voted in by the board of directors which could also expel members who failed to pay the yearly dues of 25 cents or "in cases where members become troublesome."[47]

The end of Prohibition, like the deteriorating economy, had its effect on the social structure of the resorts. The ban on alcohol was repealed on December 5, 1933, with the ratification of the Twenty-First Amendment but state laws restricting or prohibiting the sale alcohol were not affected unless the legislatures took action to accommodate the change in mores. A Walworth County survey on whether to remain dry or wet resulted in all but one of the townships voting for wet. The Wisconsin legislature acted quickly to revise its laws but not before applications for permits to sell alcohol were filed and tavern keepers began stocking liquor.[48]

With the imminent threat of the availability of legal liquor the conservative welfare groups again became aroused. In January of 1934 the dance hall rules in Walworth County were stiffened to require inspectors to visibly sport a badge or star and to wear caps designating them as officers of the law. Supervisors would be assigned to dances alphabetically rather than by proximity to the hall.[49]

At the June Walworth County board meeting thirty-five members of the Temperance Union and representatives of the Ministerial Association came armed with resolutions, amendments, and new ideas for the "control of evil" in county dance halls. One reporter described the meeting as "a mess" where the board of supervisors passed, reconsidered, and rescinded action for the control of dance halls and the sale of liquor. As a result of this wild session, those in attendance had no idea what had taken place, which motions were carried, and which demands were deferred.[50]

Since dance hall ordinances specifically prohibited the presence of alcoholic beverages, taverns with dancing rooms were initially denied permission to sell liquor. This unpopular application of the law caused most county dance hall ordinances to either be amended, repealed, or ignored. Legal liquor effectively put the dance hall inspectors out of work but created new business opportunities and transferred the locus of socialization to the tavern.

In the spring of 1934 seven liquor license applications were filed in the township, four for taverns within Pell Lake itself and the others for bars located around the edges. Stanley Walby operated the Green Dragon just off the Lake Geneva highway, W.O. Steffens had a place on Clover Road near the railroad tracks, and Herbert Schow ran a bar on Clover Road farther north.[51] William Hand operated a grocery, tavern, dance hall, gas pumps, icehouse, and restaurant at the north beach.[52] Mathew Welter, and later William Bishop, had a similar assemblage of businesses at the southern beach.

The Pell Lake pavilion continued functioning as a dance hall but, faced with competition from these taverns, most if not all with their own dancing rooms,[53] the popularity of the pavilion waned after only a few more years. On July 1, 1937, the pavilion was transformed into a roller rink with an admission price of 25 cents.[54]

Remnants of the Ridgway law remain in Wisconsin statutes as Sec. 59.56 (12), and, in the chapter titled Miscellaneous Police Provisions, Sec. 175.20.

Although dance halls are still mentioned, the fee income is now directed toward compensating the county for extraordinary governmental services involved with block parties, street fairs, or other public events such as extra police protection, traffic control, and refuse collection rather than for the hiring of inspectors.

* * *

A third wave of clubs appeared after World War II when resort communities experienced a resurgence of popularity. The middle and lower classes were once more able to afford a summer home and a second generation of families bought the cottages others had aged out of. The cost of repairs and improvements could be financed by renting the cottage out for a few weeks in the summer.

A new consumerist attitude was noticeable. Stone barbecue pits were constructed in the back yards and neighbors competed with each other for the most impressive table umbrella. Once again mothers and children stayed at the cottage all summer while the fathers toiled in the city and joined the family after work on Friday. On Saturday and Sunday, friends and relatives who did not have a summer place at Pell Lake descended on those who did.

The Pell Lake POA rebuilt the beach shelters, piers, and rafts to accommodate the constant stream of kids walking down the roads, carrying their pails and shovels and rolling inner tubes, on their way to the lake for a day of sunning and swimming. By the 1950s the pavilion had been renamed the Pelladium, was used for an occasional dance,[55] and continued to function as a roller rink most afternoons and evenings.[56] The roof of the aging building leaked but the teenagers skillfully skated around the puddles when it rained. A military surplus quonset hut, erected on North Lake Shore Drive half way between the beach and Saint Mary's church, became a snack shop called The Hut and Clover Road became home to a motor court with about half a dozen detached cabins for rent.

A Lutheran congregation was formed at a clubhouse meeting in 1947 and initially services were held in the garage of the Antemann home on Juneau Road. In the 1950s the Catholics enlarged Saint Mary's[57] and the Lutherans replaced the garage by purchasing an old schoolhouse, moving it to Clover Road, and refitting it for use as a church.[58] Steffans, having relocated his tavern business to the intersection of Thistle and Juneau, sold it to Hungarian immigrant Henry Karbiner and his wife Katie in 1947.[59] The name was changed to Henry's Tavern and the big building and its cement stairway entrance were painted a definitive green. When fathers arrived from the city on Friday evenings, families celebrated at Henry's with fish fry, beer, and a game of Skee-Ball.

The revived enthusiasm in resort activities bolstered the POAs and was reflected in the clubs. September of 1955 saw the formation of the Silver Lake Property Owners Improvement Association, a splinter group of the Interlaken POA. Renewed interest in the Pell Lake Friendship Club surfaced in 1959 when a resident wrote to the Secretary of State inquiring about the articles of incorporation. Some newly formed groups evinced a purpose more serious than mere socialization, such as the Social and Civic Club incorporated in 1949 to encourage active participation in civic as well as social activities at Lake Como Beach and the Pell Lake Businessmen's Association formed in 1952 to encourage business development and advocate for civic betterment.[60]

In these postwar years the resorts once again flourished as family getaways in warm weather. But the summer resort concept could not keep up with the continually evolving social picture. By the time Warren Smadbeck died in 1965, the original concept of the newspaper resort had long since run its course.

Owners grew older, making winter homes in Arizona or Florida more attractive than a cottage at a lake. Their children and grandchildren had other, more enticing alternatives for vacation dollars. The 1970s introduced theme parks, waterparks, and swappable time-shares. A condo at a ski resort provided a different option for a second home. Changes in transportation also contributed to the decline of the resorts as summer enclaves. Interstate highways made lakes farther north more accessible. At Pell Lake Marinette Road was renamed Pell Lake Road when Highway 12, the main approach from Illinois, was rerouted to the northeast and upgraded to super highway status, reducing Pell Lake to a name on an exit ramp for those passing by.

Constructed by the C and NW railroad in 1924, the Pell Lake depot was an impressive building measuring 20' × 50'.[61] But the growing use of automobiles resulted in fewer train passengers and, in 1941, the railroad was allowed to remove the depot and substitute a small, frame structure that was little more than a wooden shack.[62]

13. Social Considerations

When the train speed slowed to fifteen miles per hour due to poor track conditions, weekday commuters between Chicago and Pell Lake dropped to an average of six per day.[63] The railroad could not justify the expense of maintaining the tracks, the depots, and the train cars and engines and terminated the run to Pell Lake and Lake Geneva on August 9, 1975. By then even the replacement depot had disappeared and the passengers stepped out of the train into the weeds.[64]

Many cottage owners with limited retirement income sold the house in the city and moved to the summer home, winterized with indoor plumbing, a garage, an insulated attic, and a furnace. Younger workers with low income jobs found the cottages to be an inexpensive housing choice. A 1969 planning report for Pell Lake counted about 500 homes around the lake and characterized it as primarily a retirement community.[65] Pell Lake had lost its status as a summer resort.

This reshaping of the character of the communities is again mirrored in the history of the Walworth County newspaper resort clubs. When the office of the Wisconsin secretary of state purged inactive associations in 1985 the Pell Lake Businessmen's Association, Pell Lake Friendship Club, Pell Lake Social Club, and the Lake Como Beach Social and Civic Club, all fell victim and were involuntarily dissolved.

Local neighborhood clubs were no longer relevant. The POAs survived out of necessity but struggled to fulfill their community obligations

The original train depot at Pell Lake was handsomely constructed of frame and stucco with a red tile roof and a canopy at each end.

When ridership declined, the Pell Lake depot building was sold and relocated to become a private residence. It was replaced with a simple wooden shed, shown here in the early 1950s, bearing merely the name of the stop and a phone number.

to maintain the clubhouse and parkland. The Secretary of State declared both the Pell Lake POA and the Interlaken POA in bad standing in 1987 for failure to file yearly reports, and both were involuntarily dissolved in 1993. Interlaken restored its rank in 1995 and has been delinquent only twice since. The Lake Como Beach POA defaulted three times between 1998 and 2015 but in each case recovered its reputation. It took the Pell Lake POA eleven years to regain good standing.[66]

* * *

The transformation into a viable year-round community was not achieved gracefully by the newspaper colonies. The small lot size was a major handicap. Purchasers of two lots who waited too long to put up a cottage were confronted with zoning laws that rendered the lots unbuildable. Some were sold to adjacent land owners while others were just usurped by the neighbors. Here and there at Pell Lake a few of these orphaned lots still remain, often unkempt.

Some of the newspaper colonies became quite run down. Orienta Park, the 1909 development in Wichita, Kansas, exemplifies the situation. An article in the *Catholic Advance* in the mid–1960s deemed Orienta Park the "Poor Corner" of Wichita[67] and it was soon slated for urban renewal.

13. Social Considerations

A redevelopment approach similar to urban renewal was employed in 1981 at Coon Lake Beach in Minnesota. The nearby city of East Bethel acquired seventeen lots through tax forfeitures and obtained a federal grant to remove old cottages and clear abandoned lots. The lots were then offered to adjoining property owners for purchase or else combined to form large 125' × 100' parcels that sold for $7,500.[68] At least the Smadbeck grid pattern and most of the street names were preserved.

At another Minnesota resort a more drastic reconfiguration took place. A comparison of the original plat map of Carver Beach with a current map shows the street layout redesigned with completely different names. Only Highland Park Drive and Violet Road, retain both their original course and label. Even the lake was renamed, with Long Lake becoming Lotus Lake, although this change probably occurred in the 1930s.

Urban redevelopment was pursued too aggressively at the early Smadbeck vacation colony of Lakewood Pines. Warren Smadbeck had sold his leftover lots to an investment partner, Maximillian Hirshberg, in the 1950s. The land, acquired by the township through a wholesale tax foreclosure action in 1973, was bundled with other properties to become sites for affordable housing, schools, and an industrial park. This made it impossible to locate the original parcels on the tax rolls or on newly created property maps. After decades of unsuccessfully trying to identify Hirshberg's land, his descendants asserted ownership claims and obtained a ruling in their favor, exposing the township to the considerable expense of buying off their rights.[69]

* * *

No dramatic renewal changes have been attempted at Pell Lake. Some cottages remain summer homes although the lake is now little used for swimming. The year-round residents are a mix of retirees and wage earners. The land platted in the 1920s is not attractive for the building of modern, larger homes, even assuming enough adjoining lots can be obtained, since neighboring houses would be decades old and of inexpensive construction. As a result, fresh housing is mainly restricted to the fringes and Ira Pell's original farm acreage is today blanketed with newer homes.

Henry's Tavern was shuttered in 1964 when the Karbiners retired and, in time, the building was torn down leaving only the green cement steps. Those too have since disappeared. Both the big oak tree and the triangular island the tree sat on in front of the tavern at the intersection of Thistle and Juneau are gone.

The roller rink closed and was demolished in 1961.[70] The site of the original dance pavilion is now home to a few picnic tables and swing sets and bears a sign identifying it as the old Roller Rink Park. Saint Mary's parish dissolved a few years ago and the church building became a food bank and day care center. The Lutherans were more successful in sustaining their congregation and built a large new church on Pell Lake Road.

Although altered in appearance, the clubhouse still survives and continues to be used as the headquarters of the Pell Lake POA. Relieved of any function, the stone pillars remain in the yard thickly shrouded in flowering vines as if trying to hide in embarrassment.

Another puzzlement sits nearby. A dedication plaque mounted on a rock in the clubhouse yard reads, "In the 1800's this landmark was the Ira A. Pell's family homestead." Ira Pell never owned the land where Warren Smadbeck built the clubhouse nor did Smadbeck purchase any part of the Pell farm. The peculiar wording on the plaque serves both to confuse and to contribute to the history of Pell Lake.

14

Pell Lake in Context and Comparison

Viewed in the contexts of time and surroundings Pell Lake is, among all of the colonies, the archetypal example of a newspaper colony. Its existence, for nearly one hundred years, continues to exemplify Warren Smadbeck's original conception of a resort development promoted through a collaboration with a newspaper.

* * *

Pell Lake was fun—even the name itself was fun to say. Just eight letters comprising two conjoined syllables and flowing easily off the tongue. "Pell Lake" was a definite improvement over "Pells Lake" with that pesky middle "s" interrupting the three rolling consecutive "l"s. No other newspaper colony has a name as enjoyable to pronounce. Lake Louisvilla comes close but five syllables taxes the tongue and Plage Laval is a pleasurable phrase only because it is French.

Pell Lake shares its name sparingly. Among other geographical locations only Pell City, Alabama, founded in 1890 and named after local businessman George Pell, incorporates the Pell name. Few other newspaper colonies have such odd place names. Lake Louisvilla, where the last letter of Louisville was changed to create a new word, presents one example. Bolinas Beach and Estacada Beach have unusual names but both were borrowed from like-named adjoining cities. Skyland was a one-of-a-kind name but the designation largely disappeared when it became part of Ruidoso.

Rarely is the name of a newspaper used for the name of a place, but the newspaper colonies can take credit for three: Herald Harbor, Sentinel Beach, and Times Beach. Herald Harbor, which barely qualifies as a newspaper resort, is overshadowed by the much more famous Herald Square in New York. The name Sentinel Beach was used only during the two months long promotion to sell the lots and was never attached to the subdivision as a whole, rather Hudson Lake Beach remained in more popular usage. Post

171

Office Colony was certainly an unusual name, one intended to identify the subscribers rather than the publication itself, but that name too was abandoned after it served its purpose for the initial advertising campaign.

Times Beach might claim an exclusive name but for another Times Beach also deriving its name from a newspaper. Times Beach in Buffalo, New York, was not a newspaper resort or any kind of resort. It wasn't even much of a beach and, like its namesake, it too fell prey to environmental misfortune. In the early 1930s the *Buffalo Times* promoted the use of a half mile crescent of land along Lake Erie as a bathing beach. The beach operated briefly in 1935 but was soon determined to be a health hazard and was ordered closed. Nothing about its location was conducive to recreational bathing. There was no public transportation directly to the site so that bathers were required to walk for more than a mile through an area of grain elevators and other heavy industry to reach it. These close-by industries discharged waste into the harbor causing heavy pollution while break walls in the harbor made the water stagnant and encouraged algae growth.[1] For many years the city of Buffalo struggled with finding a use for the area and finally transformed it into the Times Beach Nature Preserve.

The majority of the newspaper colonies share their name with some nearby place and many of those are common or overused names. With its combination of structure and rarity, the name "Pell Lake" can be judged the most ideal for a newspaper colony.

* * *

The creation of Pell Lake took place at just the right time. It came into being at the peak of the land boom. The war had been over for several years, long enough for workers to realize an increase in both wages and leisure. The average populace could afford cars and swimsuits, and easy credit made owning a summer cottage within the range of possibility. In 1924 customers for the lots were enjoying the fruits of their labors and could not yet see the decline in the economy that was on the horizon.

Pell Lake was also developed at the most favorable time in the Smadbeck newspaper resort chronology. Bertram Mayo had died and the newspaper/real estate plan he developed was open for exploitation. Beginning with Asbury Park Estates in 1916 the Smadbeck brothers had polished their approach and honed their skills with at least fourteen resorts before Pell Lake. By then they knew just how much they could get away with to minimize their work and maximize their profits.

The advantageous time frame for Pell Lake is further illustrated by the changes that took effect after its development. In a rural world without zoning requirements real estate developers in 1924 had the freedom to operate without lot size or sanitation restrictions. Other constraints that would

14. Pell Lake in Context and Comparison

affect subsequent newspaper resorts in Walworth County had not yet been implemented, and in fact, Pell Lake itself was the impetus for several of these innovations. Out of state salesmen were able to get away with selling lots at Pell Lake without a Wisconsin realty license, single 20' × 100' lots remained salable, and outhouses continued to be allowed. Changes in all of these areas came about because the success of Pell Lake caught the attention of local real estate men and resulted in the formation of the Walworth County Real Estate Board. The Board, in turn, caused the arrest of the newspaper salesmen and managed to bring about the two-lot minimum, the requirement that outhouses be replaced with chemical toilets or septic tanks, and the adoption of a building code that provided for the appointment of an inspector and a need to obtain a construction permit.[2] Pell Lake was the last newspaper resort to escape all of these regulations.

In 1924, the year of Pell Lake's founding, Dr. Warren Smadbeck was in his prime, both personally and professionally. He maintained his wife and daughters in a lovely Manhattan townhouse on West 74th Street.[3] The home had stained glass windows on the main level and was within a block of Central Park. He shared the building with his sister and her family as well as an entourage of servants. Socially he rubbed elbows with politicians as his predecessor, Bertram Mayo had done before him. His three daughters were both lovely and spirited and it would be another ten years before the eldest would embarrass her father.[4]

Stress and angst were years away from the auspicious year of 1924 when Warren Smadbeck's worries merely involved hanging on to his fancy jewelry and nodding at the right time to make purchases at the antique auctions he frequented. Descriptions of items listed for sale in a catalog for an American Art Association auction in February of 1936 displayed the Smadbeck taste. Typical was an Italian Renaissance embroidered tapestry made of crimson Genoese velvet with heavy pile, appliquéd in thickly padded gold bullion with a bold design of huge scrolling branches of flowers and pomegranates. Described as "of Important Size" the wall hanging measured 12' × 6', more than half the width of one of his Pell Lake lots.[5] He had not repaired many teeth during his brief career as a dentist, but continued to be addressed as Dr. Smadbeck and was so titled in the auction catalogue.

By 1924 Warren Smadbeck had been developing real estate for nearly fifteen years with half of that time devoted to the newspaper colonies. Beginning in the comfort of the Jewish community, the first few colonies were with Yiddish newspapers but he soon branched out to government employees and then the general public, finding a wide market for small waterfront parcels of land. While he worked with his brother Arthur, Warren Smadbeck spearheaded the colony developments at least through Pell Lake. The economy was strong, workers had money, and indications of a depression were not so apparent. Nevertheless, his interest and activity in the newspaper colonies appear to have peaked with the formation of Pell Lake.

Beginning in 1925 the responsibility of newspaper colony creation was primarily managed by Arthur. Warren turned his attention to the two Canadian newspaper resorts, Plage Laval and Sandy Hook, and the Hotel Presidente in his beloved Cuba, providing him with the opportunity to spend more time there. With Pell Lake Warren Smadbeck reached the epitome of accomplishment with the newspaper deal. He could now pass the mantle on to his younger brother and proceed to conquer foreign locales.

* * *

The features of the Pell Lake location had distinct advantages over the resorts that were developed before it. The land had been used for farming and was level. This made it easy to plat the acreage into evenly shaped and sized lots and to convince buyers that one lot was as desirable as another, and it also simplified laying out roads. In this respect the Pell Lake area was more favorable than the recently completed colony of Knightstown Lake with its uneven, ravine-filled terrain. At 700 acres the amount of land at Pell Lake was not so expansive as to be unmanageable while not as small as such places as Lake Louisvilla with its mere 80 acres. The size of the lake and its relationship to the land was also irreproachable. Some predecessors, such as Asbury Park Estates, Colonie Estates, and Chagrin Falls Park, were not located next to water at all or were merely near water as at Marshfield Estates, Patchogue Lakes, and Lakewood Pines. Nor was the Pell Lake farmland merely a strip of land along a river as at Loveland Park, and it was not on the shore of a much larger body of water as were Lake Erie Beach, Lake Michigan Beach, and Lake Saint Croix Beach.

Pell Lake was a natural body of water, not artificially created by a dam. Its size and configuration allowed the colony to completely surround it, creating a compact self-contained community—the first newspaper resort to accomplish this feat. It even had a sand bottom and two natural beaches. While the shoreline was exclusive to the colony, the body of water was in the public domain relieving the eventual POA from the burden of maintaining the lake bed, a contrast to such places as Nassau Lake Park.

But the land and water needed for a successful newspaper resort could not be too perfect or it would be put to a better, more profitable use. The best location for a newspaper colony had imperfections that made it affordable for developers to purchase yet ones that could be effectively camouflaged. Pell Lake had just enough of the right kind of flaws to satisfy this need. The swamp north of the lake could be ignored, and the marshy areas along the western shore could be dredged. The only dam needed was a low

14. Pell Lake in Context and Comparison

one to raise the water level and minimize the marsh areas. By 1924 Warren Smadbeck had enough experience to build a model clubhouse, as well as beach houses, piers, swimming rafts, and a lakeside dance pavilion, and he added the established pattern of botanical names for the streets. Pell Lake met every requirement.

* * *

The location of Pell Lake had a significant advantage over other newspaper resort sites—it was within easy distance of Chicago, a city with the winning combination of a market of buyers and a collaborating newspaper already experienced with the promotion. Only New York had a larger population and a supply of willing publications, but that metropolis was already surrounded by oceanside resorts. Of course, there was always room for more, but Chicago offered the special circumstance of being large enough to provide an abundance of buyers while small enough for lot owners to band together in their neighborhoods off season to maintain year-round interest in the colony.

Lakewood, created by Bertram Mayo, and Lake Michigan Beach, were both Michigan newspaper resorts sponsored by the *Chicago Evening Post* that appealed more to residents on the south side of the city. The whiter, somewhat more prosperous north side of Chicago, offered a virtually untapped market for Pell Lake. Some of these residents may have taken the train to Lake Geneva for a brief outing but most could not afford to summer there. Pell Lake provided the opportunity to ride the train, depart only five miles short of the more exclusive and elite Lake Geneva, and actually own a little piece of property at a lake.

The colony was on a well-established train route from Chicago to Lake Geneva with the train tracks passing right through the resort acreage less than a third of a mile from the shore line of the lake. The railroad did not need to extend the rail line, it merely erected a depot and added a stop to its schedule.

The Smadbecks had a solid relationship with the *Chicago Evening Post*. The paper had already sponsored two resorts and its affiliate, the *Indianapolis Star*, created Knightstown Lake the year before. With several successful alliances already completed, the *Post* did not need to be convinced to enter into the arrangement. The paper was familiar with the advertising formula of frequent full-page ads and many supporting newshead articles. Both the newspaper and Warren Smadbeck knew precisely how to use that formula to escalate profit. A better partner for the Smadbecks did not exist.

By the time Pell Lake was created both parties to the alliance had a stable of experienced employees. Smadbeck had buying agents to scout out the farmland and engineers to make it look attractive. The big city offered up plenty of men hungry for commission sales work, and there was no lack of local lumberyards and builders willing to construct cottages for the lot buyers. The newspaper could provide advertising men and office rooms to house the sales staff. The business manager of the *Post*, Frank Hussey, was very familiar with the trustee ownership sequence of handling the land transfers, and he even provided his son R.B. to manage field sales for the new venture.

Any legal complications that arose were capably handled by Warren Smadbeck. By now he had enough experience to know how to deal with recalcitrant adjoining landowners and what tricks to use to avoid legal complications. The subscription premium scheme had been perfected and the result was a prototype newspaper colony. Pell Lake had everything going for it. No wonder it was a success.

* * *

In spite of being the classic newspaper colony, Pell Lake has not been the subject of a book. A few of the other colonies have been written about in the Images of America series by Arcadia Publishing, books that concentrate on photographs with sparse text, and briefly refer to the Smadbecks and the newspaper deal.

Times Beach, has been discussed in more books than any other newspaper colony. Its fame comes not from its formation as a newspaper subscription promotion but from the unfortunate circumstance of its downfall. In the 1960s a chemical company in nearby Verona, Missouri, produced substances that left a liquid residue called "still bottom." Looking for a way to rid itself of this byproduct other than through costly incineration, the chemical manufacturer contracted with a nearby solvent company to dispose of the waste. That company, in turn, subcontracted the job to Russell Bliss, a recycler of used motor oil. Bliss denied knowing that the substance he agreed to dispose of was potentially hazardous. According to one report he dipped a paper napkin in the still bottom residue, lit the napkin on fire, and concluded that it was something akin to a heavy grease.[6]

Bliss mixed these dregs with waste oil and, in 1971, sprayed the material at horse farms to keep down the dust. When horses began to die and birds dropped from the rafters, the Centers for Disease Control was alerted. It took several years for the CDC to conclude that the soil contained the toxic substance dioxin. In 1979 it was discovered that Bliss had also been spraying the dioxin laced oil on the roads at Times Beach to help with a dust problem. Much soil testing, disagreement over contamination standards, and political haggling ensued before the Environmental Protection Agency ordered Times Beach evacuated. The news that they would lose their homes came to the residents right after a devastating flood and just before Christmas in 1982.

A new EPA program nicknamed Superfund had been created two years earlier to clean up and monitor sites contaminated with hazardous waste. Times Beach became the first site to be bought out by the Superfund: its residents were paid for their homes either directly or through condemnation. Since Times Beach had half of the dioxin in Missouri and was unpopulated, it became the location of the incinerator used to dispose of all the dioxin contaminated soil in Missouri as well as the houses, businesses, and possessions of Times Beach residents. The triangular site that was Times Beach is now home to the Route 66 State Park.

All of the books that treat Times Beach as subject matter are non-fiction and all use it as an example of an environmental misfortune. Some writers argue that the dioxin contamination at Times Beach was one of the most dangerous environmental disasters to affect mankind.[7] Other authors take the position that the health scare was completely baseless,[8] while still others provide a more evenly balanced assessment of the situation.[9] None dwell on the genesis of the town, mentioning its formation as a newspaper resort only in passing if at all.

Unlike any other newspaper colony, Times Beach has found its way into the world of poetry in a book of poems that derives its title, *Times Beach*, directly from the resort and contains a poem of the same name.[10] This is narrative free verse based on real events and people; thus it cannot properly be categorized as "fiction." A more accurate description might be literary treatment in pseudo-poetic form.

The four-page poem condenses the history of Times Beach as a resort created through a newspaper promotion and its progression through the Depression and World War II into one lengthy sentence and describes Times Beach as a "breezy summer resort for the urban affluent." While the poet, John Shoptaw, has the name of the newspaper and the year it was created correct, Times Beach was not designed to appeal to the affluent. The developers lured working class buyers who could afford lots in a floodplain priced at $67.50 on a two-year installment plan and populate the lots with cottages built on stilts. Only at the end of that one long sentence does Shoptaw recognize the financial disadvantage of the residents, placing blame on the Depression and wartime gas rationing.

The poem quickly dispenses with the creation of Times Beach through its alliance between journalism and real estate and leaves the bulk of the narrative to predictably concentrate on the end of the community in an environmental calamity. But at least some literary attention is paid to Times Beach as a newspaper colony, the resort's name is adopted for both the title of the poem and the title of the book, and the book's cover is graced with a period photo of three coquettish girls draped over the entrance sign to the resort.

* * *

There are also two literary settings for works of fiction inspired by newspaper colonies. The more recent book, *Ghosting*, is set at Lake Louisvilla, although the colony is not mentioned by name. Written by an author who lives in the Louisville area and writes under the pen name Kirby Gann,[11] *Ghosting* has been widely reviewed[12] and summaries of the story are rife on the Internet. It is enough here to know that Gann's novel is a gritty tale of drugs and crime filled with unsavory people speaking unpretty words and committing deplorable acts.

The reader would not know that Lake Louisvilla was the inspiration for Lake Holloway, the setting for the book, were it not for a news item about the author printed in the Sunday Features section of Louisville's *Courier-Journal* about the time the book was released.[13] The article credits Gann with considering the current state of Lake Louisvilla, having been drained years ago, as a suitably creepy place for the events described in the novel, most notably when a particularly horrific scene makes use of a muddy sinkhole.

Nothing in *Ghosting* considers the newspaper subscription history of Lake Louisvilla. The book describes Lake Holloway as a man-made lake that was originally part of a spa retreat built for the wealthy. The resort failed financially, fire destroyed the resort hotel, and scavengers moved in when vegetation took over the cottages and roadways.[14]

This portrayal in large part accurately borrows from the history of Lake Louisvilla. There was a hotel, it did burn down after a few years, the resort eventually fell upon tough financial times, and squatters moved in as the flora proliferated. But, as with *Times Beach*, the presumed wealth of the original lot owners is misunderstood. The author is not to be criticized for the absence of truth in the telling of the story. This is a work of fiction after all, and just as Gann was free to substitute a different name for the lake, he was also free to change the circumstances of its historic development. Admittedly the story is more dramatic if the now drug-ridden and mucky Lake Holloway was first created for a privileged and moneyed class.

That makes two references, the poetic *Times Beach*, and the fictional *Ghosting*, that describe the original establishment of the community as geared toward buyers with adequate or even abundant finances. In reality, these colonies were substandard resorts, made to look good on the surface, and unlikely to attract buyers who could afford something better. These misdescriptions could be the result of inadequate research leading to a presumption of the background that the author wanted to find rather

14. Pell Lake in Context and Comparison

than what the actual facts were, or they could have been purposefully fabricated to produce maximum dramatic effect, yielding to the temptation to inflate the theatrical picture of a place as rundown, abandoned, eliminated, or drained, by contrasting it with a beginning as a playground for the elite.

* * *

A third literary treatment of a newspaper colony escapes this dichotomy by providing no history of the resort in the pages of the book. That the colony is Bolinas Beach is known because the name Bolinas is used and its geographical features are accurately described. This is the more intriguing and erudite of the novels by a writer whose works have entered the realm of neo-green cult fiction.

The author Ernest Callenbach enjoyed a career writing and teaching about film as an art form. While editing California natural history guides at the University of California Press, he became interested in environmentalism and also in the concept of simple living—minimizing possessions and practicing self-sufficiency and sustainability. Callenbach achieved notoriety as a writer and lecturer on these topics.

His utopian novel *Ecotopia: The Notebooks and Reports of William Weston*[15] was ideally suited in time and topic to the developing environmental movement of the mid-1970s. Callenbach coined Ecotopia as the name of a nation organized when Northern California, Oregon, and Washington seceded from the United States to become an independently governed and environmentally conscious breakaway country. To protect itself against reunification and infiltration by nonbelievers, Ecotopia was closed to visitors and to communications with outsiders until Weston, an international affairs reporter working for the fictional *Times-Post*, was granted leave to enter in anticipation that he would come to understand and appreciate the Ecotopian way of life and report his findings to the wider world.

Using diary entries and dispatches to his employer as a literary device, Weston describes life in a self-supporting society where nearly everything, including human waste, is recycled and all energy is powered by the sun. The book presents the practices employed by the Ecotopians as achievable, providing a framework for structuring a nation governed by ecological sustainability. Callenbach devotees so thoroughly embraced his eco-friendly principles that they even recycled his book by means of an Ecotopian lending library.[16]

Neither Bolinas nor Bolinas Beach is anywhere mentioned in *Ecotopia*. Nor do the physical descriptions of the sites described in the novel comport with that of the Bolinases. All that is reserved for Callenbach's subsequent novel, *Ecotopia Emerging*,[17] a prequel to *Ecotopia*, where the author identifies Bolinas, both by name and description, as the headwater of his utopian ecological society.

Callenbach may not have fully appreciated how appropriate his choice of Bolinas was as the setting for *Ecotopia Emerging*. In an interview given thirty years after the release of the prequel and shortly before his death, he commented that he set one of the scenes in the book at Bolinas because he liked being there—it was brave and thrilling the way it protruded out into the ocean with the reef running in one direction and the beach in the other.[18] This explanation seriously downplays the important role Bolinas played in the book.

The "seaside town of Bolinas on the northern California coast" is pinpointed at the very beginning of *Ecotopia Emerging*. One of the primary characters in the book, a teenage inventor named Lou Swift, lives there in a sprawling house built by hand by her parents. The author does not distinguish between Bolinas, the older town next to the sea, and the newspaper colony of Bolinas Beach up on the mesa, an easily forgivable transgression since, by mid-twentieth century, the residents themselves no longer made a distinction, other than location, between the mesa and the earlier downtown business district.[19]

Nevertheless, the house Lou Swift lives in is clearly on the mesa. Callenbach tells his readers that when the house was built there was a road running in front of it and now the road had mostly dropped away leaving only a footpath.[20] Satellite views of Bolinas Beach indicate that he was describing a home facing Ocean Parkway, the waterside street platted by Arthur Smadbeck,[21] portions of which no longer exist due to erosion of the cliffside.

The isolation of Bolinas definitely added to its attraction as the setting for the birthplace of the Ecotopian concept. With only one road into the area requiring a twenty-minute drive along perilous rocky cliffs, the Ecotopians could easily establish a guard post to fend off the governmental contingents sent to challenge their activities. Additionally, the residents of Bolinas are reported to be reclusive. A few years after the release of *Ecotopia Emerging*, an article in the *Los Angeles Times* described how the highway signs pointing to the town were routinely removed by those living there to discourage discovery of their little seaside hamlet. This news item also highlighted the relaxed lifestyle of the inhabitants, painting the women as "wearing '60s-style long, full Earth Mother skirts,"[22] a picture that comports with Callenbach's depiction of Bolinas residents at an outdoor party dressed in homemade "cloaks, capes, ornamented vests, spectacularly gaudy shirts" and skirts worn with dramatic hats and elegant boots, some outfits tight and revealing, others loose, flowing and dramatic.[23] The Ecotopian culture also hints at an absence of clothing, an attitude entirely compatible with the recognition of Bolinas Beach as one of the best locations for nude sunbathing north of San Francisco.[24]

Marguerite Harris, one of the leading counterculturists of Bolinas Beach, described the ideology of the community leadership there in the early 1970s as containing "elements of the radical 'New Left' movement of the sixties, environmental protectionism, agrarian romanticism, and parallels to the American populist movement."[25] This played out for Harris and three of her counterparts when they won seats on the Bolinas Community Public Utility District in 1971. These "radical protectionists" immediately enacted a resolution placing a moratorium on water service for all new construction with the intent to curtail growth.

Callenbach was certainly familiar with the physical characteristics of Bolinas but he may not have been fully aware of the substantial evidence backing up his representation of the character of the inhabitants and the shape of its society. Nevertheless, the isolation of this seaside hamlet together with its counterculture population—reclusive and self-reliant individuals possessing a pioneering spirit—rendered Bolinas an appropriate place to identify as a fictional hotbed of sustainability and survivalism.

All three of these literary newspaper colonies—Times Beach, Lake Louisvilla, and Bolinas Beach—found their way into American literature for an environmental reason: Times Beach because its demise was considered an environmental disaster, Lake Louisvilla because its draining left a sinkhole, and Bolinas Beach because of its remote location and the attitude of its residents toward preserving nature. In his *Times Beach* poem Shoptaw mentions the newspaper promotion to sell the lots but this is not vital to his writing. No association between Lake Holloway and a newspaper is cited by Gann in his novel *Ghosting*. In Callenbach's books the involvement of a newspaper is relegated to having the fictional *Times-Post* assign a reporter to investigate and report on Ecotopia. This leaves the newspaper colony origins of the three colonies in the periphery at best.

Pell Lake has never inspired a published poem. Nor are its physical attributes so distinctive that a novelist might consider using it as a setting for a grisly act. It is not isolated and has not nurtured a population so progressive as to cause it to be idealized as an inspiration for a movement. Pell Lake has not yet and most likely never will achieve cult status and it is unlikely that anyone would mistake its origins as having been aimed at a wealthy populace.

* * *

Pell Lake began as the quintessential newspaper colony and its trajectory has been quite uneventful compared with many of the other resorts. Its course of development did not match the sinewy drama of Lake Louisvilla,

Times Beach, or Bolinas Beach. Yet, this very uneventfulness is what makes Pell Lake unique—among all the colonies it has come closest to preserving the original character of the newspaper resort.

The physical properties of the lake have endured unaffected by the passage of time primarily due to its being a natural body of water. Aside from the low dam Warren Smadbeck installed to raise the lake level, Pell Lake has survived essentially as created by nature. Unlike a man-made lake there is no large dam to be maintained and no cause to drain the lake. The marshy pond that is Pell Lake continues to exist basically as it was in Warren Smadbeck's time, needing only dredging and weed cutting from time to time.

The land also remains as Warren Smadbeck left it. The only significant effort at redevelopment occurred in the 1990s when, amid much controversy, the Pell Lake Sanitary District was formed and sewerage and water service was installed. Nevertheless, outhouse structures at Pell Lake continue to outlive their functionality. The lots have not been reconfigured, Pell Lake is not considered urban enough to be affected by urban renewal, it has not been absorbed into a larger city, and the attempts to incorporate the colony into a municipality have been unsuccessful. Only in recent years has the Village of Bloomfield been formed linking Pell Lake more closely with the land adjoining it.

Being part of the Village of Bloomfield has resulted in some administrative changes, but this consolidation with the surrounding farmland has had little operative effect on the character of the resort. Pell Lake has been home to the Bloomfield Town Hall at least since 1915, predating the development of the community by Smadbeck. In that year a new town hall building was constructed near the crossing of the highway to Lake Geneva and the north and south road[26] to which Warren Smadbeck would attach the name "Clover." The hall sat, and its modern replacement still sits, on a small triangle skirted around by Smadbeck's development. The Bloomfield Town Board accommodated the development of Pell Lake from its inception first by quickly approving the plat maps and later by cooperating with such activities as cleaning and dredging the lake,[27] thereby demonstrating that the governance of the resort has always been intermingled with that of the township. Technically, now only the lake itself officially bears the name "Pell Lake" but common usage continues to apply that name to the community.

Pell Lake has been spared the redesigning experienced by other newspaper colonies. The established legal structure endures with the POA continuing to have ownership of the shared properties. Although the dance pavilion turned roller rink fell out of use and was razed, the POA maintains the land as a park along with the adjacent beach areas. The clubhouse stands where Smadbeck built it and is one of the few, and perhaps the only, original clubhouse used solely for its intended purpose throughout its existence. The POA somehow manages to come up with enough money to keep the building operational as its headquarters without renting it out for weddings or other functions. The POA does not sell memberships to use the lake, has imposed no special assessments, and retains and abides by the original legal formula.

There have been no changes in the road pattern laid out by Smadbeck, and only one road has been renamed. Many original cottages linger on and, while some have been added onto and modernized beyond recognition, a few early bungalows can be found lurking, unaltered, among the trees and bushes. The lake continues to be used for boating and fishing although the quality of the water has curtailed swimming and snowmobilers now replace the ice skaters.

No longer primarily a summer community, the population of retirees and wage earners now living at Pell Lake nevertheless sustain its working-class demographic. There has been no upgrade in the level of wealth, nor has there been any change in the characteristics of the residents. Pell Lake has failed to become a hotbed of environmental activism, a nudist retreat, a home for hippie types, a cult group breeding ground, or a home to any other atypical behavior.

* * *

Both written and pictorial documentation of Pell Lake give it an advantage over many other newspaper colonies in a bid for qualifying as the prototype newspaper resort. The wealth of archived information about the creation and progress of the colony begins with the advertisements and their corresponding advertorials. A full run of the *Chicago Evening Post* exists both in hard copy at the Chicago History Museum and on microfilm at Chicago's Harold Washington Library Center, making available every ad placed by Warren Smadbeck and every *Post* promotional article relating to Pell Lake.

Similar newspaper information exists for several other newspaper colonies but Pell Lake has further newspaper resources. It is positioned in close proximity to Lake Geneva, a considerably larger city with a newspaper of its own continuously from 1872 to the present. If one resort city can have another resort city as a suburb, then Pell Lake has that relationship with Lake Geneva and is treated as such by the local press. Pell Lake was and is important enough to justify reports of newsworthy proceedings taking place there while being small enough to invite articles about incidental events, thus providing a comprehensive account of activity in the community.

For instance, articles such as "Improvements at Pells Lake Going Forward Steadily: New Scow Being Built to Carry Dredging Machine"[28] and "Pell Lake Community Forging Ahead"[29] report on the major efforts involved in building a scow to dredge the lake, while "Pell Lake Group Having Good Time and Working Hard"[30] tells about efforts to find an appropriately distinguished name for the scow and raise money for the "dredge fund." One front page article in the *Lake Geneva News Tribune*, "Valuation of City for Next Year is Lower,"[31] tells of the legal action taken against Warren Smadbeck to recover unpaid income taxes, and another, "Motor Trip to the North Woods,"[32] chronicles the vacation plans of POA officers and their hunting and fishing expectations. A report that a local resident pled guilty to making moonshine in violation of the Prohibition law[33] is judged newsworthy and so is a report that the "ice [on Pell Lake] is as smooth as glass."[34]

Even the newspaper colony positioned most similarly to Pell Lake fails to garner the same attention. Like Pell Lake, the advertisements and newsheads exist for Lake Como Beach, also located in Walworth County, Wisconsin, also developed as a newspaper colony with the *Chicago Evening Post*, and also near enough to Lake Geneva to be the subject of its news reporting. But Lake Como Beach was developed after Pell Lake and, constituting only a fraction of the lakeshore of the much larger Lake Como, is less self-contained. As a result, it receives sparser attention in the local paper and, rather than being treated individually, is often slighted in comparison with Pell Lake.[35]

Newspapers are not the sole source of written documentation about Pell Lake. Given its existence as a natural body of water the lake has been mapped for nearly two hundred years. Of course, as with all other similarly created communities, the county register of deeds maintains plat maps and land records. In spite of the disappearance of the embarrassing minutes of the POA proceedings concerning the visit of the Negro boys to the beach in 1950, an abundance of other written documents remains. The archives of the state historical society preserve corporate records of club organizations in addition to documents and correspondence relating to Smadbeck's petition to build the dam and the marshland owners' petition to stop him. The clerk of courts office maintains court files in proceedings ancillary to the taxation lawsuit. These records provide a wealth of information about how the Smadbecks plied their trade. If such chronicles exist for any other colony they have not yet been uncovered.

In addition, among all the Smadbeck newspaper colonies Pell Lake excels at visual documentation of its formative years. Scenes from the resorts were often included in the large newspaper advertisements and articles, but most of these pictures reproduce very poorly and are all but useless

14. Pell Lake in Context and Comparison

as image references. Postcards provide a much richer vein of information to document what the colonies looked like at the time of, or shortly after, their development. Again, its proximity to Chicago placed Pell Lake in a favorable position for attention of this type.

At the beginning of the twentieth century the thriving postcard photograph business was most active in the Midwest where Chicago dominated the field with more than a dozen photographers producing greeting cards bearing pictures of the city. Among the Chicago photographers, the C.R. Childs Company owned by Charles Childs produced the greatest quantity of postcards overall and provided vast coverage of the various Chicago neighborhoods.[36]

By the mid-1920s Childs expanded his territory to include more rural, resort locations. He sent photographers out on trains to capture the sights, turn the images into picture cards, and market them through local store owners.[37] Vacationers, anxious to report their holiday experiences to friends and relatives, provided a ready market for the scenic cards.

Childs' photography spanned northern Illinois and southern Wisconsin, chunks of Indiana and Michigan, and a few counties in Iowa. Minnesota was ignored, obviously too far distant for his traveling picture takers.[38] The borders of his photographic range limit Childs' scenes of newspaper colonies to Pell Lake, Lake Como Beach, and Lake Michigan Beach. Interlaken was within the geographical area but its late development, distance from a rail line, and lack of scenic interest suggest Childs never got there.

Located along a direct train route from the city, Pell Lake was a particular beneficiary of Childs' efforts. The photographer did not have far to walk from the train depot to the beach areas, the most popular spot for photos. In contrast the second Wisconsin newspaper resort, Lake Como Beach, was far more difficult for a photographer to reach. The train stop at Lake Como dated back to 1888 when the C and NW Railway extended service to Williams Bay. At the time of the development of Lake Como Beach by Arthur Smadbeck, the railroad constructed a new platform a mere tenth of a mile further east of the prior one and mounted an old baggage car body to serve as a depot. A seven- or eight-mile bus ride was required to reach the colony, a situation that was not very welcoming to train riding photographers. A similar handicap affected Lake Michigan Beach where the rail route from Chicago was less direct and nearly twice the distance compared to Pell Lake.

The C.R. Childs Company photographed Pell Lake on at least two occasions. One early postcard can reliably be dated to 1924. The card bears a numerical coding assigned to the nearby town of Genoa Junction which changed its name to Genoa City in 1924, suggesting that the photograph was not taken later than that year. Subsequent Childs' cards of Pell Lake bear a numerical prefix assigned specifically to Pell Lake. Other cards have subject matter and postmarks indicating that they were photographed in 1926 or 1927.

Pell Lake's lone serious rival as a repeated photographic subject in its early days is Beachwood, the resort created by Bertram Mayo in 1914 with the help of his friend Addison Nickerson. Nickerson served as the engineer for the development, was used as a stepping stone in the chain of ownership, and built many of the structures at the resort. He assembled an album, now maintained by the Beachwood New Jersey Historical Archive, that contains photos taken by a professional photographer, depicting the earliest bungalows as well as the community buildings. This photographic assemblage, together with the Pell Lake postcards, comprises the richest sources of early images of newspaper colonies.

Considered in the context of both time and space, Pell Lake, the resort community with the uniquely funny name, is unmatched as a newspaper colony. It was created at the most advantageous time for the newspaper deal and was ideally positioned in proximity to both a big city with a newspaper experienced in the promotion and a nearby upper-class resort. Pell Lake and the land around it, never having been subject to environmental disaster, restructuring, or drastic demographic alteration, has remained constant in character. Added to this assemblage of assets is an abundance of newspaper documentation, archival materials, and early pictorial representations. Compared with all other newspaper resorts, Pell Lake remains the most authentic newspaper colony.

Conclusion

In a piece titled "Miscellany" in the *Rushville Republican*, on November 18, 1954, Cy McIlwain wrote about the plans to rehabilitate Knightstown Lake. Recounting its development thirty years earlier, he referred to "postage stamp" lots sold through a "slicker" promotion and recalled that "a lot of people were burned up and yelled 'swindle' when the deal folded."

Bertram Mayo's practices at Beachwood were classified as fraud by investigative reporter Victor Watson. Words and phrases such as "suckers," being "stung," "one born every minute," and "scoundrels" peppered his testimony at the U.S. House Committee hearings in 1916. A profile of Mayo describes him with the terms "charlatan" and "crook."[1]

In early September of 1930 a group of Pell Lake property owners met to discuss their dissatisfaction with the *Chicago Evening Post* promotion, complaining that the descriptions of the resort in the ads were far different from reality. They grumbled that the water level had receded leaving piers on dry ground and reducing the lake to a mere frog pond.[2]

A few weeks later a meeting was held at the Lake Como Beach clubhouse attended by sixty-five lot owners, as well as Walworth County District Attorney Arthur Thorson and Frank Bentley, an investigator for the Wisconsin Real Estate Brokers Board. Having selected their lots from a plat at the *Post*'s Chicago office, some investors discovered, upon visiting the site, that the waterfront land they chose faced marsh rather than open water. A long list of grievances was presented, including the failure to provide a promised beach, insufficient electrical service, and poorly constructed culverts, dams, and roads.[3]

* * *

Victor Watson's accusations of fraud were not pursued. Likewise, there was little the investigator for the Real Estate Brokers Board could do to satisfy the complaining lot customers at Pell Lake and Lake Como Beach. He spoke of revoking any licenses to sell real estate that the *Post* held in Wisconsin and of preventing further promotion in the state.[4] The Board did have one victory. In early October 1929 it refused to issue a license to John J. Gordon of Chicago who sought to sell lots at Interlaken, the third of the *Chicago Evening Post*'s newspaper colonies in Walworth County. The denial was based on the advertised sale of 20' lots and that the *Post* was not the real owner although the ads gave that impression. Gordon threatened to bring an action in federal court seeking a mandatory injunction requiring the Board to issue the license,[5] but with the start of the Depression a few weeks later he probably did not carry out the threat.

The Real Estate Brokers Board continued to be watchful. Between 1930 and 1932 six people from Illinois were charged with selling real estate in Walworth County without a Wisconsin license. At least two of the arrests took place at Pell Lake.[6] But these remedies were all prospective. Recovering damages for past harm was a much more troublesome undertaking.

Fraud is difficult to prove and the developers would be quick to place blame on the fast-talking sales agents. The written contract between the newspaper and the lot buyer promised little more than a deed to a lot and specifically denied liability for any "verbal statements or representations or written alterations."[7] Buyers had scant basis for dissatisfaction with the location of the lots if they failed to view the land before purchasing it. Even if actionable misrepresentation could be established, the monetary damages would likely not exceed the price paid for the lots and collecting on a judgment would present another challenge since the developers divested themselves of available local assets.

* * *

Without doubt Warren Smadbeck was a sophisticated and shrewd businessman. Hiding behind the veneer of a newspaper, he bought substandard land near inferior bodies of water, disguised the faults, and employed puffery, hyperbole, and aggressive sales tactics to snag buyers. Along the way he made lavish assurances knowing that he likely would not be called upon to keep them. His actions in this regard at Pell Lake demonstrate the extremes of his cunning.

Surrounded by swamp on three sides, Pell Lake was far from an ideal recreational haven. Dr. Smadbeck nevertheless made it look good, at least long enough to sell the lots, by constructing a dam to raise the water level, a feat he accomplished by providing ditches and drainage to satisfy the demands of the owners of adjoining marshland. But the pugnacious developer did not stop there. In addition to constructing the drainage system he agreed not only to maintain it, but to maintain it in perpetuity.

Then he went even farther. To secure the vow to forever keep the drainage pipes in good repair, Smadbeck granted the marsh owners a lien on all land he owned in Pell Lake. Ostensibly this was a broad assurance.

Conclusion

The lien covered the clubhouse and the lots it sat on, the dance pavilion and its site, all the parkland and the bathing houses erected there, as well as any unplatted land.

Smadbeck was not done yet. He further expanded his guarantees by making the lien enforceable against all future owners of the land, even specifying that the proposed POA would be bound by the mortgage when the organization was formed and the land was ultimately deeded to it.

Certainly Frank Hussey, trustee for the *Chicago Evening Post*, must have known of this handicap on the parkland since his son, R.B. Hussey is listed as a witness to Warren Smadbeck's agreement with the landowners. Far more doubtful is whether the information was relayed to the organizers of the Pell Lake POA when Hussey deeded the land to it in January of 1926. There is no language in the deed mentioning the lien.[8] An examination of the title would have revealed the obligation, but the POA, grateful for the property that the *Post* had so generously given to it at no charge, probably did not engage an abstractor for this purpose.

It can be confirmed that William McManus, president of the Pell Lake POA in the early 1930s, did not know that the land it owned had been pledged as security by Smadbeck. McManus, during the course of his correspondence with the state regarding lake levels, asked the Public Service Commission to identify the party responsible for maintaining the drainage system. Innocent of the knowledge that the POA owned the parkland, the secretary of the commission answered the question in late fall of 1932 by sending to McManus a copy of the agreement between Smadbeck and the marsh owners and suggesting that the POA look to the owner of the parkland to pay for needed repairs to the pump and tile drains.[9]

And so, in accepting title to the parkland, the POA unwittingly assumed the responsibility of fulfilling the promises made by Smadbeck to the landowners. This information came to the POA just as it was in the midst of cooperating with District Attorney Thorson in the seemingly fruitless effort to collect tax money from the Smadbecks. It was obvious that the POA would be unsuccessful in seeking recourse against the developer.

The marshland owners were likewise without a meaningful remedy. They could pursue the POA for the cost of repairing the drain pipes, but the POA had little or no cash money. The parkland, with aging structures and the decline in the price of real estate in general, was of negligible value. In effect Warren Smadbeck tricked the POA by giving it land saddled with obligations, and he also tricked the land owners by giving them a lien worth very little. He correctly calculated that the Smadbeck consortium would never have to make good on his liberal promises.

* * *

The newspapers, as the middlemen, were complicit in the scheme. They loaned their addresses and offices to the developers to be used as real estate sales headquarters. Their employees willingly served as go-betweens transmitting the lots from the developers to the subscribers. In their quest for subscriptions and advertising money they donned the mantle of speculators and allowed their reputations to be exploited.

Frank Hussey had his name on every deed to a Pell Lake lot. Both he and Carroll Shaffer, as well as the *Chicago Evening Post*, were named as parties in the legal actions brought by Thorson on behalf of the Pell Lake lot owners seeking property attachments. R.B. Hussey was on-site hawking lots, even submitting to arrest for doing so, and he lent his signature to a dubious agreement that handicapped the Pell Lake POA.

When the Smadbecks took over from Mayo they reshaped the association between the developers and the press into one that was deeper and more intimate. The interplay between the developers and the newspapers reached a new extreme with the formation of Mirror Holding Corporation, a real estate company spun off from a newspaper. A publication was no longer used merely to advertise real estate but had itself assumed the role of a developer.

* * *

Hampered by inconsistent bragging, there is no reliable accounting of the number of communities sold through the newspaper deal. In 1952 the *New York Times* told of 155 developments established by Home Guardian.[10] A few years later the *Philadelphia Inquirer* reported on the 87th development created by Warren and Arthur Smadbeck.[11] In 1956 the brothers were applauded for selling 700,000 lots in thirty states[12] and in 1965 for founding 60 colonies in the United States and Canada,[13] a figure that was also claimed by Arthur in a 1957 interview.[14]

Of course, not all Smadbeck developments were newspaper colonies and not all newspaper colonies were brought about by the Smadbecks. Approximately fifty newspaper resorts are identified in this book, but there are certainly others not recognized here. For example at Deal Beach Estates, adjacent to Asbury Park, the land was owned by Home Guardian and lots were transferred to buyers by Henry J. Auth, business manager of the *Newark Star Eagle*, acting as a trustee.[15] There is also Lakehurst in Ocean County, New Jersey, an area immediately north of Horicon Lake, mapped out in the Smadbeck pattern with a Lakeshore Drive and botanically named streets. It is known that the Smadbecks owned property in this area.[16] No advertisements or other information about the development of Deal Beach Estates or Lakehurst as a newspaper colony have been located.

Conclusion

At some colonies there is only a vague awareness of the newspaper subscription premium origin while at others it has been subsumed completely, upstaged by modern day struggles to survive as a tenable community. A website devoted to Lake Erie Beach political issues asserts that the community was "established by the Murphy family in 1924."[17] In fact, Eugene C. Murphy was the business manager for the *Buffalo Courier*[18] and served as the trustee conduit between Smadbecks' Home Guardian and the newspaper lot buyers.

At Lake Saint Croix Beach in Minnesota, the trustee was John A. Gobeil of the *Saint Paul News*. A recent summary plan for the area suggests that Warren Smadbeck conveyed the lots to Gobeil to satisfy an outstanding advertising bill, an interpretation that connects newspaper advertising with development of the resort but exhibits a glaring misconception of the relationship.[19]

The newspaper subscription past of additional communities will emerge as more digitized newspapers become available. Perhaps the information provided here will enable others to recognize clues in their neighborhoods and be spurred to research local land records and restore their communities' newspaper resort credentials.

* * *

So was it all a hoax? A swindle? Was the sales jargon all flimflam and hokum? Were the lot buyers bilked, hoodwinked, and hornswoggled? Were they defrauded? Or were they just naive? For all of their trickery, shiftiness, and shenanigans, the developers and the newspapers likely did nothing wrong, or at least nothing that was legally actionable, or at least nothing that was legally actionable with recoverable damages.

Not all buyers of newspaper resort lots were dissatisfied. Many, perhaps those with realistic expectations, were pleased with their inexpensive purchase of a little bit of land in the country. If the water levels of the lakes receded, they either did not notice or did not care and they were oblivious to leaking pipelines, broken pumps, and crumbling dams. They built their cottages, fished and swam, puttered around, and showed off their summer playground to friends.

The newspaper/real estate alliance was uniquely suited to the Roaring Twenties. Before then publications lacked the ability to handle this breed of advertisement, real estate developers were as yet unprepared, and the populace was not financially ready. In the years following the 1920s newspapers had lost their status as the primary source of information for the working classes, the economy deteriorated, social attitudes changed, and laws and regulations affecting zoning, the environment, and disclosure were imposed.

Conclusion

That the alliance between newspapers and developers will never be replicated makes the story of the quaint origin of these colonies all the more special. To view the newspaper deal as teetering on the brink of being a swindle only serves to embellish the remarkable history of the newspaper resorts of the 1920s.

Appendix: Resort Locator

Appendix: Resort Locator

State/County	Colony	Year	Coordinates	Developer	Newspaper
California/Los Angeles	Beverly Glen	1911	34.099894, -118.443713	Mayo	Sunset magazine
California/Marin	Bolinas Beach	1927	37.899467, -122.704474	Smadbeck	San Francisco Bulletin
California/Sonoma	Cazadero Redwoods	1910	38.513564, -123.112984	Mayo	Oakland Enquirer/Sunset magazine
Canada/Manitoba	Sandy Hook	1927	50.544826, -96.981599	Smadbeck	Winnipeg Evening Tribune
Canada/Quebec	Plage Laval	1926	45.559606, -73.865390	Smadbeck	La Patrie
Florida/Highlands	Avon Park Lakes	1957	27.630251, -81.544810	Smadbeck	Chamber of Commerce
Florida/Manatee	Palmetto Point	1954	27.556292, -82.568975	Smadbeck	Chamber of Commerce
Florida/Sarasota	South Venice	1953	27.054042, -82.425065	Smadbeck	Chamber of Commerce
Florida/St. Johns	St. Augustine South	1953	29.848973, -81.315744	Smadbeck	Florida Speaks magazine
Indiana/Henry	Knightstown Lake	1923	39.801855, -85.504157	Smadbeck	Indianapolis Star/ Muncie Star
Indiana/Lake	Post Office Colony, The Shades	1913	*41.385458, -87.423458	Trend Magazine	Trend Magazine
Indiana/LaPorte	Hudson Lake	1927	41.718307, -86.553710	Illges	Southtown Economist
Indiana/LaPorte	Sentinel Beach	1927	41.717718, -86.541695	Illges?	The Sentinel
Indiana/LaPorte	Southtown Beach	1938	41.561353, -86.553099	Gustavus	Southtown Economist
Kansas/Sedgwick	Orienta Park	1909	37.654156, -97.364047	Kansas Land Imp. & Dev.	Kansas Magazine
Kentucky/Oldham	Lake Louisvilla	1924	38.319236, -85.515229	Smadbeck	Louisville Post/Louisville Herald

Appendix: Resort Locator

State/County	Colony	Year	Coordinates	Developer	Newspaper
Maryland/Anne Arundel	Herald Harbor	1924	39.049044, -76.577998	Snodgress, Shelton, Eddy	Washington Herald
Maryland/Anne Arundel	Woodland Beach	1931	38.934630, -76.549093	Smadbeck	Washington Post
Maryland/Kent	Chesapeake Landing	1962	39.270414, -76.167750	Smadbeck	Chamber of Commerce
Massachusetts/Middlesex	Long Lake Beach	1925	42.533561, -71.472639	Smadbeck	Boston Post
Massachusetts/Plymouth	Marshfield Estates	1920	42.109235, -70.688873	Smadbeck	Boston Evening Record
Massachusetts/Worcester	Lake Sam-O-Set	1926	42.491015, -71.757521	Smadbeck	none
Michigan/Berrien	Lake Michigan Beach	1922	42.224761, -86.373446	Smadbeck	Chicago Evening Post
Michigan/Berrien	Madron Lake	1929	*41.871351, -86.414395	Smadbeck	Chicago Jewish Chronicle
Michigan/Muskegon	Lakewood	1912	43.377028, -86.246262	Mayo	Chicago Evening Post
Michigan/Sanilac	Great Lakes Beach	1930	43.214728, -82.522972	Smadbeck	Detroit Daily
Minnesota/Anoka	Coon Lake Beach	1925	45.308226, -93.158218	Smadbeck	
Minneapolis Daily Star Minnesota/Carver	Carver Beach	1927	44.881989, -93.544312	Smadbeck	Minneapolis Daily Star
Minnesota/Washington	Lake St. Croix Beach	1924	44.920910, -92.763446	Smadbeck	St.Paul News
Missouri/St. Francois	Iron Mountain Lake	1939	37.684587, -90.621518	Smadbeck	none
Missouri/St. Louis	Times Beach	1925	38.508346, -90.603288	Smadbeck	St. Louis Times
Nebraska/Douglas	King Lake	1925	41.315241, -96.297783	Smadbeck	Omaha Daily News
New Jersey/Burlington	Brown's Mills-in-the-Pines	1916	39.974083, -74.576001	Mayo	Philadelphia Press

Appendix: Resort Locator

State/County	Colony	Year	Coordinates	Developer	Newspaper
New Jersey/Cape May	Sea Isles Estates	1927	39.192103, -74.818711	Griffith	Sunday Star
New Jersey/Cumberland	Beach Club Lake	1927	39.337502, -75.047203	Smadbeck	Philadelphia Record
New Jersey/Cumberland	Laurel Lake	1927	39.336961, -75.032944	Smadbeck	Philadelphia Record
New Jersey/Monmouth	Asbury Park Estates	1916	40.225886, -74.028643	Smadbeck	Jewish Daily News
New Jersey/Monmouth	Deal Beach Estates	1918	*40.229820, -74.023225	Probably Smadbeck	Newark Star Eagle?
New Jersey/Morris	Lake Parsippany	1931	40.852973, -74.445723	Smadbeck	Daily Mirror
New Jersey/Ocean	Beachwood	1914	39.941664, -74.186921	Mayo	New York Tribune
New Jersey/Ocean	Cedarwood Park	1926	*40.054577, -74.130384	Hudson Dispatch?	Hudson Dispatch
New Jersey/Ocean	Lakehurst	?	40.011392, -74.322084	Probably Smadbeck	?
New Jersey/Ocean	Lakewood	1919	*40.069834, -74.217906	Smadbeck	Jewish Daily News
New Jersey/Ocean	Lakewood Gardens	1925	40.085968, -74.145478	Hudson Dispatch?	Hudson Dispatch
New Jersey/Ocean	Lakewood Pines	1921	*40.069834, -74.217906	Smadbeck	The Chief
New Jersey/Passaic	Upper Greenwood Lake	1932	41.460819, -73.658081	Smadbeck	Daily Mirror
New Jersey/Salem	Penn Beach	1925	39.646952, -75.528027	Smadbeck	Philadelphia Record
New Jersey/Sussex	Sparta Lake	1928	41.047297, -74.563497	Smadbeck	Paterson Press Guardian
New Mexico/Lincoln	Skyland	1928	33.325061, -105.659719	Smadbeck	El Paso Herald/El Paso Times
New York/Albany	Colonie Estates	1920	*42.748578, -73.754079	Smadbeck	Troy Record
New York/Erie	Lake Erie Beach	1922	42.628094, -79.088368	Smadbeck	Buffalo Courier/Buffalo Enquirer

Appendix: Resort Locator

State/County	Colony	Year	Coordinates	Developer	Newspaper
New York/Orange County	Walton Lake/Round Island Lake	1928	41.311920, -74.218415	Wadsworth	Paterson Evening News
New York/Putnam	Lake Carmel	1930	41.460819, -73.658081	Smadbeck	Daily Mirror
New York/Putnam	Putnam Lake	1931	41.471741, -73.543751	Smadbeck	Daily Mirror
New York/Rensselaer	Nassau Lake Park	1924	42.538770, -73.600653	Smadbeck	Knickerbocker Press/ Albany Evening News
New York/Suffolk	Fire Island Pines	1952	40.665054, -73.069175	Smadbeck	none
New York/Suffolk	Mastic Beach	1926	40.760998, -72.847318	Smadbeck	Brooklyn Citizen
New York/Suffolk	Mastic Park	1920	40.800087, -72.840370	Smadbeck	Brooklyn Citizen
New York/Suffolk	Montauk Beach	1932	41.020232, -71.988489	Smadbeck	Daily Mirror
New York/Suffolk	North Shore Beach	1928	40.953510, -72.929967	Smadbeck	Daily Mirror
New York/Suffolk	Patchogue Lakes	1919	40.788170, -73.021605	Smadbeck	Brooklyn Citizen
New York/Suffolk	Sound Beach	1929	40.962795, -72.970224	Smadbeck	Daily Mirror
New York/Westchester	Sherman Park	1891	41.112842, -73.792976	Louis Smadbeck	none
Ohio/Clark	Crystal Lakes	1925	39.886946, -84.023853	Smadbeck	Dayton Journal/Dayton Herald
Ohio/Fairfield	Fairfield Beach	1926	39.912724, -82.475654	Smadbeck	Columbus Dispatch
Ohio/Geauga	Chagrin Falls Park	1921	41.414158, -81.388797	Smadbeck	Jewish World
Ohio/Warren & Hamilton	Loveland Park	1924	39.294720, -84.260589	Smadbeck	Commercial Tribune
Oregon/Clackamas	Estacada Lake	1928	45.285468, -122.336764	Smadbeck	Portland Telegram
Pennsylvania/Greene	Waynesburg Lakes	1962	39.974028, -80.182470	Smadbeck	Chamber of Commerce

Appendix: Resort Locator

State/County	Colony	Year	Coordinates	Developer	Newspaper
Texas/Galveston	Clear Lake Shores	1927	29.543265, -95.031839	Smadbeck	Houston Post Dispatch
Wisconsin/Walworth	Interlaken	1929	42.733623, -88.572683	Smadbeck	Chicago Evening Post
Wisconsin/Walworth	Lake Como Beach	1926	42.611523, -88.483699	Smadbeck	Chicago Evening Post
Wisconsin/Walworth	Lake Ivanhoe	1926	42.579975, -88.340719	Brumfield, Watson, Anglin	none
Wisconsin/Walworth	Pell Lake	1924	42.542241, -88.346604	Smadbeck	Chicago Evening Post

*Location Approximate

Chapter Notes

Introduction

1. Throughout the book persons of African American descent are referred to as "Negro" or "colored." These terms were frequently used by the black population in the 1920s to describe themselves: "colored" is incorporated into the name of the National Association for the Advancement of Colored People and both words were in common usage in its magazine, *The Crisis*.

Chapter 1

1. Albert Clayton Beckwith, ed., *History of Walworth County Wisconsin*, Indianapolis: B. F. Bowen, 1912, 1:41.
2. *Public Land Survey, Bloomfield Township, T1N R18E Interior Field Notes* (Board of Commissioners of Public Lands, 1836).
3. *General Instructions*, Surveyor General of Wisconsin and Iowa (1846), 344.
4. 1810 U.S. Census, *Population Schedule*, Clarendon, Rutland County, Vermont, 267.
5. Marvin Blanchard, History of Centerville, New York, Chicago: deposited in the cornerstone of the Centerville United Methodist Church, copied by Lois Fiegl, Town Historian, 1908: 13, 17.
6. Moses M. Strong, *History of the Territory of Wisconsin, From 1836 to 1848*, Madison: Democrat Printing, 1885, 219.
7. The transfer of ownership from Stacy to Pell occurred so quickly that the deed predated the issuance of the land patent itself by several weeks. Loren Stacy Patent, March 3, 1843, Bureau of Land Management, General Land Office, Certificate 8954; Stacy to Pell, Walworth County Register of Deeds (WCRD), Deeds, January 27, 1843, 3:46, Elkhorn, Wisconsin.
8. *Map of Walworth County, Wisconsin*, Elkhorn: Redding and Watson, 1857, sheet 5.
9. A comparison of the production value of the Pell farm with that of other owners of similar acreage in the township demonstrates that Ira Pell's performance as a farmer was mediocre. 1870 U.S. Census, *Schedule 3—Productions of Agriculture*, Bloomfield, Walworth County, Wisconsin, Post Office Genoa.
10. "Ira A. Pell came in 1842, and settled on Section 15, near the lake which now bears his name. He died in 1870. His widow and two sons still live on the claim." *History of Walworth County Wisconsin*, Chicago: Western Historical, 1882, 838; "Ira A. Pell (1800–1871), namesake of the lakelet in section 15, married Mary L. (1816–1883), daughter of Ephraim and Alida Farmer," Beckwith, *History of Walworth County*, 1:230.
11. Headstone, Bloomfield Cemetery, Pell Lake.
12. Ginny Hall, *Meandering Around Walworth County: An Auto Tour Guide*, Bloomfield and Linn Township: Friends of the Lake Geneva Public Library, 2009, 2:12. *Exploring Walworth County: A Hands-On Guide to the Past & Present of Walworth County, Wisconsin*, Elkhorn: Walworth County Sesquicentennial Committee, 1998, unpaginated.
13. Pre 1907 Wisconsin Death Records, 1:153, Nelson Pell, January 16, 1882; Register of Deaths 1900–1908, 3:167 (District Court, Marshall County, Marshalltown, Iowa), O. C. Pell, December 3, 1901.
14. Pell to Hafs, WCRD, Deeds, November 2, 1883, 68:613.

15. *Map of Walworth County, Wisconsin* (Everts, Baskin and Stewart, 1873).

16. Although the name of the lake is possessive, it was routinely printed without an apostrophe.

17. Jacob Schmadbeck, Middleton, 1860, Connecticut Wills and Probate Records 1860, Middleton, v. 22, 105, Connecticut State Library, Hartford.

18. 1860 U.S. Census, *Population Schedule*, Cromwell, Middlesex County, Connecticut, p. 38, lines 4–10.

19. Mineral patents to David Abraham, Henri Leonce Frassinet, Samuel Freudenthal, and Louis Smadbeck, February 6, 1892, Bureau of Land Management, General Land Office, Serial Nos. AZAZAA 012869 (Mexican lode) and AZAZAA 012870 (Emelia lode).

20. Index to New York City Marriages 1866–1937, October 9, 1883, Certificate No. 27937, New York City Municipal Archives.

21. Philip H. Horne, *Mount Pleasant: The History of a New York Suburb and Its People*, Hawthorne, NY: self-published, 1971, 37. Sherman Park has been re-identified with the names Hawthorne and Thornville.

22. *Annual Report of the Superintendent of Banks for the Year 1893*, James P. Lyon, State Printer (Albany, 1894), 679–681. See also "Sherman Park's Guests," (*New York*) *Evening World*, December 8, 1891, 3.

23. Horne, *Mount Pleasant*, 37; "Coliseum Leader Sold Suburbs, but Stayed in New York Himself," *New York Times*, April 29, 1956, 75.

24. "An Incomparable New York Suburb," *(New York) World*, March 22, 1895, 14.

25. 1905 New York State Census, New York County, Borough of Manhattan, p. 12, lines 18–24; "Warren Smadbeck, 80, Is Dead; Suburban Real Estate Developer," *New York Times*, July 30, 1965, 25.

26. New York Wills and Probate Records 1659–1999, Surrogates Court, Record of Wills, v. 915, p. 111.

27. Passenger List of Vessels Arriving at New York, New York, 1820–1957; arrived April 6, 1910, on the SS *Moltke* from Havana, List 11, lines 11–13; arrived November 8, 1910 on the SS *Kronprinzessin Cecilie* from Bremen, List 2, lines 7–9.

28. City of New York Department of Health, Certificate and Record of Death, No. 4547, Louis Smadbeck, New York City Municipal Archives.

Chapter 2

1. The local newspaper began incorporating the name change into its news reports in late October 1924. Compare "Linn-Bloomfield," *Lake Geneva (Wisconsin) News*, October 23, 1924, 4, referring to Pells Lake with "West Geneva," *Lake Geneva News*, October 30, 1924, 9, referencing Pell Lake.

2. Julius Freudenthal was a noteworthy character in his own right. He was one of the principals in the Longfellow mine and became wealthy when it was sold. A casualty of the Panic of 1893, he was the subject of a lengthy article on the front page of the *New York Times* and in newspapers across the country when, in 1896, he avoided creditors by disappearing, leaving his son Ludwig exposed for some of his debt. "J. Freudenthal Missing," *New York Times*, July 12, 1896, 1; "Business Troubles," *New York Times*, July 15, 1896, 11.

3. Holtzheimer to Freudenthal, WCRD, Deeds, 174:79; Kull to Freudenthal, 174: 80–81.

4. Kull to Freudenthal, WCRD, Deeds, date unreadable, 174:170; Reeves to Freudenthal, July 19, 1924, 174:276; Hibbard to Freudenthal, August, 14, 1924, 174:332.

5. Freudenthal to Smadbeck, WCRD, Deeds, May 2, 1924, 175: 413, 415, 418; June 16, 1924, 175:416; July 25 1924, 174:284; August 16, 1924, 174:383; September 20, 1924, 175:635; December 5, 1924, 176:319.

6. Lee E. Lawrence, "The Wisconsin Ice Trade," *Wisconsin Magazine of History* 48, no. 4 (Summer 1965).

7. Consumers Company to Freudenthal, WCRD, Deeds, May 15, 1924, 175:319.

8. "Start Work to Enlarge Pell Lake," *Lake Geneva (Wisconsin) News Tribune*, March 11, 1926, 1.

9. WCRD, Plats, Pell Lake Subdivision Section 1, July 16, 1924, 3:77; Section 2, July 16, 1924, 3:77A; Section 3, August, 5, 1924, 3:78; Section 4, August 23, 1924, 3:79; Section 5, September 2, 1924, 1:89; Section 6, September 29, 1924, 1:90A; Section 7, October 10, 1924, 2:11A; Section A, August 23, 1924, 3:78A; Section B, October 10, 1924, 2:11.

10. *Sixty-Fifth Annual Report of the Chicago and North Western Railway Company, Year Ending December 31, 1924* (C and NW Railway Company, 1924), 14.
11. *McHenry (Wisconsin) Plaindealer*, April 9, 1925, 7; Display Ad, *Chicago Evening Post*, June 4, 1925, 5.
12. "Subdivision at Lake Como To Be Largest Yet," *Lake Geneva News Tribune*, December 3, 1925, 1.
13. Twenty-four-hour electric service arrived at Pell Lake in 1929. "Areas Are Using More Electricity," *Oshkosh Daily Northwestern* (Oshkosh, Wisconsin), December 31, 1929, 18.
14. *Appointment of U.S. Postmasters, 1832-1971*, 92:458.
15. "Short Notes," *Lake Geneva News Tribune*, July 5, 1928, 8.
16. *Lake Geneva News Tribune*, August 6, 1925, 1.
17. *Lake Geneva News Tribune*, November 19, 1925, 1.
18. *Lake Geneva News Tribune*, May 28, 1925, 7.
19. Pell Lake Property Owners Association, Wisconsin Department of Financial Institutions (WDFI), December 18, 1925, Entity ID 6P02082.
20. Hussey to Pell Lake Property Owners Association, WCRD, Deeds, January 7, 1926, 193:231.
21. Smadbeck to Jonap, WCRD, Deeds, February 23, 1927, 193:345.
22. Sitterle's Subdivision, WCRD, Plats, November 7, 1924, 2:13; Sitterle's Addition, August 13, 1925, Plats, 2:19.
23. Pell Lake Highlands, WCRD, Plats, June 12, 1925, 1:99.
24. "Kimball Sells Part of Farm at Pells Lake," *Lake Geneva News Tribune*, April 9, 1925, 1.
25. Leon Sex was also responsible for resort developments at Lily Lake, Lakemoor, and Channel Lake, all in northern Illinois. None of his projects were tied to newspaper subscriptions.
26. Pell Lake Addition, WCRD, Plats, June 17, 1925, 8:29.
27. "Buy Site for Splendid Hotel at Pell Lake," *Lake Geneva News Tribune*, March 18, 1926, 1; See also Robert Streit to The Public, WCRD, Farm Names, February 1, 1926, 1:89.
28. Display Ad, *Chicago Evening Post*, June 4, 1925, 5.

29. "Bloomfield," *Lake Geneva News Tribune*, February 19, 1925, 2.
30. Pell Farm Annex, WCRD, Plats, September 29, 1925, 2:21A.
31. Motorists had to wait until August 12, 1928 for the last stretch of concrete paving, between McHenry and Richmond, Illinois, to be opened to traffic. "Short Route to Chicago Opened to Traffic Sunday," *Lake Geneva News Tribune*, August 16, 1928, 1.
32. Conversation with Art Oster, August 25, 2019.
33. *McHenry Plaindealer*, June 11, 1925, 1, and April 9, 1925, 7.
34. "An Opportunity," *Lake Geneva News Tribune*, April 9, 1925, 6.
35. "Business Men Report Good Season Despite Poor Weather," *Lake Geneva News Tribune*, September 16, 1926, 1.
36. "Will Collect $175,000 For Taxes in City," *Lake Geneva News Tribune*, January 14, 1926, 1.

Chapter 3

1. Kathleen Drowne and Patrick Huber, *The 1920s: American Popular Culture Through History*, Westport, CT: Greenwood Press, 2004, 103–04.
2. The last lot was sold on June 27, 1919. Horne, *Mount Pleasant*, 38.
3. *New York Times*, December 19, 1909, 15.
4. Articles of Incorporation, New York Department of State, Division of Corporations (NYDS), DOS ID 30431.
5. *Rosenbaum v. Sarasohn, Reports of Cases Heard and Determined in the Appellate Division of the Supreme Court of the State of New York*, v. 184 (1918): 204–09.
6. "Unique Real Estate Offer," *Arkansas City Daily Traveler*, July 16, 1909, 6.
7. Display Ad, *Hutchinson (Kansas) News*, September 15, 1909, 11; See also "Orient Shop News," *Kansas Magazine* 3, no. 3 (March 1910).
8. See, e.g., Display Ads, *Wichita Beacon*, August 13, 1909, 9; *Wichita Daily Eagle*, September 4, 1909, 6; *Hutchinson News*, September 10, 1909, 9.
9. Display Ad, *Kansas Magazine* 3, no. 2 (February 1910).
10. Massachusetts Town and Vital Records, Boston Births 1865, Bertram Mayo, No. 1010.

11. 1870 U.S. Census, *Population Schedule*, Boston, Suffolk County, Massachusetts, 134, line 15.
12. "Wholesale clothing," *Boston Directory*, Boston, Sampson, Murdock, 1889, 825; "Clothier," *Directory of Dedham and Westwood*, North Cambridge: Edward A. Jones, 1899, 66.
13. *Boston Directory*, Boston: Sampson, Murdock, 1894, 907.
14. "Over Five Hundred Citizens Help to Boom the Interests of Oakland," *San Francisco Call*, April 4, 1904, 7.
15. *Husted's Oakland, Alameda & Berkeley Directory for the Year 1906*, Oakland: F. M. Husted, 1906, 323.
16. William Mill Butler, ed., *Beachwood Borough Directory and Who's Who*, New York: Blanchard Press, 1924, 133.
17. "To Bore For Oil," *Evening Bee* (Sacramento), August 9, 1907, 6.
18. "To Prospect Big Tract for Oil: Betts Thinks He Has Struck It Rich and Plans Development," *Evening Bee*, July 8, 1907, 6; "Looking For Oil: Prospecting Will Be Carried on with Vigor," *Evening Bee*, July 22, 1907, 7.
19. "Articles of Incorporation," *Prescott (Arizona) Morning Courier*, December 18, 1906, 4.
20. "They Call Him 'The Miracle Man' of the Oil Fields," *National Magazine* 50 (April, 1921–May, 1922), 329.
21. "Diamond Drill at Goldfield District," *Salt Lake Tribune*, June 16, 1913, 12.
22. 1910 U.S. Census, *Population Schedule*, Oakland, Alameda County, California, sheet 13B, line 71.
23. "Realty Company Formed," *San Francisco Call*, February 17, 1907, 43; Display Ad, *San Francisco Call*, March 31, 1907, 41.
24. "Real Estate Transfers," *Petaluma (California) Argus*, February 25, 1910, 2 (80 acres); Chapman to Bartlett, March 14, 1910, Deed Book 263:189 (120 acres), and May 4, 1910, Deed Book 263:263 (160 acres), Sonoma County Recorder, Santa Rosa, California. Deeds often state the price as "one dollar and other valuable compensation" to indicate that it was a bargained transaction without specifying the amount paid. The purchase price can sometimes be computed based on the affixed revenue stamps. Neither situation applies here and the wording in the two referenced deeds suggests that the $10.00 figure listed was the actual purchase price.
25. "Meeting of Supervisors," *Healdsburg (California) Enterprise*, July 9, 1910, 3.
26. See, e.g., Bartlett to Foster, May 5, 1910, Sonoma County Recorder, Deed Book 286:230.
27. Display Ad, *Sunset* 25, no. 3 (September, 1910).
28. Leslie E. Smirnoff, "A Cultural Resources Inventory and Management Plan for Sonoma Land Trust's Little Black Mountain Property" (master's thesis, Sonoma State University, 2009), 58.
29. Sonoma County Archives, Assessor Records 1873–1983, accessed July 13, 2018: http://www.sonoma.lib.ca.us/history/archive/?p=collections/findingaid&id=25&q=&rootcontentid=63,; "Assessment Practices Survey and Assessor's Response: Sonoma County" (Assessment Standards Division, Property Tax Department, California State Board of Equalization, 1989), 20.
30. See, e.g., "Lots Cost Little; See Picture Show," *Oregon Daily Journal*, November 25, 1911, 6; "They Will Bite," *Petaluma (California) Daily Courier*, June 4, 1912, 8.
31. "Old Adage That Suckers Abound," *Butte (Montana) Inter Mountain*, October 25, 1912, 2.
32. "Told Land is Worthless," *The Petaluma Argus*, August 22, 1923, 10.
33. Sec. 532c of the Code reads: "Any person, firm, corporation or copartnership who knowingly and designedly offers or gives with winning numbers at any drawing of numbers or with tickets of admission to places of public assemblage, any lot or parcel of real property and charges or collects fees in connection with the transfer thereof, is guilty of a misdemeanor."
34. Smirnoff's "A Cultural Resources Inventory" contains a history of Little Black Mountain land ownership that specifically includes the Mayo/Bartlett acreage.
35. "Daniels Named On Prison Board," *Oakland Tribune*, December 10, 1925, 1.
36. "Walton Disciples Return From Trip," *Berkeley Daily Gazette*, May 10, 1909, 2.
37. Barton Phelps, *A Place in the Canyons*, Menlo Park, CA: Sunset Books, 2013, unpaginated, accessed July 11, 2018: http://bpala.com/wp-content/uploads/2012/05/Arroyo-Garden-Book-SM.pdf.

38. 1911 Los Angeles City Directory (Los Angeles City Directory Company, 1911), 968.
39. Display Ad, *Los Angeles Herald*, May 4, 1911, 7.
40. Classified Ad, *Los Angeles Herald*, October 22, 1910, 14. Parts of Beverly Glen remain a construction challenge. A home that managed to circumvent these problems is Arroyo House. See Phelps, *A Place in the Canyons*.
41. "Former Governor Pardee and Wife Visiting Here," *Los Angeles Herald*, June 8, 1911, 12.
42. "Beverly Glen on Map Most Charming Region," *Los Angeles Herald*, May 14, 1911, Sec. 3, 3.

Chapter 4

1. *Chicago Evening Post*, 5.
2. June 18, 1912, 9; June 21, 1912, 14.
3. June 3, 1912, 9.
4. *Chicago Evening Post*, Announcement, May 22, 1912, 5; C. W. Redfern, "Lakewood, Transformed Wilderness, Shows Possibilities of Lake Resorts," *Muskegon (Michigan) News Chronicle*, June 3, 1912, 8.
5. "First Street Railway Ever Operated in State Summer Resort Begins Operations," *Muskegon (Michigan) Chronicle*, October 27, 1913, 8.
6. Lakewood Street Railway Company Articles of Incorporation, Michigan Department of Licensing and Regulatory Affairs, July 31, 1913, ID No. 800170911; *Ninth Annual Report of the Michigan Railroad Commission for the Year Ending December 31, 1915*, 123.
7. "Sells Resorters Lumber" *Muskegon Chronicle*, February 12, 1913, 5.
8. Classified Ads, *Muskegon Chronicle*, June 7, 1913, 6; July 1, 1913, 6; July 15, 1914, 6.
9. "Judge Sullivan Cuts Jury's Verdict, Holds Sum Allowed Excessive," *Muskegon Chronicle*, February 16, 1914, 1.
10. Stanley D. Brown was an attorney who specialized in newspaper law and served as general counsel for the *Tribune*. Obituary, *Ithaca Journal*, October 24, 1967, 7.
11. See, e.g., "Summer Homes Offered Readers," *New York Tribune*, November 18, 1914, 5.
12. *H. Snowden Marshall: Hearings Before the Committee on the Judiciary*, 64th Cong. (1916).
13. *Marshall Hearings*, 987–88.
14. "Postal Probe of Lakewood Resort Fizzles," *Muskegon Chronicle*, July 20, 1915, 9.
15. *Marshall Hearings*, 963, 969.
16. *Marshall Hearings*, 32–34.
17. "Kill Resolution to Impeach Marshall," *New York Times*, July 12, 1916, 6; see also *Marshall v. Gordon*, 243 U.S. 521 (1917).
18. Butler, *Beachwood Borough Directory*, 22.
19. Butler, *Beachwood Borough Directory*, 48.
20. Butler, *Beachwood Borough Directory*, 22.
21. *New York Tribune*, December 15, 1916, 6; December 12, 1917, 9; January 5, 1919, Part 2, 5.
22. A series of articles by Erik Weber ably describes the entire Beachwood saga—Mayo's background, his relationship with Nickerson, the circumstances surrounding the purchase of the land, the articles in the *Tribune* and the *Courier*, and the investigations into the mail fraud charges. Weber's history also includes many early photographs. "Building Beachwood, Parts I, II, III, and IV," *Riverside Signal* 1, issues 6–9 (February 25–April 21, 2011).
23. Marie F. Reynolds, *Browns Mills*, Charleston: Arcadia Publishing, 2000, 7, 81, 107.
24. Reynolds, *Browns Mills*, 90–92.
25. Butler, *Beachwood Borough Directory*, 132.
26. "Likes Florida's Climate," *Tampa Morning Tribune*, December 10, 1913, 7; "A Significant Incident," *Tampa Morning Tribune*, December 12, 1913, 8.
27. "Picturesque New Jersey," *Jersey City News*, January 21, 1905, 1.
28. Leland M. Williamson, et al., eds., *Prominent and Progressive Pennsylvanians of the Nineteenth Century*, Philadelphia: Record Publishing, 1898, v. 3, 317–19.
29. "Brown's Mills To Be Made Into Summer Resort," *Trenton Times*, March 2, 1903, 5.
30. Editorial, *Trenton Times*, March 10, 1903, 4.
31. "Plan $50,000 Hotel at Brown's Mills," *Woodbury (New Jersey) Daily Times*, April 30, 1903, 1.

32. "Brown's Mills Improvements," *Trenton Times*, January 6, 1905, 3.
33. Display Ad, *Philadelphia Inquirer*, February 28, 1905, 12.
34. Proclamation, *Trenton Sunday Advertiser*, April 14, 1907, 17.
35. "Ex-Senator Pfeiffer Goes in Bankruptcy," *Trenton Sunday Advertiser*, December 3, 1905, 5.
36. "New Corporations," *Trenton Evening Times*, March 5, 1910, 9.
37. "Pines Resort Sold at Master's Sale," *Trenton Evening Times*, June 3, 1916, 5.
38. "Browns Mills," *Allentown (New Jersey) Messenger*, September 28, 1916, 5.
39. "Doing Things at Browns Mills," *Allentown Messenger*, January 18, 1917, 4; "Browns Mills," *Allentown Messenger*, February 22, 1917, 8.
40. "Likes Florida's Climate," *Tampa Morning Tribune*.
41. "A Significant Incident," *Tampa Morning Tribune*.
42. "Two Elections Claim Attention of Voters," *Tampa Morning Tribune*, February 1, 1914, 2.
43. "Tarpon Springs," *Tampa Morning Tribune*, December 8, 1915, 11.
44. "Tarpon Springs," *Tampa Morning Tribune*, January 27, 1916, 7.
45. "Two Elections Claim Attention of Voters," *Tampa Morning Tribune*.
46. "Send a Car of Oranges to Poor," *Tampa Daily Times*, February 20, 1915, 20.
47. "Tarpon Bank Increases its Capital by Double," *Tampa Morning Tribune*, January 14, 1916, 12.
48. "Arrested at Tarpon on Incendiary Charge," *Tampa Morning Tribune*, January 15, 1916, 9.
49. "The Florida Press," *Tampa Morning Tribune*, May 3, 1917, 6.
50. *Marshall Hearings*, 934.
51. U.S. World War I Draft Registration Cards, No. 21, June 5, 1917, Burlington County, New Jersey.
52. Bertram C. Mayo, will dated December 18, 1914, Ocean County Courthouse Wills and Probate Records, 1917–1921, v. 17, pp. 112–40, Tom's River, New Jersey.
53. Mayo, codicil to will dated May 1, 1915, pp. 125–26.
54. Display Ad, *Union Postal Clerk* 9, no. 10 (October 1913), 8.
55. "Sues Publishers for $20,000," *Chicago Daily Tribune*, January 14, 1914, 11.
56. Display Ad, September 3, 1914, 7.
57. *Copyright Entries, Part 1, Group 2*, Washington, D.C., Copyright Office (1916): 333.
58. North Carolina Death Certificates, State Board of Health, Bureau of Vital Statistics, Bertram Chapman Mayo, Register No. 444, Buncombe County, North Carolina.
59. "Rides in Plane to Study Lines for Speed Boat," *Saint Petersburg Daily Times*, January 25, 1920, 3.
60. "To Purchase Lots," *Los Angeles Times*, January 3, 1920, 1.
61. "Many Realty Deals in Tarpon Springs," *Tampa Morning Tribune*, March 16, 1920, 9.
62. "Real Estate Transfers," *New York Times*, January 12, 1919, RE 9.
63. "Tarpon Springs," *Tampa Sunday Tribune*, June 29, 1919, 4B.
64. Mayo, codicil to will dated January 9, 1920, p.132.
65. North Carolina Death Certificates, No. 444.
66. 1920 U.S. Census, *Population Schedule*, Los Angeles, Los Angeles County, California, p. 43A, line 48.
67. "Estates Appraised," *New York Herald*, April 6, 1921, 18.
68. North Carolina Death Certificates, No. 444.

Chapter 5

1. North Carolina Death Certificates, No. 444.
2. U.S. Passport Applications, No. 134875, January 27, 1921.
3. U.S. World War I Draft Registration Cards, No. 44, June 5, 1917, New York, New York.
4. Frank Presbrey, *The History and Development of Advertising*, Garden City, NY: Doubleday, Doran, 1929, 126. There were two other paid advertisements in the same paper but not for the sale of goods. Rather they offered rewards for the capture of a thief and the return of stolen articles.
5. Presbrey, *The History and Development of Advertising*, 260.
6. See *Who's Who in Advertising*, Detroit: Business Service Corporation, Detroit, 1916, 10–11.

7. *The Elementary Laws of Advertising: And How to Use Them*, Chicago: Novelty News Press, 1913, 89–98.
8. Henry S. Bunting, *The Premium System of Forcing Sales: Its Principles, Laws and Uses*, Chicago: Novelty News Press, 1913.
9. Bunting, *Elementary Laws of Advertising*, 89–98.
10. William R. Scott, *Scientific Circulation Management for Newspapers*, New York: Ronald Press Company, 1915, 174–75.
11. John E. Kennedy, *Reason-Why Advertising*, Chicago: Judicious Advertising.
12. Display Ad, *Judicious Advertising* (October 1911), 86.
13. Presbrey, *The History and Development of Advertising*, 294.
14. *(Riverhead, New York) County Review*, October 19, 1944, 13.
15. No effort has been made here to investigate the business relationship between the various newspapers that sponsored colonies and those that merely advertised the promotions. Quite possibly many of these publications operated under a common corporate roof.
16. Display Ad, *(Albany, New York) Times Union*, May 28, 1920, 16.
17. Display Ad, *Schenectady (New York) Gazette*, November 23, 1920, 12.
18. Display Ad, *(Albany) Times Union*, June 24, 1920, 14.
19. Display Ad, *Boston Post*, July 30, 1920, 6.
20. Display Ad, *Boston Post*, May 22, 1921, 28.
21. Display Ads, *Boston Post*, 1921: April 19, 22; April 21, 7; April 23, 3; April 28, 17.
22. Display Ad, *Dunkirk (New York) Evening Observer*, July 8, 1922, 14.
23. "High School Teacher Asks for His Grapes," *Buffalo Commercial*, August 25, 1922, 3.
24. Lake Michigan Beach is also known as Hagar Shores.
25. "Deputy Sues Land Holder," *(Benton Harbor, Michigan) News-Palladium*, December 7, 1925, 3.
26. Masthead, *Indianapolis Sunday Star*, May 13, 1923, 8.
27. "R. B. Hussey Dies of Heart Disease," *Indianapolis Star*, May 16, 1929, 12.
28. Lots could also be purchased with a subscription to the *Muncie (Indiana) Star*.
29. "Cottage Is Built Among Tree Tops," *Indianapolis Star*, October 9, 1923, 9.
30. *Chicago Evening Post*, August 6, 1924, 11.
31. *Buffalo Enquirer*, July 27, 1922, 3.
32. *Minneapolis Daily Star*, August 6, 1925, 1.
33. *Chicago Evening Post*, August 5, 1924, 4.
34. *Chicago Evening Post*, July 18, 1924, 1.
35. "Post's Pell Lake Resort Develops Another Booster," *Chicago Evening Post*, July 25, 1924, 3.
36. Act of August 24, 1912, 37 *U.S. Statutes at Large*, Section 2, 539 at 554. For a discussion of the history and effectiveness of the law see Linda Lawson, *Truth in Publishing: Federal Regulation of the Press's Business Practices, 1880-1920*, Carbondale: Southern Illinois University Press, 1993.
37. "No Blanket Ruling on Marking Reading Notices 'Adv.,'" *Printers Ink* (December 28, 1916), 74.
38. "Start Work to Enlarge Pell Lake," *Lake Geneva News Tribune*.
39. Display Ad, *Dayton Herald*, 16–17.
40. "Crystal Lakes People Organize Improvement Club," *Dayton Herald*, November 17, 1925, 14.
41. Photos of Lake Louisvilla can be viewed at Historic Photos of Louisville Kentucky and Environs: The Suburbs—Northeast, accessed February 24, 2020: http://historiclouisville.weebly.com/northeast.html, and at University of Louisville Archives and Special Collections, accessed February 10, 2018: https://digital.library.louisville.edu/cdm/search/searchterm/lake%20louisvilla/field/all/mode/all/conn/and/order/nosort/ad/asc/cosuppress/0.
42. The estimated number of acres for four developments initiated in 1924 are Loveland Park 750; Lake Louisvilla 80; Lake Saint Croix Beach 300; and Pell Lake 700. Acreage is not available for Nassau Lake Park.

Chapter 6

1. Mark Sullivan, *Our Times 1900-1925, The War Begins 1909-1914*, Vol. 4, New York: Charles Scribner's Sons, 1932, 88–93.
2. *Marshall Hearings*, 986.
3. Notice, *New York Tribune*, May 5, 1915, 3.
4. *Marshall Hearings*, 922, 932.

Notes—Chapter 6

5. Honor Built Bungalow Ad, March 9, 1916, 6; Nickerson Glenn Building Ad, March 11, 1916, 6; Rohdenburg Ad, March 17, 1916, 7.
6. *New York Tribune*, July 27, 1919, 11.
7. Will Irwin, "The American Newspaper, XIV—The Press of Two Cities," *Collier's* 47 (1911): no. 18:13.
8. Will Irwin, "The American Newspaper, II—The Dim Beginnings," *Collier's* 46 (1911): no. 18:14.
9. Irwin, The Dim Beginnings, 15–16.
10. William R. Scott, *Scientific Circulation Management*, 17.
11. Lawson, *Truth in Publishing*, 48–49.
12. Scott, *Scientific Circulation Management*, 27–29.
13. Will Irwin, "The American Newspaper, I—'The Power of the Press,'" *Collier's* 46 (1911): no. 20:15.
14. Irwin, Will, "The American Newspaper, IX—The Advertising Influence," *Collier's* 47 (1911): no. 10:15.
15. Irwin, "The Advertising Influence," 16.
16. For a thorough discussion of the intertwining of second-class mailing status with premiums, circulation, and advertorials see Richard B. Kielbowicz, *A History of Mail Classifications and Its Underlying Policies and Purposes* (Postal Rate Commission Report), July 17, 1995.
17. 37 U.S. Statutes at Large, chap. 389, sec. 2, 539 at 554.
18. *Lewis Publishing Co. v. Morgan*, 229 U.S. 288 (1913).
19. Lawson, *Truth in Publishing*, 90.
20. Algernon Tassin, "Dollars and Display: The Earnings of Advertising Men," *The Bookman* (September 1910), 26, https://www.google.com/books/edition/The_Bookman/SItHAQAAMAAJ?hl=en&gbpv=1&dq=tassin+dollars+and+display&pg=PR6&printsec=frontcover.
21. Sullivan, *Our Times, The War Begins*, 96.
22. Richard Kluger, *The Paper: The Life and Death of the New York Herald Tribune*, New York: Alfred A. Knopf, 1986, 182, 190.
23. Scott, *Scientific Circulation Management*, 150.
24. Masthead, *New York Tribune*, January 3, 1915, 10.
25. Kluger, *The Paper*, 190.
26. *New York Tribune*, September 10, 1915, 14.
27. Notice, March 31, 1915, 5.
28. *Marshall Hearings*, 974–75.
29. *Rosenbaum v. Sarasohn*, 207. This was not the only time the Smadbecks were content to have the other party to an agreement compose the provisions—a business practice that often worked to the developers' advantage.
30. Display Ad, *Minneapolis Daily Star*, August 20, 1925, 11.
31. See generally Presbrey, *The History and Development of Advertising*, 244–52.
32. "Star Readers' Resort Grows," *Minneapolis Daily Star*, August 12, 1925, 5.
33. The Meramec River Route 66 Bridge was constructed in 1931–32 to accommodate the rerouting of Route 66.
34. Display Ad, *(Wilmington, Delaware) News Journal*, June 4, 1925, 15.
35. "Pinto Says King Lake Well Water Is Unfit," *Omaha World-Herald*, July 21, 1925, 1.
36. "King Lake Promoters May Dig Two Wells," *Omaha World-Herald*, July 25, 1925, 8.
37. "Lake Has Water and Bullheads Again," *Omaha World-Herald*, November 21, 1934, 3.
38. Display Ad, *Minneapolis Star*, August 5, 1925, 9.
39. *Omaha World-Herald*, July 16, 1926, 14.
40. See Gregg M. Turner, *The Florida Land Boom of the 1920s*, Jefferson, NC: McFarland, 2015.
41. *Chicago Evening Post*, May 31, 1926, 3.
42. *Columbus Evening Dispatch*, August 5, 1926, 1.
43. "Laurel Lake is Beautiful Spot," *Millville (New Jersey) Daily Republican*, May 23, 1927, 1. See also Display Ad, *Millville Daily Republican*, June 2, 1927, 9.
44. "Work Progressing on Laurel Lake Tract," *Millville Daily Republican*, May 16, 1927, 1.
45. "Temporarily Halt Work at Laurel Lake," *Millville Daily Republican*, June 5, 1929, 1.
46. Display Ad, *(Camden, New Jersey) Morning Post*, May 11, 1929, 15.
47. "Buyers Flooding City With Bids for Laurel Lake Lots," *Millville Daily Republican*, August 9, 1946, 1.
48. Display Ad, *Philadelphia Record*, 30–31.

49. "Laurel and Beach Club Lakes Were Incorporated," *Millville Daily Republican*, November 26, 1929, 1.
50. Display Ad, *Brooklyn Daily Eagle*, June 8, 1919, 32.
51. *Dunkirk Evening Observer*, July 14, 1922, 6.
52. *County Review*, April 7, 1927, 15.
53. Display Ad, *Minneapolis Star*, July 28, 1927, 15.
54. Display Ad, *Philadelphia Inquirer*, March 20, 1928, 18.
55. "To Build Summer Homes at Much Lower Figure," *Buffalo Enquirer*, July 29, 1922, 2.
56. "Sale of Lots at Lake Erie Beach and Building Operations Beat All Records," *Buffalo Enquirer*, June 24, 1922, 4.
57. See "Charges King Lake Agent Didn't Aid Kin," *Omaha World-Herald*, July 28, 1925, 7; Classified Ad, *Chicago Tribune*, July 8, 1925, 33.
58. Bolinas Beach Display Ad, *Oakland Tribune*, May 12, 1927, 17.
59. Display Ad, *Delaware County Daily Times*, June 21, 1927, 4.
60. See "New Development on Pleasant Lake," *Elkhorn (Wisconsin) Independent*, June 26, 1930, 1.
61. "Thousands Visit Daily Star Summer Resort at Coon Lake," *Minneapolis Star*, August 10, 1925, 3.
62. "Next Week Will See Several Homes Begun at Lake Erie Beach," *Buffalo Enquirer*, June 17, 1922, 4.
63. Coon Lake Display Ad, *Minneapolis Star*, August 10, 1925, 5.
64. Display Ad, *Indianapolis Star*, February 23, 1924, 10.
65. Display Ad, *Indianapolis Star*, April 18, 1925, 14.
66. *San Anselmo (California) Herald*, February 25, 1927, 7.
67. Display Ad, *Oakland Tribune*, May 11, 1927, 20.
68. Marguerite Kirk Harris, "Radical Environmental Protectionism in a Small Community: A Study of the Bolinas Water Moratorium," (master's thesis, Montana State University, Bozeman, 1977), 22.
69. Harris, "Radical Environmental Protectionism," 21.
70. Display Ad, *El Paso Herald*, April 4, 1928, 8–9; "Skyland To Be Community Mountain Camp Village 135 Miles from Here," *El Paso Herald*, April 4, 1928, 1, 10.
71. "Business Houses Being Built at Ruidoso Skyland," *El Paso Herald*, April 19, 1928, 4.
72. "Skyland to Get New Dance Hall," *El Paso Herald*, May 14, 1928, 9.
73. "Ferry Approaches Are in Bad Shape," *Galveston Daily News*, August 23, 1927, 1.
74. 1860 U.S. Census, *Population Schedule*; Cromwell, Middlesex County, Connecticut, p. 38, dwelling 293, line 4.
75. Dorothy Ingersoll Zaykowski, *Sag Harbor: The Story of an American Beauty*, Sag Harbor: Sag Harbor Historical Society, 1991, 116.
76. Warren Jay Smadbeck, U.S. Passport Applications, No. 134875, January 27, 1921.
77. Display Ad, *(Montreal, Quebec) Gazette*, July 23, 1926, 6. Plage Laval incorporated as a town in 1932, annexed adjoining communities in 1950, and changed its name to Laval-Ouest in 1952.
78. Display Ad, *Winnipeg Evening Tribune*, August 2, 1927, 6–7.
79. "Over $4,500 Now," *Evening World*, July 28, 1893, 4.
80. "Dr. Smadbeck, Millionaire, Sends Orphans to Circus," *Winnipeg Evening Tribune*, August 5, 1927, 5; "Children Visit Circus, Guests of Millionaire, Dr. and Mrs. Smadbeck, of Sandy Hook Fame, Entertain 137 Tots," *Winnipeg Evening Tribune*, August 8, 1927, 8.
81. Display Ad, *(Paterson, New Jersey) Morning Call*, July 25, 1928, 20.
82. Display Ad, *Chicago Daily Tribune*, July 9, 1929, 18.
83. "Would Change Name of Russel's Lake," *Elkhorn Independent*, March 5, 1925, 1.
84. Wandawega Historical Society, Elkhorn, Wisconsin: The Wandawega Hotel (Circa 1925–1942), accessed February 22, 2020: http://www.wandawegahistory.org/index#/the-wandawega-hotel.
85. The name was changed to Great Lakes Shores in 1936.
86. Display Ad, *(Port Huron, Michigan) Times Herald*, July 2, 1930, 22.

Chapter 7

1. See Raymond B. Vickers, *Panic in Paradise, Florida's Banking Crash of 1926*, Tuscaloosa: University of Alabama Press, 1994, 5.

2. "Radio Corporation Sells 950 Acres in Rocky Point," *County Review*, May 5, 1927, 17.
3. Display Ad, *New York Times*, June 12, 1930, 15.
4. Great Lakes Beach Display Ad, *Port Huron Times-Herald*, July 2, 1930, 22.
5. Display Ad, *New York Times*, June 17, 1928, RE 5.
6. Articles of Incorporation, NYDS, DOS ID 40805.
7. McGolrick Realty was another entity associated with the creation of numerous summer communities in the New York area. Using the name State Line Golf and Country Club, McGolrick and the Smadbecks cooperated in buying up farmland and developing resorts including Lake Carmel, Putnam Lake, and Lake Peekskill, all in Putnam County. Lake Peekskill, however, absent a subscription requirement, does not meet the criterion of a newspaper colony. Display Ad, *Brooklyn Daily Eagle*, May 5, 1929, 23.
8. The original plat maps need to be examined to ascertain that these were the original names of the streets and not later changes.
9. Display Ad, *New York Times*, June 10, 1931, 49.
10. Montauk Beach Property Owners Association, accessed February 24, 2020: http://www.mbpoa.com/about-us.
11. Index to New York City Marriages, March 27, 1911, Certificate No. 7168.
12. Classified Ad, *New York Times*, August 5, 1918, 16.
13. 1930 U.S. Census, *Population Schedule*, New York County, New York, p. 20B, lines 51–58.
14. "Wills for Probate," Madeline Smadbeck, *New York Times*, January 10, 1935, 40.
15. "Mrs. Fay Wed to Dr. Smadbeck," *New York Times*, December 19, 1935, 30.
16. "2-Day Art Auction Realizes $38,038 Here," *New York Times*, February 16, 1936, N8.
17. *Reno-Gazette Journal*, July 17, 1943, 10.
18. "Smadbeck-Shear," *New York Times*, October 8, 1919, 19.
19. Classified Ad, *New York Times*, March 29, 1922, 39.
20. "Smadbeck's Boat Wins Opening Regatta Heat," *Brooklyn Citizen*, August 5, 1927, 3.
21. 1930 U.S. Census, *Population Schedule*, New York County, New York, p. 12B, lines 51–58.
22. "Coliseum Leader Sold Suburbs," *New York Times*, April 29, 1956, 75.
23. Cobey Black, "A Gentleman with Vision," *Honolulu Star Bulletin*, August 26, 1957, 15.
24. "Avon Park C. of C. Sponsors Low Cost Lot Sales," *Saint Petersburg Times*, January 6, 1957, 10-F.
25. "Wills for Probate," *New York Times*, July 1, 1913, 17.
26. *In the Matter of the Claim of Warren and Arthur Smadbeck, Inc. under the International Claims Settlement Act of 1949*, Claim No. CU 2465, Decision No. CU 967, Foreign Claims Settlement Commission of the United States, April 22, 1970.
27. "Warren Smadbeck, 80, Is Dead," *New York Times*, July 30, 1965.
28. Peter B. Flint, "Arthur Smadbeck, 90, Ran Coliseum," *New York Times*, September 7, 1977, 55.
29. Daily Mirror Subscription Contract, June 13, 1928, North Shore Beach Property Owners Association, History, accessed February 20, 2018: http://www.northshorebeach.org/history. While the payment plan was a great aid to the buyers, it seriously impedes research of the land records. There is no public record of the date of the purchase contracts and the deeds were not issued until the final payment was made, often two years later. These circumstances prohibit an accurate determination of just how quickly the lots sold and requires reliance on information contained in the articles and ads, information that was no doubt hyped by the sellers.
30. Display Ad, *Modesto News-Herald*, February 1, 1929, 11.
31. "King Lake Lots Sold," *Omaha World-Herald*, July 24, 1929, 3.
32. Diane Stallings, "Skyland Development Reflects Ruidoso History," *Ruidoso News*, September 19, 1991, 10A.
33. Deed information is both incomplete and contradictory. Not all deeds disclose the amount of acreage transferred and revenue stamps are unreadable on others.
34. "Beach on Meramec," *Washington (Missouri) Citizen*, August 14, 1925, 4.
35. Display Ad, *Brooklyn Daily Eagle*, October 29, 1922, 22.

36. Display Ad, *Buffalo Courier-Express*, June 23, 1932, 7.
37. Display Ad, *Modesto (California) News-Herald*, February 1, 1929, 11.
38. Display Ad, *San Anselmo Herald*, November 16, 1933, 3.
39. Display Ad, *Fitchburg Sentinel*, June 9, 1933, 15.
40. Display Ad, *Long Island Daily Press*, May 18, 1936, 3.
41. "Real Estate on Which 1934 Taxes Have Not Been Paid to Be Sold by Collector Harnden July 23," *Fitchburg Sentinel*, July 1, 1935, 12.
42. "Committee to Study Welfare Plan Elsewhere," *Fitchburg Sentinel*, November 13, 1935, 12.
43. See, e.g., *Lake Louisvilla (Louisville) Courier-Journal*, April 15, 1935, 23; Fairfield Beach, *Lancaster (Ohio) Eagle-Gazette*, March 24, 1938, 15–21; Loveland Park, *Cincinnati Enquirer*, April 10, 1944, 30–31.
44. *General Index Book 25 C*, 1930–1933, WCRD.
45. "County Worries Over Lake Taxes," *Janesville (Wisconsin) Daily Gazette*, November 22, 1930, 17.
46. *Lake Geneva News Tribune*, September 11, 1930, 4.
47. *Pell Lake Property Owners Association v. Chicago Evening Post*, File No. 10547, and *Roy Thompson v. Chicago Evening Post*, File No. 10584, Walworth County Wisconsin, Clerk of Circuit Court Archives, Elkhorn (1930).
48. Smadbeck to Jonap, WCRD, Deeds, February 23, 1927, v. 193, 345.
49. *Pell Lake POA v. Chicago Evening Post* and *Roy Thompson v. Chicago Evening Post* (1934).
50. "U.S. World War II Draft Registration Cards, 1942," Serial No. 1520, Local Draft Board 7, April 27, 1942, Philadelphia, Pennsylvania.
51. Jonap to Schulze, WCRD, Deeds, June 7, 1937, 249; 278.
52. 1930 U.S. Census, *Population Schedule*, Queens County, New York, 15A, line 14; 1940 U.S. Census, *Population Schedule*, Queens County, New York, p. 5B, line 53.
53. Display Ad, *Orlando Sentinel*, July 25, 1954, 18-D.
54. Display Ad, *(Hagerstown, Maryland) Morning Herald*, January 24, 1956, 7.
55. Arthur Juntunen, "$200 Lots Start Town," *Detroit Free Press*, March 14, 1954,

29. See South Venice Civic Association, "A History of South Venice Beach," accessed February 25, 2020: http://southvenicebeach.org/a-history-of-south-venice-beach/.
56. Walter Powers, "Sarasota Board Seeks Ervin Ruling on Venice Chamber's Part in Realty Promotion," *Tampa Morning Tribune*, February 3, 1953, 11.
57. "Centreville C. of C. Wary of Real Estate Proposal," *(Wilmington, Delaware) News Journal*, April 29, 1959, 29.
58. Steve Raymond, "Giant Ad Drive to Launch New Palmetto Development," *Tampa Daily Times*, January 31, 1955, 5.
59. "Avon Park Chamber Sponsors Realty Project to Encourage New Residents," *Tampa Sunday Tribune*, January 6, 1957, 9-B.
60. "Centreville C. of C. Wary of Real Estate Proposal," *News Journal*; "Shore Lots on Sale," *The (Baltimore) Sun*, August 26, 1962, Sec. c, 4.
61. "Housing Set for Greene," *(Uniontown, Pennsylvania) Evening Standard*, October 27, 1962, 4.
62. *(Greenfield, Indiana) Daily Reporter*, February 18, 1927, 4.
63. "New Castle News," *(Richmond, Indiana) Palladium-Item*, November 18, 1959, 10.
64. "New Castle News," July 12, 1961, 12.
65. Display Ad, *(Muncie, Indiana) Star Press*, August 31, 1961, 34.
66. "Knightstown Will Develop Lake Site Just East of Town," *Rushville (Indiana) Republican*, September 1, 1961, 2.
67. Frank Salzarulo, "Old Subdivision and New Vision," *Indianapolis News*, June 25, 1962, 3.

Chapter 8

1. Evelyn Hachey, *History of Lake Samoset* (Leominster Historical Society, 1956), unpaginated.
2. Littleton Historical Society, *Littleton*, Charleston: Arcadia Publishing, 2002, 71.
3. Display Ad, *Fitchburg Sentinel*, July 16, 1926, 15.
4. Display Ad, *Fitchburg Sentinel*, July 14, 1926, 9.
5. Display Ad, *Jewish Daily News*, February 21, 1919, 10–11.
6. Display Ad, *Philadelphia Inquirer*, July 17, 1921, 21.

7. Display Ad, *Jersey Journal*, June 4, 1921, 5.
8. Display Ad, *Brooklyn Daily Eagle*, November 17, 1922, 3.
9. Display Ad, *Jersey Journal*.
10. "Pittsburgh Firm to Begin Tests of Missouri Iron Ore Tomorrow," *Saint Louis Post-Dispatch*, March 27, 1942, 20; "Mountain Lake Tract in Ozarks to Be Subdivided," *Saint Louis Post-Dispatch*, June 4, 1939, 24.
11. Display Ad, *Saint Louis Post-Dispatch*, June 9, 1939, 17.
12. Display Ad, *Saint Louis Post-Dispatch*, August 8, 1943, 9.
13. Iron Mountain Lake Property Owners Association, Articles of Incorporation, July, 22, 1954, Missouri Secretary of State, Charter No. 00000214.
14. Michael Shaw, "Brooklyn Goes Broke, Files for Bankruptcy," *Saint Louis Post-Dispatch*, October 15, 2003, 25.
15. Fire Island Pines Historical Preservation Society, "Fire Island and Lone Hill," accessed September 25, 2020: https://web.archive.org/web/20140111213934/, www.fiphps.org/time-line/fire-iisland-and-the-lone-hill.
16. "Sites Available on Fire Island," *Long Island Star Journal*, July 31, 1953, 12.
17. Alfred G. Aronowitz, "Fire Island," *New York Post*, July 31, 1959, 34.
18. "100-Unit Co-op Approved for Fire Is. Pines," *(New York) Daily News*, February 15, 1960, B1.
19. Aronowitz, "Fire Island," *New York Post*.
20. Diane Ketcham, "At the Pines, Sadness Amid the Splendor," *New York Times*, August 1, 1993, Sec.13, 9.
21. Display Ad, *(Wilmington, Delaware) Evening Journal*, June 6, 1927, 18–19.
22. Display Ad, *(Wilmington, Delaware) Every Evening*, September 1, 1927, 3.
23. "Carroll Griffith Ended Own Life, Theory of Police," *Wilmington (Delaware) Morning News*, September 11, 1931, 1–2.
24. *Wilmington Morning News*, March 4, 1932, 15.
25. Al Chase, "Plan $500,000 Building at Indiana-43D," *Chicago Daily Tribune*, May 13, 1927, 28.
26. Display Ad, *(Chicago) Sentinel*, May 13, 1927, 16–17, 37.
27. Hudson Lake Beach, LaPorte County Recorder, Plats, November 2, 1927, Doc. 2003 P-06018, LaPorte, Indiana.
28. Display Ad, *(Chicago) Southtown Economist*, July 10, 1928, 8.
29. Display Ad, *Southtown Economist*, June 19, 1928, 13.
30. *Southtown Economist*, August 9, 1927, 6.
31. *Sentinel*, May 27, 1927, 14.
32. "Morris Eller Dies at 77; Long in City Politics," *Chicago Daily Tribune*, November 23, 1943, 16.
33. *The Sentinel Presents 100 Years of Chicago Jewry*, Chicago: Sentinel Publishing, 1948, 11.
34. LaPorte County Recorder, Deeds, November 30, 1927, Doc. 149–051, LaPorte, Indiana.
35. Southtown Beach, LaPorte County Recorder, Plats, May 14, 1938, Doc. 2003 P-07103, LaPorte, Indiana.
36. "Work for Police Station Lodgers: Swift & Co. Employ 300 Cutting Ice at Fish Lake," *Chicago Sunday Tribune*, January 19, 1896, l.
37. "Mill Creek," *South Bend Daily Tribune*, September 22, 1899, 6.
38. "Nothing But Muck," *South Bend Tribune*, August 21, 1903, 2.
39. Display Ad, "The People Who Work With Swift & Company," *Moline (Illinois) Daily Dispatch*, April 9, 1919, 13.
40. Display Ad, *Southtown Economist*, July 24, 1938, 9.
41. Display Ad, *Chicago Daily Tribune*, May 30, 1947, 28.
42. "Exclusive Summer Home Colony in the Making in Monroe Lake Region," *Paterson (New Jersey) Evening News*, August 30, 1928, 1.
43. Display Ad, *Paterson Evening News*, August 31, 1928, 13.
44. Display Ad, *Paterson Evening News*, May 17, 1929, 20.
45. Display Ad, *Jersey Journal*, November 11, 1924, 19.
46. Display Ad, *Jersey Journal*, September 13, 1926, 6.
47. Edward L. Walsh, "Parkway Paved Way for Brick's Growth," *Asbury Park Press*, March 2, 1986, H1; Brick Township Historical Society, Brick, New Jersey, Education, A Brief History of Brick Township, accessed February 25, 2020: https://bricktownshiphistoricalsociety.com/education/.
48. See, e.g., Display Ad, *Jersey Journal*, August 9, 1927, 7.

49. Display Ad, *Jersey Journal*, October 14, 1930, 9.
50. "Brick Residents Ask Improvements," *Asbury Park Evening Press*, October 8, 1931, 2.
51. "Lot Buyers Find Streets Costly," *Asbury Park Press*, October 6, 1932, 1.
52. "Drum Point Road Building Approved," *Asbury Park Evening Press*, December 21, 1933, 14.

Chapter 9

1. Ben Procter, *William Randolph Hearst: Final Edition. 1911-1951*, Oxford: Oxford University Press, 2007, 5.
2. William R. Scott, *Scientific Circulation Management*, 157.
3. Ben Procter, *William Randolph Hearst: The Early Years, 1863-1910*, Oxford: Oxford University Press, 1998, 143.
4. "Building Up the Circulation," *Fourth Estate* (March 27, 1915), 25.
5. Lawson, *Truth in Publishing*, 47; see also "Barrett Tells of Mob Attack," *Chicago Daily Tribune*, April 14, 1914, 15; "Circulation War Started by American," *(Chicago) Day Book*, June 9, 1914, 29; "Chicago Newspaper Gunmen Methods Hit Cleveland—Mayor Puts Kibosh On," *Day Book*, November 27, 1914, 8.
6. Will Irwin, "The American Newspaper, IV—The Spread and Decline of Yellow Journalism," *Collier's* 46 (1911): no. 24:36.
7. Will Irwin, "The American Newspaper, III—The Fourth Current," *Collier's* 46 (1911): no. 22:14-15.
8. Will Irwin, "The American Newspaper, X—The Unhealthy Alliance," *Collier's* 47 (1911): no. 11:28.
9. Irwin, "The Unhealthy Alliance," 29, 31.
10. Ferdinand Lundberg, *Imperial Hearst: A Social Biography*, New York: Random House, 1936, 249-50.
11. Will Irwin, "The American Newspaper, III—The Fourth Current," *Collier's* 46 (1911): no. 22:15; Irwin, "The American Newspaper, X—The Unhealthy Alliance," *Collier's* 47 (1911) no. 11:17-18.
12. See, e.g., photo captioned "The Mayor, Committee and Naval Officers at City Hall," *New York Tribune*, May 30, 1913, 4.
13. Milton Mayer, *Robert Maynard Hutchins: A Memoir*, Berkeley: University of California Press, 1993, 149.
14. Louis Pizzitola, *Hearst Over Hollywood: Power, Passion, and Propaganda in the Movies*, New York: Columbia University Press, 2002, 99.
15. Lundberg, *Imperial Hearst*, 248.
16. "'I Do Not Read Hearst Papers' Case is Reviewed," *New York Tribune*, November 10, 1918, 20.
17. "Arrest of Nathan Vidaver," *(New York) Sun*, March 5, 1908, 2.
18. Lundberg, *Imperial Hearst*, 117.
19. Procter, *Hearst: The Early Years*, 222.
20. Kluger, *The Paper*, 186.
21. *Marshall Hearings*, 919.
22. *Marshall Hearings*, 973.
23. *Marshall Hearings*, 976.
24. *Marshall Hearings*, 983.
25. *New York Tribune*, September 10, 1915, 14.
26. *Marshall Hearings*, 990, 995.
27. "Buchanan and Seven Others Are Indicted," *Rockford (Illinois) Morning Star*, December 29, 1915, 1.
28. "Jurors Defend Marshall's Acts," *New York Tribune*, February 29, 1916, 3.
29. *Marshall Hearings*, 1001, 1005-06.
30. *Marshall Hearings*, 923, 939.
31. *Marshall Hearings*, 926.
32. *Marshall Hearings*, 970.
33. *Marshall Hearings*, 925, 991-92.
34. *New York Tribune*, April 25, 1916, 5.
35. *Extension of Remarks of Hon. Frank Buchanan of Illinois, Appendix to The Congressional Record*, 64th Cong. (1916), 1660-61.
36. "Marshall Escapes Impeachment Trial," *Sun*, July 12, 1916, 5.
37. *Marshall v. Gordon*, 531-32.
38. "Marshall Loses His Habeas Corpus Writ," *Watertown (New York) Daily Times*, July 19, 1916, 1.
39. "Illinois for Hughes," *Rockford (Illinois) Daily Register-Gazette*, November 8, 1916, 1.
40. "Rintelen, Lamar and Martin Guilty in Munition Plot," *New York Tribune*, May 21, 1917, 1.
41. "H. S. Marshall Dies' Famous as Lawyer," *New York Times*, May 30, 1931, 9.
42. "Arrests Due When O'Leary Comes To-day," *New York Tribune*, June 18, 1918, 6.
43. "From Overalls to Congress and Then Back to Overalls," *Rockford (Illinois) Republic*, February 8, 1918, 8.

44. "Those Screams? Oh, a Wife Got an Eye on Her Rival," *Chicago Sunday Tribune*, August 25, 1918, 5.
45. "Renew Labor Feuds, 1 Dead," *Chicago Daily Tribune*, January 8, 1924, 1.
46. "Frank Buchanan, Ex-Labor Leader, Politician, Dies," *Chicago Daily Tribune*, April 19, 1930, 20.
47. "H. S. Marshall Dies," *New York Times*, May 30, 1931.
48. Secretary of State, Corporations of New Jersey; List of Certificates Filed During the Years 1915–16 (1917), 51.
49. Butler, *Beachwood Borough Directory*, 47.
50. "Browns Mills," *Allentown Messenger*, February 22, 1917.
51. "Beachwood as It Is," *New York Tribune*, May 12, 1916, 8.
52. "What the Camera Tells of Improvements at Beachwood, The Tribune's Land Project," *New York Tribune*, Graphic Section, May 14, 1916, unpaginated.
53. *New York Tribune*, September 14, 1917, 1.
54. *New York Tribune*, September 16, 1917, 1.
55. *New York Tribune*, September 23, 1917, 1; *New York Tribune*, September 30, 1917, 1.
56. *New York Tribune*, April 28, 1918, Section III, 1.
57. *New York Tribune*, September 21, 1918, 8.
58. "Washington Herald Is a Hearst Newspaper," *Fourth Estate* (November 18, 1922), 2.
59. "Magazines," *Advertising & Selling* (May 1923), 42.
60. Gloria Ryan Spence, "The History of Herald Harbor, MD. (1924–1984)," Herald Harbor Citizen's Association, accessed February 25, 2020: https://www.heraldharborcommunity.com/history.
61. Spence, "The History of Herald Harbor"; Daniel de Vise, "Once a Daring Marketing Scheme, Arundel Colony Now a Realtor's Dream," *Washington Post*, July 23, 2005, accessed February 25, 2020: https://www.washingtonpost.com/archive/local/2005/07/23/once-a-daring-marketing-scheme-arundel-colony-now-a-realtors-dream/b6210f54-832a-4dc3-b1b4-5b15ef59b05a/.
62. Spence, "The History of Herald Harbor."
63. "Sixth District Advertising Men Meet Next Week," *Appleton (Wisconsin) Post Crescent*, March 19, 1927, 3.
64. See, e.g., Display Ad, *Washington Post*, July 11, 1924, 8.

Chapter 10

1. *Manitowoc (Wisconsin) Herald-News*, July 24, 1925, 3.
2. "Form County Real Estate Board Here," *Elkhorn Independent*, May 6, 1926, 1; "County Realtors Hit 20 Foot Lots," *Elkhorn Independent*, May 20, 1926, 1.
3. "State Stops Sale of Small Sized Lots," *Lake Geneva News Tribune*, May 27, 1926, 1.
4. "Investigate Lot Sales Plan of Chicagoans," *Milwaukee Journal-Sentinel*, May 25, 1926, p. 4; "Gets License to Sell Lots on Lake Como," *Milwaukee Journal-Sentinel*, May 26, 1926, 2.
5. *Big Blue v. Knightstown Lake*, Case No. 74 C 116, Henry County, Indiana, Clerk of Courts.
6. Eldon Pitts, "Misunderstanding: Knightstown Lake Won't be Shut Down," *Muncie Star*, May 15, 1992, 7.
7. Sheldon Shafer, "Residents of Lake Louisvilla Fear State Officials May Pull the Plug," *(Louisville) Courier-Journal*, June 22, 1981, Sec. B, 3.
8. Brien Shea, "Residents Lament Loss of Lake, Drainage Mess," *Courier-Journal*, October 25, 1989, p 5. Also see photo captioned "Mud Wrestling," *Courier-Journal*, October 18, 1989, 10.
9. Michele Kurtz, "State to Sell Lake Louisvilla Sites; Some Leery," *Courier-Journal*, July 18, 1990, 7.
10. Eldon Pitts, "Residents Want County to Take Control of Lake," *Star Press*, September 28, 1996, 19.
11. Eldon Pitts, "Dispute Over Who Owns Raysville Lake in Court," *Star Press*, April 11, 1997, 7.
12. "Living Dangerously: Ownership Dispute Has Stymied Repair of Knightstown Dam," *Star Press*, December 28, 1999, 1.
13. *Phase 1 Inspection Report, National Dam Safety Program, Beaver Dam, NJ 00077* (Department of the Army Corps of Engineers, Philadelphia, 1979), 3. This report states that the Beach Club Lake dam failed on November 14, 1927, a date that

appears fallacious since lot sales at Beach Club Lake were actively promoted between May and November of 1929.

14. "Buyers Flooding City," *Millville Daily Republican*.

15. "Laurel Lake Dam May Cost $30,000," *Millville Daily Republican*, May 13, 1957, 1.

16. "County Items," *(Lake Geneva, Wisconsin) Herald*, May 23, 1885, 1.

17. *Charles B. Gleason v. Warren Smadbeck*, W.P. 209; Petition of Warren Smadbeck, W.P. 211; *Opinion and Decisions of the Railroad Commission of Wisconsin*, v. 29 (1930), 499.

18. *McHenry Plaindealer*, October 16, 1924, 6; "Twelve Cases Are Scheduled Before R. R. Commission," *Wausau (Wisconsin) Daily Record-Herald*, October 21, 1924, 16.

19. W.P. 211 and W.P. 209, Stipulation, WCRD, Mortgages, March 27, 1925, 147:409.

20. *Opinion and Decisions of the Railroad Commission of Wisconsin*, Memorandum of Decision, June 11, 1925, 499–500.

21. "Face Charges in Fatality," *Plainfield (New Jersey) Courier-News*, January 24, 1952, 20.

22. *DNR Water Regulations Dam Correspondence*, Pell Lake Dam 64.19, Steinmetz to Railroad Commission letter, September 25, 1928, item 2102051, Wisconsin Historical Society (WHS) Archives.

23. The letters written by McManus to the PSC could not be located. Only the letters from the PSC responding to McManus's inquiries survive. *Dam Correspondence*, May 16, 1931 to July 11, 1934, items 2102053 to 2102075.

24. *Dam Correspondence*, item 2102063, November 1, 1932.

25. *Dam Correspondence*, item 2102071, April 13, 1933; item 2102077, March 1, 1937.

26. *Dam Correspondence*, item 2102080, April 11, 1962.

Chapter 11

1. At a few resorts the owners' association was called the Improvement Association.

2. Lake Como Beach POA, Entity ID L012564, WDFI.

3. *Official Year Book and Directory of the Lake Como Beach Property Owners Association for the Year 1929*.

4. Linda Godfrey, "The Como Clubhouse," *(Delevan, Wisconsin) Week*, June 13, 1993, 36–38.

5. "KL Owners' Board," *Indianapolis Star*, July 16, 1925, 14.

6. "Knightstown May Have Bathing Pool," *Indianapolis Star*, July 11, 1927, 18.

7. Erie County Clerk, Deeds, February 8, 1924, v. 1739, 88, Buffalo, New York.

8. Erie County Clerk, Deeds, February 15, 1924, v. 1739, 91.

9. Erie County Clerk, Deeds, August 26, 1932, v. 2348, 250.

10. By this time both Smadbecks had died and Home Guardian Company had been dissolved. The agreement was signed by Willard Bleyer, the last vice president of Home Guardian and nephew of Warren and Arthur.

11. Erie County Clerk, Deeds, Agreement April 21, 1987, 9709:304 and Deed May 7, 1987, 319, Buffalo, NY.

12. *Lake Erie Beach Property Owners Association v. Nowak*, 275 New York Appellate Division 990 (1994).

13. Elmer Ploetz, "Town of Evans Chided by Both Sides in Lake Erie Beach Park Flap," *Buffalo News*, September 13, 2001, accessed February 15, 2020: https://buffalonews.com/2001/09/13/town-of-evans-chided-by-both-sides-in-lake-erie-beach-park-flap/.

14. See Lake Erie Beach Park, accessed February 25, 2020: http://lakeeriebeachpark.org.

15. "There'll Be New Town Up Lake Michigan Beach Way Some Day," *News-Palladium*, January 1, 1938, 23.

16. Lisa W. Foderaro, "Long Island Village Votes to Disband 6 Years After Incorporating," *New York Times*, November 26, 2016, A19.

17. "Residents of Lake Louisvilla Fear State Officials May Pull the Plug," *Courier-Journal*.

18. *Staff Report to the Planning Commission, Kidson Appeal*, Application No. CC98–02, Marin County Community Development Agency, October 10, 2005.

19. Peter Fimrite, "Bolinas Oceanfront Parcel $3.9 Million, No Building," *San Francisco Chronicle*, March 29, 2011, accessed February 9, 2018: https://www.sfgate.com/

science/article/Bolinas-oceanfront-parcel-3-9-million-no-2377069.php.

20. Nels Johnson, "For Sale: A Mile of Marin County Coastline," *Marin Independent Journal (California)*, March 13, 2011, accessed February 25, 2020: https://www.marinij.com/2011/03/13/for-sale-a-mile-of-marin-county-coastline/.

21. County of Marin Assessor, Parcel Nos. 191-300-01, 192-233-01, 192-243-01, 192-253-01, and 192-263-01, accessed February 9, 2020: https://www.marincounty.org/depts/ar/divisions/assessor/search-assessor-records.

22. "Property Owners Report Given at Pell Lake," *Lake Geneva Regional News*, March 3, 1960, sec. 2, 7.

23. William Westhoven, "Lake Parsippany Debates Mandatory Assessments," *(Rockaway, New Jersey) Daily Record* January 29, 2017, accessed February 25, 2020: http://www.dailyrecord.com/story/news/2017/01/29/lake-parsippany-debates-mandatory-assessments/97081520/.

24. *Purzycki v. Lake Parsippany*, Case No. C-2-17, Superior Court of New Jersey, Chancery Division, Morris County (2017).

25. *Purzycki v. Lake Parsippany*, Amended Complaint.

26. *Purzycki v. Lake Parsippany*, Judgment, October 7, 2019.

27. Chris Schultz, "Voters Reject Pell Lake Incorporation," *Week*, February 25, 2001, 5A.

28. Steve Targo, "Chairman's Reaction Recalls How It All Began," *Lake Geneva Regional News*, December 8, 2011, 7A.

29. Lisa Seiser, "Voters Back New Village," *Lake Geneva Regional News*, November 10, 2011, 9A.

Chapter 12

1. Elliott Rudwick, *Race Riot at East Saint Louis July 2, 1917*, Carbondale: Southern Illinois University Press, 1964.

2. "Real Estate Man for Fair Play," *New York Age*, July 12, 1917, 8.

3. "New Recreation Center," *(Fort Myers, Florida) News-Press*, May 12, 1954, 3.

4. *New York Herald*, May 3, 1921, 23.

5. William M. Tuttle, Jr., *Race Riot: Chicago in the Red Summer of 1919*, Champaign: University of Illinois Press, 1970, 3-6.

6. *Buchanan v. Warley*, 245 U.S. 60 (1917).

7. *Corrigan v. Buckley*, 271 U.S. 323 (1926).

8. Osborne to Hibbard, WCRD, Deeds, January 22, 1927, v.193, 221.

9. Sex to Bobula, WCRD, Deeds, July 29, 1927, 185:153.

10. Hussey to Jensen, WCRD, Deeds, March 1, 1927, 196:145 (Pell Lake); Shaffer to Tangas, WCRD, Deeds, October 21, 1927, 190:132 (Lake Como Beach).

11. Interlaken Inc. to Turnquist, WCRD, Deeds, August 7, 1933, 229:34.

12. Jack Mason, *Last Stage for Bolinas*, Inverness, CA: North Shore Books, 1973, 88; Stallings, "Skyland Development Reflects Ruidoso History," *Ruidoso News*, September 19, 1991, 10A.

13. John E. Ryckman, "Post Opens New Vacation Paradise at Pell Lake, Wis.," *Chicago Evening Post*, July 16, 1924, 3.

14. "Ku Klux Lodge Being Formed?" *Lake Geneva News*, May 24, 1923, 1.

15. "Klan Holds Initiation Near Genoa Junction," *Lake Geneva News*, September 6, 1923, 1.

16. Robert A. Goldberg, "The Ku Klux Klan in Madison, 1922-1927," *Wisconsin Magazine of History* 58, no. 1 (Autumn 1974), 31.

17. Robert S. Allen, "Wisconsin Joins Move to Curb Masked Bodies," *Wisconsin State Journal*, January 23, 1923, 1; "Legislature to See Onslaught on Ku Klux," *(Madison, Wisconsin) Capital Times*, January 8, 1923, 1.

18. "Anti-Klan Bill Meets Death by Governor's Veto," *Wisconsin Rapids Daily Tribune*, June 1, 1923, 1.

19. Samuel Gonzales, "A Black Community in Rural Wisconsin: A Historical Study of Lake Ivanhoe," (master's thesis, University of Wisconsin, Whitewater, 1972), 34.

20. "$150,000 Offered for Wandawega Lake Land by Negroes," *Elkhorn Independent*, May 7, 1925, 1.

21. Gonzales, "A Black Community," 33.

22. Gonzales, "A Black Community," 5-6.

23. Gonzales, "A Black Community," 9-10.

24. 1920 U.S. Census, *Population Schedule*, Chicago, Cook County, Illinois, p. 4B, line 57.

25. U.S. World War I Draft Registration

Cards, Serial No. 5221, Order No. 4710, September 9, 1918, Chicago, Illinois.

26. Gonzales, "A Black Community," 37–39.

27. Gonzales, "A Black Community," 36.

28. "Negroes Plan Colony Near Lake Geneva," *Lake Geneva News*, May 28, 1925, 1.

29. Gonzales, "A Black Community," 35–36.

30. Gonzales, "A Black Community," 41.

31. Lake Ivanhoe, WCRD, Plats, July 26, 1926, v. 3, 92.

32. Gonzales, "A Black Community," 43–46.

33. Stedman to Boger, WCRD, Deeds, April 5, 1927, 193:554.

34. Gonzales, "A Black Community," 100.

35. "Pledges Fight to Remove Pell Lake 'Restriction,'" *Janesville Daily Gazette*, 7.

36. "Discrimination at Pell Lake," *Janesville Daily Gazette*, August 1, 1950, 6.

37. "Incident at a Lake," *Wisconsin State Journal*, August 7, 1950, 4.

38. Gonzales, "A Black Community," 61.

39. "Finds Pell Lake Beach Privately Owned; New Signs," *Janesville Daily Gazette*, August 15, 1950, 9.

40. Gonzales, "A Black Community," 61; See also Wilkes to Gage, WCRD, Deeds, July 21, 1951, 430:371.

41. Gonzales, "A Black Community," 62.

42. Steve Targo, "Time to Follow Rules," *Lake Geneva Regional News*, July 8, 2010, 6; See also Steve Targo, "E. coli in Pell Lake?" *Lake Geneva Regional News*, August 12, 2010, 6.

43. Butler, *Beachwood Borough Directory*, 48.

44. Butler, *Beachwood Borough Directory*, 152.

45. "Advertising Mr. Hyde," *The Crisis* (March 1915), 236.

46. Butler, *Beachwood Borough Directory*, 116.

47. Butler, *Beachwood Borough Directory*, 4, 48.

48. *Philadelphia Inquirer*, July 16, 1944, 43. Whether or not this community was developed and its name have not been determined.

49. Andrew Wiese, *Places of Their Own: African American Suburbanization in the Twentieth Century*, Chicago: University of Chicago Press, 2004, 70.

50. *Cleveland Plain Dealer*, June 16, 1922, 27.

51. *Cleveland Plain Dealer*, July 14, 1922, 26.

52. Wiese, *Places of Their Own*, 70.

53. Wiese, *Places of Their Own*, 72.

54. 1920 U.S. Census, *Population Schedule*, Akron, Summit County, Ohio, p. 1A, lines 63–64.

55. Anderson Hitchcock, *We've Always Been Free: Poems, Reveries, Short Stories, Photos and Other Musings of Growing Up in Chagrin Falls Park, Ohio*, Bloomington: iUniverse, 2012, unpaginated.

56. While cross burning is generally associated with the Ku Klux Klan, it has been used to protest a Jewish presence.

57. For example Hitchcock states that Samuel Rocker was also the publisher of the *Negro Digest*. Rocker died in 1936 and the *Negro Digest* was founded by John H. Johnson in 1942. Also, Hitchcock may have meant to refer to the *Cleveland Gazette* rather than the *Cleveland Spectator*, as no evidence of a publication with the latter name could be found.

58. "New Jersey Firm Buys Farms on Madron Lake," *News-Palladium*, May 21, 1928, 14.

59. "Plat of Madron Lake Filed Today," *News-Palladium*, February 28, 1929, 6.

60. "Buchanan Township," *(Saint Joseph, Michigan) Herald-Press*, April 10, 1937, 10.

61. "Buchanan Sees Resort Boom," *Herald-Press*, December 31, 1928, 67.

62. *News Palladium*, September 15, 1930, September 6 and 22, 1930, 5.

63. *Herald-Press*, December 19, 1945, 11.

Chapter 13

1. Display Ad, *Dayton Herald*, August 9, 1927, 5.

2. Display Ad, *Boston Post*, June 2, 1920, 2. In *Marshfield, a Town of Villages, 1640–1990*, the authors identify the home converted to the Marshfield Estates clubhouse as the "old Kent house." Cynthia Hagar Krusell and Betty Magoun Bates (Historical Research Associates, Marshfield Hills, Massachusetts, 1990), 128.

3. "Barn Becomes Clubhouse," *Herald-Press*, June 28, 1928, 10.

4. "Skyland to Be Community Mountain

Camp Village 135 Miles from Here," *El Paso Herald*, April 4, 1928. The building now houses the Ruidoso Women's Club. Stallings, "Skyland Development Reflects Ruidoso History."

5. Alicia Gooden, "'If the Walls Could Talk,'" *Galveston Daily News*, March 20, 1999, 1, 12.

6. The Village Green, Nassau Village Beautification Committee (New York), August 2016, accessed February 25, 2020: http://nebula.wsimg.com/a0d05874ae59450a2ba506a80bd8944c?AccessKeyId=3150E8AC5058496F1B24&disposition=0&alloworigin=1.

7. Linda Godfrey, "The Como Clubhouse," *(Delevan, Wisconsin) Week*, June 13, 1993, 36–38.

8. *Purzycki v. Lake Parsippany*, Amended Complaint.

9. "Ridgway Dance Bill Passed by Supervisors," *Elkhorn Independent*, November 22, 1923, 1, 10.

10. Elisabeth I. Perry, "'The General Motherhood of the Commonwealth': Dance Hall Reform in the Progressive Era," *American Quarterly* 37, no. 5 (Winter 1985), 719–33.

11. "Moonshine, Social Diseases in Trail of Unregulated Dance Hall is Told to Committee," *Capital Times*, February 14, 1923, 2.

12. Perry, "'The General Motherhood of the Commonwealth,'" 721.

13. "Blaine Signs Bill Giving to Counties Rule of Dance Hall," *Stevens Point (Wisconsin) Daily Journal*, June 7, 1923, 6. The Ridgway bill became codified in Wisconsin statutes as Sec. 59.08 (8) in the chapter on counties, and as Secs. 351.57 and 351.58 in the chapter titled "Offenses on Chastity, Morality and Decency."

14. *Proceedings of the Walworth County Board of Supervisors for the Year 1923*, November Session, 23–26.

15. "Argument Seems To Be All Against 'Pass-out' Checks in the Rural Dance Halls," *Sheboygan (Wisconsin) Press-Telegram*, November 26, 1923, 3.

16. "Women Score Conditions in Dance Halls," *Capital Times*, June 25, 1924, 8.

17. "Board Asks Repeal of State Blue Laws," *(Neenah, Wisconsin) Daily News Times*, November 19, 1925, 1.

18. "Dance Inspectors Hold Meeting Saturday P.M." *Elkhorn Independent*, May 14, 1925, 1.

19. "Roadhouses to Come Under County Dance Hall Measure," *Green Bay (Wisconsin) Press Gazette*, May 27, 1925, 1.

20. "Master Legal Minds Define Roadhouses," *(Neenah, Wisconsin) Daily News*, January 19, 1924, 3.

21. "Dance Regulation," *(Hurley, Wisconsin) Montreal River Miner*, February 18, 1927, 2.

22. "Shearer Knocks Blaine Tactics," *Racine (Wisconsin) Journal News*, June 13, 1925, 5.

23. "Inspector Was Drunk at Dance," *Menasha (Wisconsin) Record*, November 17, 1927, 1.

24. "Improve Dance Halls by Inspection," *Montreal River Miner*, December 25, 1925, 1.

25. "Kewaunee County Will Not Repeal Dance Ordinance," *Green Bay Press Gazette*, April 7, 1925, 4.

26. "Roadhouses to Come Under County Dance Hall Measure," *Green Bay Press Gazette*, May 27, 1925, 1.

27. "Moonshine, Social Diseases," *Capital Times*, February 14, 1923, 2; "Kewaunee County Will Not Repeal," *Green Bay Press Gazette*, April 7, 1925, 4.

28. "Dance Regulation," *Montreal River Miner*, February 18, 1927, 2.

29. "Insure Dance Inspectors—A Risky Job," *Sheboygan (Wisconsin) Press*, November 20, 1925, 13.

30. "Klansmen Raid Dutch Mill at Delavan Lake," *Lake Geneva News*, July 10, 1924, 1.

31. "Call Sheriff to Stop Zenda Dance Fight," *Lake Geneva News Tribune*, March 19, 1925, 1.

32. "Dance Inspectors Hold Meeting," *Elkhorn Independent*, May 14, 1925, 1.

33. "Bloomfield," *Lake Geneva News Tribune*, August 13, 1925, 2.

34. W.P. 211 and W.P. 209, Stipulation, WCRD, Mortgages, March 27, 1925, 147:409.

35. "County News: Caldwell," *Racine-Journal News*, May 14, 1926, Sec. 2, 10.

36. *Eau Claire (Wisconsin) Leader*, November 18, 1925, 2.

37. "Sauk County Repeals Dance Restrictions," *Capital Times*, January 18, 1924, 9.

38. "Improve Dance Halls by Inspection," *Montreal River Miner*, December 25, 1925, 1.

39. "Pass Out Check Plank Is Asked," *Eau Claire Leader*, September 27, 1924, 3.
40. "Officials Say Dance Hall Ordinance Has Been Success Here," *Elkhorn Independent*, November 26, 1925, 1, 8.
41. "Laurel Lake Is Beautiful Spot," *Millville Daily Republican*, May 23, 1927, 1.
42. University of Louisville Archives and Special Collections: https://digital.library.louisville.edu/cdm/search/searchterm/lake%20louisvilla/field/all/mode/all/conn/and/order/nosort/ad/asc/cosuppress/0.
43. Display Ad, *(Montreal, Quebec) Gazette*, June 17, 1927, 5.
44. "Pell Lake Group Having Good Time and Working Hard," *Lake Geneva News Tribune*, August 20, 1931, 4.
45. W. L. Hand, "Pell Lake," *Regional News*, November 23, 1933, 15.
46. W. L. Hand, "Pell Lake," *Regional News*, November 9, 1933, 15.
47. Corporate Records, Box 044, File No. P002835, Pell Lake Social Club; File No. P002851, Pell Lake Friendship Club, WHS Archives.
48. "Police Seize 75 Cases of Rum, But Release It," *Capital Times*, December 11, 1933, 2.
49. "Walworth Co. Board Meets Here Tuesday," *Elkhorn Independent*, January 11, 1934, 8.
50. "County Board in Wild Session on Dance Ordinance," *Elkhorn Independent*, June 14, 1934, 1.
51. Notice, *Regional News*, May 17, 1934, 16.
52. Classified Ad, *Chicago Daily Tribune*, April 18, 1937, 58.
53. W. L. Hand, "Pell Lake," *Regional News*, November 9, 1933.
54. "A Picture of the Past," *Lake Geneva Regional News*, October 12, 2006, Sec. D, 1.
55. "Bloomfield Firemeni's [sic] Dance Saturday," *Lake Geneva Regional News*, August 7, 1952, 6.
56. Display Ad, *Lake Geneva Regional News*, July 12, 1956, sec. 2, p. 4.
57. *Antioch (Illinois) News*, September 10, 1959, 5.
58. "Pell Lake Lutherans to Rededicate Church," *Lake Geneva Regional News*, June 8, 1978, 15.
59. Steffens to Karbiner, WCRD, Deeds, August 6, 1947, 371;207.
60. Corporate Records, 0108, File No. S008993, Silver Lake POA; Box 044, File No. P002851, Pell Lake Friendship Club; Box 033, File No. L003582, Lake Como Beach Box h Social and Civic Club; Box 0045, File No. P004120, Pell Lake Businessmen, WHS Archives.
61. *Sixty-Fifth Annual Report of the Chicago and North Western Railway Company, Year Ending December 31, 1924* (C and NW Railway Company, 1924), 14.
62. "Okeh [sic] Removal," *Wisconsin Rapids Daily Tribune*, September 8, 1941, 7.
63. "Railroad Sets Terms on Keeping State Run," *Milwaukee Sentinel*, February 28, 1975, Sec. 2, 13.
64. P. L. Behrens, *Steam Trains to Geneva Lake*, Hebron, IL: self-published, 2002, 136.
65. *Pell Lake, Walworth County: An Inventory With Planning Recommendations*, Lake Use Report No. FX-37, DNR, 1969, 9.
66. Pell Lake POA, Entity ID 6P02082; Interlaken POA, Entity ID 6I03143; Lake Como Beach POA Entity ID L012564; WDFI.
67. "Sewing Class Conducted for Needy," July 30, 1965, 5.
68. "Anoka County History: Coon Lake Beach Neighborhood," *ABC Newspapers* (Coon Rapids, Minnesota), November 19, 2013, accessed February 25, 2020: http://abcnewspapers.com/2013/11/19/anoka-county-history-coon-lake-beach-neighborhood/.
69. Joyce Blay, "Judge Rules Time Out for Condemnation Negotiations after Lakewood Foreclosure Fumble," July 10, 2015, accessed October 18, 2017: http://www.joyceblaynewsandviews.com/freedomofthepress/blog1.php/judge-rules-time-out-for (site discontinued).
70. P. C. Laycock, "Pell Lake News," *Lake Geneva Regional News*, November 30, 1961, Sec. 2, p. 5.

Chapter 14

1. George Wyatt, "Hazards Weigh Heavily Against Revival of Times Beach," *Buffalo Courier Express*, February 3, 1953, 15.
2. "Adopt Sanitary and Building Code for Subdivisions," *Lake Geneva News Tribune*, June 24, 1926, 1.
3. 1925 New York State Census 1925, Manhattan County, City of New York, p. 3, lines 43–49.
4. "Love Affairs of Cuban Count Stir

New York Society," *Kingston (New York) Daily Freeman*, January 4, 1934.

5. Anderson Galleries, *Italian and French Furniture, Works of Art, Decorations*, New York, 1936, No. 82, unpaginated. Exhibition catalog.

6. Robert Emmet Hernan, *This Borrowed Earth: Lessons from the 15 Worst Environmental Disasters Around the World*, New York: Palgrave Macmillan, 2010, 92.

7. Hernan, *This Borrowed Earth*, 91–100.

8. Adam J. Lieberman and Simona C. Kwon, *Facts Versus Fears: A Review of the Greatest Unfounded Health Scares of Recent Times* (American Council on Science and Health, 2004), 32–34.

9. Daniel A. Vallero and Trevor M. Letcher, *Unraveling Environmental Disasters*, Waltham, MA: Elsevier, 2013, 117–19.

10. John Shoptaw, *Times Beach*, Notre Dame: University of Notre Dame Press, 2015, 120.

11. Kirby Gann, *Ghosting*, New York: Ig Publishing, 2012.

12. See, e.g., Keith Dixon, "Debt of Honor," *New York Times Book Review*, June 3, 2012, 43.

13. Matt Frassica, "The Gift of Ghosting," *(Louisville) Courier-Journal*, May 20, 2012, sec. 1, 4.

14. Gann, *Ghosting*, 41.

15. Ernest Callenbach, *Ecotopia: The Notebooks and Reports of William Weston*, Berkeley: Banyan Tree Books, 1975.

16. Elaine Woo, "Ernest Callenbach Dies at 83; Wrote Environmental Novel 'Ecotopia,'" *Los Angeles Times*, April 25, 2012, accessed November 13, 2019: https://www.latimes.com/local/obituaries/la-me-ernest-callenbach-20120425-story.html.

17. Ernest Callenbach, *Ecotopia Emerging*, Berkeley: Banyan Tree Books, 1981.

18. David Kupfer, "An Ecotopian Life: Interview with Ernest Callenbach," *Bay Nature Magazine* (July–September 2012), 21.

19. Harris, "Radical Environmental Protectionism," 22.

20. Callenbach, *Ecotopia Emerging*, 12.

21. An early plat map for Bolinas Beach is reproduced in Harris, "Radical Environmental Protectionism," 20.

22. John Hurst, "'Still Not Here': Reclusive Hamlet of Bolinas Trying to Blend Life Styles of Hippies of the '60s, Old-Timers," *Los Angeles Times*, July 8, 1984, 3.

23. Callenbach, *Ecotopia Emerging*, 214.

24. "Sunbathing in the Buff: Where to Go From Here," *San Francisco Examiner*, September 12, 1979, 21.

25. Harris, "Radical Environmental Protectionism," Abstract.

26. "Nearly Completed," *Lake Geneva Herald*, September 17, 1915, 1.

27. See "Project to Drag Pell Lake to Get Under Way Soon," *Regional News*, June 20, 1935, 6.

28. *Lake Geneva News Tribune*, August 6, 1931, 1.

29. *Lake Geneva News Tribune*, August 27, 1931, 5.

30. *Lake Geneva News Tribune*, August 20, 1931, 4.

31. *Lake Geneva News Tribune*, November 20, 1930, 1.

32. *Lake Geneva News Tribune*, August 13, 1931, 1.

33. "Pell Lake Man Pleads Guilty to Liquor Charge," *Lake Geneva News Tribune*, May 15, 1930, 1.

34. "Town Talk," *Lake Geneva News Tribune*, December 22, 1927, 5.

35. See, e.g., "Como Beach Is Turned Over to Lot Purchases," *Lake Geneva News Tribune*, December 9, 1926, 1.

36. LeRoy Blommaert and Perry Casalino, *This is a Real Photograph: The Life and Work of Photographer Charles R. Childs* (Blurb, 2012), 9; Abigail Foerstner, "History by Mail: Photo Postcards Are Snapshots of Time Gone By," *Chicago Tribune*, January 2, 1994, Arts Sec. 13, p. 12.

37. Blommaert, *This Is a Real Photograph*, 44.

38. Blommaert, *This Is a Real Photograph*, 19–20.

Conclusion

1. Randall Gabrielan, *Birth of the Jersey Shore: The Personalities and Politics That Built America's Resort*, Charleston: The History Press, 49.

2. "Charge Chicago Evening Post with Misrepresentation," *Elkhorn Independent*, September 25, 1930, 1, 8.

3. "Lot Promotion Interests State," *Milwaukee Journal*, September 28, 1930, 14; "Como Property Owners Complain of Empty Promises," *Elkhorn Independent*, October 2, 1930, 1, 10.

4. "Como Owners Complain Post

Misrepresented," *Lake Geneva News Tribune*, October 2, 1930, 1.

5. "Badger Real Estate Law Due for U.S. Court Test," *Wisconsin State Journal*, October 13, 1929, 1, 4.

6. *Sheboygan Press*, May 2, 1932, 2.

7. Daily Mirror Subscription Contract: http://www.northshorebeach.org/history.

8. Hussey to Pell Lake Property Owners Association, WCRD, Deeds, 193:231.

9. *Dam Correspondence*, item 2102065, November 9, 1932; item 2102067, December 1, 1932.

10. "Subdivision Is Set at Barnes Landing," July 13, 1952, Sec. W, 1.

11. "Chester Harbor Selling Fast," *Philadelphia Inquirer*, October 4, 1959, 17.

12. "Coliseum Leader Sold Suburbs," *New York Times*, April 29, 1956, 75.

13. "Warren Smadbeck, 80, Is Dead," *New York Times*, *New York Times*, July 30, 1965.

14. Black, "A Gentleman with Vision," *Honolulu Star-Bulletin*, August 26, 1957.

15. Real Estate Transfers, *Asbury Park Evening Press*, July 11, 1918, 6; *Editor and Publisher* (New York), January 22, 1921, 23.

16. Realty Transfers, *Asbury Park Press*, September 1, 1936, 16.

17. Lake Erie Beach Park: http://lakeeriebeachpark.org/park-history.

18. A. Gordon Bennett, "Buffalo Newspapers Since 1870," *Adventures in Western New York History* 21 (Buffalo and Erie County Historical Society, 1974), 9.

19. "City of Lake Saint Croix Beach 2030 Update to The 2008 Comprehensive Plan, 5" (no author, publisher, or date provided), Lake Saint Croix Beach Government, accessed February 12, 2018: http://www.lscb.govoffice.com/vertical/sites/%7B856291CF-9A76-464F-A302-062ABA3D2465%7D/uploads/%7B60EFF372-A58F-4089-B9C9-D7E84F09FCCB%7D.PDF (site discontinued).

Bibliography

ABC Newspapers (Coon Rapids, Minnesota): "Anoka County History: Coon Lake Beach Neighborhood" 19 November 2013, accessed February 25, 2020: http://abcnewspapers.com/2013/11/19/anoka-county-history-coon-lake-beach-neighborhood/.

Advertising & Selling. "Magazines" (May 1923).

Allentown (New Jersey) Messenger: "Browns Mills" 28 September 1916; "Doing Things at Browns Mills" 18 January 1917; "Browns Mills" 22 February 1917.

Anderson Galleries. *Italian and French Furniture, Works of Art, Decorations.* New York, 1936, No. 82. Exhibition catalog.

Antioch (Illinois) News: 10 September 1959.

Appleton (Wisconsin) Post Crescent: "Sixth District Advertising Men Meet Next Week" 19 March 1927.

Appointment of United States Postmasters, 1832–1971.

Arkansas City Daily Traveler: "Unique Real Estate Offer" 16 July 1909.

Asbury Park Evening Press: Real Estate Transfers 11 July 1918; "Brick Residents Ask Improvements" 8 October 1931; "Drum Point Road Building Approved" 21 December 1933.

Asbury Park Press: "Lot Buyers Find Streets Costly" 6 October 1932; Edward L. Walsh, "Parkway Paved Way for Brick's Growth" 2 March 1986; Realty Transfers 1 September 1936.

Baehr, Harry W., Jr. *The New York Tribune Since the Civil War.* New York: Dodd, Mead. 1936.

Beckwith, Albert Clayton, ed. *History of Walworth County Wisconsin.* Indianapolis: B. F. Bowen & Company. 1912.

Behrens, P. L. *Steam Trains to Geneva Lake.* Hebron, IL: self-published. 2002.

Bennett, A. Gordon. "Buffalo Newspapers Since 1870." *Adventures in Western New York History* 21. Buffalo and Erie County Historical Society, 1974.

Berkeley Daily Gazette: "Walton Disciples Return from Trip" 10 May 1909.

Big Blue v. Knightstown Lake, Case No. 74 C 116, Henry County, Indiana, Clerk of Courts.

Blanchard, Marvin. History of Centerville, New York. Chicago: deposited in the cornerstone of the Centerville United Methodist Church, copied by Lois Fiegl, Town Historian. 1908.

Blay, Joyce. "Judge Rules Time Out for Condemnation Negotiations after Lakewood Foreclosure Fumble" 10 July 2015, accessed October 18, 2017: http://www.joyceblaynewsandviews.com/freedomofthepress/blog1.php/judge-rules-time-out-for (site discontinued).

Blommaert, LeRoy, and Perry Casalino. *This Is a Real Photograph: The Life and Work of Photographer Charles R. Childs.* Blurb Inc., 2012.

Board of Commissioners of Public Lands. *Public Land Survey, Bloomfield Township, T1N R18E Interior Field Notes* (1836).

Boston Directory. Boston: Sampson, Murdock & Co., 1884, 1889.

Boston Post: Display Ads 2 June 1920, 30 July 1920, 22 May 1921, 19 April 1921, 21 April 1921, 23 April 1921, 28 April 1921.

Brick Township Historical Society, Inc. Brick, New Jersey, Education, A Brief History of Brick Township, accessed February 25, 2020: https://bricktownshiphistoricalsociety.com/education/.

Brooklyn Citizen: "Smadbeck's Boat Wins Opening Regatta Heat" 5 August 1927.

Brooklyn Daily Eagle: Display Ads 8 June 1919, 29 October 1922, 17 November 1922, 5 May 1929.

Buchanan, Frank. *Extension of Remarks, Appendix to The Congressional Record*, 64th Cong. (1916).

Buchanan v. Warley, 245 U.S. 60 (1917).

Buffalo Commercial: "High School Teacher Asks for His Grapes" 25 August 1922.

Buffalo Courier Express: Display Ad 23 June 1932; George Wyatt, "Hazards Weigh Heavily Against Revival of Times Beach" 3 February 1953.

Buffalo Enquirer: "Next Week Will See Several Homes Begun at Lake Erie Beach" 17 June 1922; "Sale of Lots at Lake Erie Beach and Building Operations Beat All Records," 24 June 1922; "Investors Seize Opportunity at Lake Erie Beach" 27 July 1922; "To Build Summer Homes at Much Lower Figure" 29 July 1922.

Buffalo News: Elmer Ploetz, "Town of Evans Chided by Both Sides in Lake Erie Beach Park Flap" 13 September 2001, accessed February 15, 2020: https://buffalonews.com/2001/09/13/town-of-evans-chided-by-both-sides-in-lake-erie-beach-park-flap/.

Bunting, Henry Stanhope. *The Elementary Laws of Advertising: And How to Use Them*. Chicago: Novelty News Press, 1913.

Bunting, Henry Stanhope. *The Premium System of Forcing Sales: Its Principles, Laws and Uses*. Chicago: Novelty News Press, 1913.

Burke, Ruth, and Rebecca Collins. *Around Clear Lake*. Charleston: Arcadia Publishing, 2013.

Butler, William Mill, ed. *Beachwood Borough Directory and Who's Who*. New York: Blanchard Press, 1924.

Butte (Montana) Inter Mountain: "Old Adage That Suckers Abound" 25 October 1912.

California Penal Code, Sec. 532c.

Callenbach, Ernest. *Ecotopia Emerging*. Berkeley: Banyan Tree Books, 1981.

Callenbach, Ernest. *Ecotopia: The Notebooks and Reports of William Weston*. Berkeley: Banyan Tree Books, 1975.

Capital Times (Madison, Wisconsin): "Legislature to See Onslaught on Ku Klux" 8 January 1923; "Moonshine, Social Diseases in Trail of Unregulated Dance Hall is Told to Committee" 14 February 1923; "Sauk County Repeals Dance Restrictions" 18 January 1924; "Women Score Conditions in Dance Halls" 25 June 1924; "Police Seize 75 Cases of Rum, But Release It" 11 December 1933.

Catholic Advance: "Sewing Class Conducted for Needy," 30 July 1965.

Cheli, Guy, *Putnam County*. Charleston: Arcadia Publishing, 2004.

Chicago Daily Tribune: Classified Ad 18 April 1937; Display Ads 3 September 1914, May 30, 1947; "Sues Publishers for $20,000" 14 January 1914; "Renew Labor Feuds, 1 Dead" 8 January 1924; Al Chase, "Plan $500,000 Building at Indiana-43D" 13 May 1927; 9 July 1929; "Frank Buchanan, Ex-Labor Leader, Politician, Dies" 19 April 1930; "Morris Eller Dies at 77; Long in City Politics" 23 November 1943.

Chicago Evening Post: Announcements 22 May 1912, 18 June 1912, 21 June 1912; Display Ad 4 June 1925; "On to Lakewood! Slogan of Fire Fans" 3 June 1912; "Barrett Tells of Mob Attack" 14 April 1914; John E. Ryckman, "Post Opens New Vacation Paradise at Pell Lake, Wis." 16 July 1924; "Pell Lake Solves Vacation Issue; Ends Big Mutiny" 18 July 1924; "Post's Pell Lake Resort Develops Another Booster" 25 July 1924; "Father Visits Pell Lake and Purchases Lots" 5 August 1924; "Land of Sunshine at Pell Lake Beckons to You" 6 August 1924; "Lake Como Beauty Appreciated by New Lot Owners" 31 May 1926.

Chicago Sunday Tribune: "Work for Police Station Lodgers: Swift & Co. Employ 300 Cutting Ice at Fish Lake" 19 January 1896; "Those Screams? Oh, a Wife Got an Eye on Her Rival" 25 August 1918.

Chicago Tribune: Classified Ad 8 July 1925; Abigail Foerstner, "History by Mail: Photo Postcards Are Snapshots of Time Gone By" 2 January 1994.

Cincinnati Enquirer: 10 April 1944.

Cleveland Plain Dealer: Display Ads 16 June 1922, July 14, 1922.

Columbus Evening Dispatch: "Dispatch Offers Summer Home Sites for $69.50" 5 August 1926.

Connecticut Wills and Probate Records, 1860, Middleton, v. 22, Connecticut State Library, Hartford.

Copyright Entries, Part 1, Group 2

(Washington, D.C., Copyright Office, 1916).
Corrigan v. Buckley, 271 U.S. 323 (1926).
County Review (Riverhead, New York): 7 April 1927; "Radio Corporation Sells 950 Acres in Rocky Point" 5 May 1927; 19 October 1944.
Courier-Journal (Louisville): Photo 18 October 1989; 15 April 1935; Sheldon Shafer, "Residents of Lake Louisvilla Fear State Officials May Pull the Plug" 22 June 1981; Brien Shea, "Residents Lament Loss of Lake, Drainage Mess" 25 October 1989; Michele Kurtz, "State to Sell Lake Louisvilla Sites; Some Leery" 18 July 1990; Frassica, Matt, "The Gift of Ghosting" 20 May 2012.
Crisis. "Advertising Mr. Hyde" (March 1915).
Daily News (Neenah, Wisconsin): "Master Legal Minds Define Roadhouses" 19 January 1924.
Daily News (New York): "100-Unit Co-op Approved for Fire Is. Pines" 15 February 1960.
Daily News Times (Neenah, Wisconsin): "Board Asks Repeal of State Blue Laws" 19 November 1925.
Daily Record (Rockaway, New Jersey), William Westhoven, "Lake Parsippany Debates Mandatory Assessments" 29 January 2017, accessed February 25, 2020: http://www.dailyrecord.com/story/news/2017/01/29/lake-parsippany-debates-mandatory-assessments/97081520/.
Daily Reporter (Greenfield, Indiana): 18 February 1927.
Davies, Pearl Janet. Real Estate in American History. Washington, D.C.: Public Affairs Press, 1958.
Day Book (Chicago): "Circulation War Started by American" 9 June 1914; "Chicago Newspaper Gunmen Methods Hit Cleveland—Mayor Puts Kibosh On" 27 November 1914.
Dayton Herald: Display Ads 14 July 1925, 9 August 1927; "Crystal Lakes People Organize Improvement Club" 17 November, 1925.
Delaware County Daily Times: Display Ad 21 June 1927.
Detroit Free Press: Arthur Juntunen, "$200 Lots Start Town" 14 March 1954.
Directory of Dedham and Westwood. North Cambridge, MA: Edward A Jones, 1899.

DNR Water Regulations Dam Correspondence, Pell Lake Dam 64.19, Wisconsin Historical Society Archives.
Donatiello, Gene, and John Leavey. Brick Township. Charleston: Arcadia Publishing, 2012.
Donovan, Gwen. Sparta. Charleston: Arcadia Publishing, 2010.
Drowne, Kathleen, and Patrick Huber. The 1920s: American Popular Culture Through History. Westport, CT: Greenwood Press, 2004.
Drye, Willie. For Sale—American Paradise: How Our Nation Was Sold an Impossible Dream in Florida. Guilford, CT: Lyons Press, 2016.
Dunkirk (New York) Evening Observer: Display Ads 8 July 1922, 14 July 1922.
Dunn, Walter S. Walworth County. Charleston: Arcadia Publishing, 1998.
Eau Claire (Wisconsin) Leader: "Pass Out Check Plank Is Asked" 27 September 1924; "Tramp, Tramp, Tramp: County Board Marks Time with Dance Ordinance and Renews Griefs of Yester Year" 18 November 1925.
Eisenstadt, Peter ed. The Encyclopedia of New York State. Syracuse: Syracuse University Press, 2005.
El Paso Herald: Display Ad 4 April 1928; "Skyland to Be Community Mountain Camp Village 135 Miles From Here" 4 April 1928; "Business Houses Being Built at Ruidoso Skyland" 19 April 1928; "Skyland to Get New Dance Hall" 14 May 1928.
Elkhorn (Wisconsin) Independent: "Ridgway Dance Bill Passed by Supervisors" 22 November 1923 "Would Change Name of Russel's Lake" 5 March 1925; "$150,000 Offered for Wandawega Lake Land by Negroes" 7 May 1925; "Dance Inspectors Hold Meeting Saturday P.M." 14 May 1925; "Officials Say Dance Hall Ordinance Has Been Success Here" 26 November 1925; "Form County Real Estate Board Here" 6 May 1926; "County Realtors Hit 20 Foot Lots," 20 May 1926; "New Development on Pleasant Lake" 26 June 1930; "Charge Chicago Evening Post with Misrepresentation" 25 September 1930; "Como Property Owners Complain of Empty Promises" 2 October 1930; "Walworth Co. Board Meets Here Tuesday" 11 January 1934; "County Board in Wild Session on Dance Ordinance" 14 June 1934.

Erie County Clerk, Deeds, Buffalo, NY.
Evening Bee (Sacramento): "To Prospect Big Tract for Oil: Betts Thinks He Has Struck It Rich and Plans Development" 8 July 1907; "Looking for Oil: Prospecting Will Be Carried on with Vigor" 22 July 1907; "To Bore for Oil" 9 August 1907.
Evening Journal (Wilmington, Delaware), Display Ad 6 June 1927.
Evening Standard (Uniontown, Pennsylvania): "Housing Set for Greene" 27 October 1962.
Evening World (New York): "Over $4,500 Now" 28 July 1893.
Every Evening (Wilmington, Delaware), Display Ad 1 September 1927.
Exploring Walworth County: A Hands-On Guide to the Past & Present of Walworth County, Wisconsin. Elkhorn: Walworth County Sesquicentennial Committee, 1998.
Fire Island Pines Historical Preservation Society. "Fire Island and Lone Hill," accessed September 25, 2020: https://web.archive.org/web/20140111213934/:///www.fiphps.org/time-line/fire-iisland-and-the-lone-hill.
Fitchburg (Massachusetts) Sentinel: Display Ads, 14 July 1926, 16 July 1926, 9 June 1933; "Real Estate on Which 1934 Taxes Have Not Been Paid to Be Sold by Collector Harnden July 23" 1 July 1935; "Committee to Study Welfare Plan Elsewhere" 13 November 1935.
Fourth Estate. "Building Up the Circulation" (March 27, 1915); "Washington Herald Is a Hearst Newspaper" (November 18, 1922).
Fowler, Nath'l C., Jr. *Fowler's Publicity*. Boston: Publicity Publishing, 1900.
Gabrielan, Randall. *Birth of the Jersey Shore: The Personalities and Politics That Built America's Resort*. Charleston: History Press, 2015.
Galveston Daily News: "Ferry Approaches are in Bad Shape" 23 August 1927; Alicia Gooden, "'If the Walls Could Talk'" 20 March 1999.
Gann, Kirby. *Ghosting*. New York: Ig Publishing, 2012.
Gazette (Montreal, Quebec): Display Ads 23 July 1926, 17 June 1927.
Gleason, Charles B. v. Warren Smadbeck, W.P. 209, *Opinion and Decisions of the Railroad Commission of Wisconsin*, v. 29 (1930).
Gonzales, Samuel. "A Black Community in Rural Wisconsin: A Historical Study of Lake Ivanhoe." Master's thesis. Whitewater: University of Wisconsin, 1972.
Green Bay (Wisconsin) Press Gazette: "Kewaunee County Will Not Repeal Dance Ordinance" 7 April 1925; "Roadhouses to Come Under County Dance Hall Measure" 27 May 1925.
Hachey, Evelyn. *History of Lake Samoset*. Leominster Historical Society, 1956.
Hall, Ginny. *Meandering Around Walworth County: An Auto Tour Guide*. Bloomfield and Linn Township: Friends of the Lake Geneva Public Library, 2009.
Harris, Marguerite Kirk, "Radical Environmental Protectionism in a Small Community: A Study of the Bolinas Water Moratorium." Master's thesis, Bozeman: Montana State University. 1977.
Headstone: Ira A. Pell. Bloomfield Cemetery. Pell Lake, Wisconsin.
Healdsburg (California) Enterprise: "Meeting of Supervisors" 9 July 1910.
Herald (Lake Geneva, Wisconsin): "County Items" 23 May 1885; "Nearly Completed" 17 September 1915.
Herald-Press (Saint Joseph, Michigan): "Barn Becomes Clubhouse" 28 June 1928; "Buchanan Sees Resort Boom" 31 December 1928; "Buchanan Township" 10 April 1937; 19 December 1945.
Hernan, Robert Emmet. *This Borrowed Earth: Lessons from the 15 Worst Environmental Disasters Around the World*. New York: Palgrave Macmillan, 2010.
History of Walworth County Wisconsin. Chicago: Western Historical Co., 1882.
Hitchcock, Anderson. *We've Always Been Free: Poems, Reveries, Short Stories, Photos and Other Musings of Growing Up in Chagrin Falls Park, Ohio*. Bloomington: iUniverse, 2012.
Honolulu Star Bulletin: Cobey Black, "A Gentleman with Vision" 26 August 1957.
Horne, Philip H. *Mount Pleasant: The History of a New York Suburb and Its People*. Hawthorne, NY: self-published. 1971.
Husted's Oakland, Alameda & Berkeley Directory for the Year 1906. Oakland: F. M. Husted, 1906.
Hutchinson (Kansas) News: Display Ads 10 September 1909, 15 September 1909.
Indianapolis News: Frank Salzarulo, "Old Subdivision and New Vision" 25 June 1962.

Indianapolis Star: Display Ads 23 February 1924, 18 April 1925; "Cottage Is Built Among Tree Tops" 9 October 1923; "KL Owners' Board" 16 July 1925; "Knightstown May Have Bathing Pool" 11 July 1927; "R. B. Hussey Dies of Heart Disease" 16 May 1929.

Indianapolis Sunday Star: Masthead 13 May 1923.

Irwin, Will. "The American Newspaper, I—'The Power of the Press,'" *Collier's* 46 (1911): no. 20; "II—The Dim Beginnings," *Collier's* 46 (1911): no.18; "III—The Fourth Current," *Collier's* 46 (1911): no. 22; "IV—The Spread and Decline of *Yellow Journalism*," *Collier's* 46 (1911): no. 24; "IX—The Advertising Influence," *Collier's* 47 (1911): no. 10; "X—The Unhealthy Alliance," *Collier's* 47 (1911) no. 11; "XIV—The Press of Two Cities," *Collier's* 47 (1911): no. 18.

Ithaca (New York) Journal: Obituary, 24 October 1967.

Janesville (Wisconsin) Daily Gazette: "County Worries Over Lake Taxes" 22 November 1930; "Discrimination at Pell Lake" 1 August 1950; "Pledges Fight to Remove Pell Lake 'Restriction'" 1 August 1950; "Finds Pell Lake Beach Privately Owned; New Signs" 15 August 1950.

Jenkins, Paul B., *The Book of Lake Geneva*. Chicago: University of Chicago Press, 1922.

Jersey City News: "Picturesque New Jersey" 21 January 1905.

Jersey Journal: Display Ads 4 June 1921, 11 November 1924, 13 September 1926, 9 August 1927, 14 October 1930.

Jewish Daily News: Display Ad 21 February 1919.

Judicious Advertising: Display Ad (October 1911), 86.

Kansas Magazine: Display Ad 3 no. 2 (February 1910); "Orient Shop News" 3, no. 3 (March 1910).

Kennedy, John E. *Reason-Why Advertising*. Chicago: Judicious Advertising.

Kielbowicz, Richard B. *A History of Mail Classifications and Its Underlying Policies and Purposes*. Postal Rate Commission Report, 17 July 1995.

Kingston (New York) Daily Freeman: "Love Affairs of Cuban Count Stir New York Society" 4 January 1934.

Kluger, Richard. *The Paper: The Life and Death of the New York Herald Tribune*. New York: Alfred A. Knopf, 1986.

Kozelnik, Scott M. *Lakewood*. Charleston: Arcadia Publishing, 2000.

Krusell, Cynthia Hagar, and Betty Magoun Bates. *Marshfield, a Town of Villages, 1640-1990*. Marshfield Hills, MA: Historical Research Associates. 1990.

Kupfer, David. "An Ecotopian Life: Interview with Ernest Callenbach." *Bay Nature Magazine* (July–September 2012).

Lake Erie Beach Park, accessed February 25, 2020: http://lakeeriebeachpark.org.

Lake Erie Beach Property Owners Association v. Nowak, 275 New York Appellate Division 990 (1994).

Lake Geneva (Wisconsin) News: "Ku Klux Lodge Being Formed?" 24 May 1923; "Klan Holds Initiation Near Genoa Junction" 6 September 1923; "Klansmen Raid Dutch Mill at Delavan Lake" 10 July 1924; "Linn-Bloomfield" 23 October 1924; "West Geneva" 30 October 1924; "Negroes Plan Colony Near Lake Geneva" 28 May 1925.

Lake Geneva (Wisconsin) News Tribune: "Bloomfield" 19 February 1925; "Call Sheriff to Stop Zenda Dance Fight" 19 March 1925; "Kimball Sells Part of Farm at Pells Lake" 9 April 1925; "An Opportunity" 9 April 1925; "Talk About Sunny Florida; Take a Look at Pell Lake Resort" 28 May 1925; "Twenty-Eight Subdivisions on Walworth County Lakes" 6 August 1925; "Bloomfield" 13 August 1925; "Wisconsin's Land Boom" 19 November 1925; "Subdivision at Lake Como To Be Largest Yet" 3 December 1925; "Will Collect $175,000 For Taxes in City" 14 January 1926; "Start Work to Enlarge Pell Lake" 11 March 1926; "Buy Site for Splendid Hotel at Pell Lake" 18 March 1926; "State Stops Sale Of Small Sized Lots" May 27, 1926; "Adopt Sanitary and Building Code for Subdivisions" June 24, 1926; "Business Men Report Good Season Despite Poor Weather" 16 September 1926; "Como Beach Is Turned Over to Lot Purchasers" December 9, 1926; "Town Talk" 22 December 1927; "Short Notes" 5 July 1928; "Short Route to Chicago Opened to Traffic Sunday" 16 August 1928; "Pell Lake Man Pleads Guilty to Liquor Charge" 15 May 1930; 11 September 1930; "Como Owners Complain Post Misrepresented" 2 October 1930; "Valuation of City for Next Year is Lower" 20 November 1930; "Improvements at Pells

Lake Going Forward Steadily: New Scow Being Built to Carry Dredging Machine" 6 August 31; "Motor Trip to the North Woods" 13 August 1931; "Pell Lake Group Having Good Time and Working Hard" 20 August 1931; "Pell Lake Community Forging Ahead" 27 August 1931.

Lake Geneva (Wisconsin) Regional News: Display Ad 12 July 1956; Notice 17 May 1934; W. L. Hand, "Pell Lake" 9 November 1933; W. L. Hand, "Pell Lake" 23 November 1933; "Project to Drag Pell Lake to Get Under Way Soon" 20 June 1935; "Bloomfield Firemeni's [sic] Dance Saturday" 7 August 1952";Property Owners Report Given at Pell Lake" 3 March 1960; P. C. Laycock, "Pell Lake News" 30 November 1961; "Pell Lake Lutherans to Rededicate Church" 8 June 1978; "A Picture of the Past" 12 October 2006; Steve Targo, "Time to Follow Rules" 8 July 2010; "E. coli in Pell Lake?" 12 August 2010; Lisa Seiser, "Voters Back New Village" 10 November 2011; Steve Targo, "Chairman's Reaction Recalls How It All Began" 8 December 2011.

Lake Saint Croix Beach Government: "City of Lake Saint Croix Beach 2030 Update to The 2008 Comprehensive Plan, 5" accessed February 12, 2018: http://www.lscb.govoffice.com/vertical/sites/%7B856291CF-9A76-464F-A302-062ABA3D2465%7D/uploads/%-7B60EFF372-A58F-4089-B9C9-D7E84F09FCCB%7D.PDF. (site discontinued).

Lancaster (Ohio) Eagle-Gazette: 24 March 1938.

LaPorte County Recorder, LaPorte, Indiana.

Lawrence, Lee E. "The Wisconsin Ice Trade." *Wisconsin Magazine of History* 48, no. 4 (Summer 1965) 257–67.

Lawson, Linda. *Truth in Publishing: Federal Regulation of the Press's Business Practices, 1880–1920*. Carbondale: Southern Illinois University Press, 1993.

Lewis Publishing Co. v. Morgan, 229 U.S. 288 (1913).

Lieberman, Adam J., and Simona C. Kwon. *Facts Versus Fears: A Review of the Greatest Unfounded Health Scares of Recent Times*. New York: American Council on Science and Health, 2004.

Littleton Historical Society. *Littleton*. Charleston: Arcadia Publishing, 2002.

Long Island Daily Press: Display Ad 18 May 1936.

Long Island Star Journal: "Sites Available on Fire Island" 31 July, 1953.

Los Angeles Times: Elaine Woo, "Ernest Callenbach Dies at 83; Wrote Environmental Novel 'Ecotopia'" 25 April 2012, accessed November 13, 2019: https://www.latimes.com/local/obituaries/la-me-ernest-callenbach-20120425-story.html.

Los Angeles City Directory 1911. Los Angeles: City Directory Company, 1911.

Los Angeles Herald: Classified Ad 22 October 1910; Display Ad 4 May 1911; "Beverly Glen on Map Most Charming Region" 14 May 1911; "Former Governor Pardee and Wife Visiting Here" 8 June 1911.

Los Angeles Times: "To Purchase Lots" 3 January 1920; John Hurst, "'Still Not Here': Reclusive Hamlet of Bolinas Trying to Blend Life Styles of Hippies of the '60s, Old-Timers" 8 July 1984.

Louisville Kentucky and Environs, Historic Photos: The Suburbs—Northeast, accessed February 24, 2020: http://historiclouisville.weebly.com/northeast.html.

Lundberg, Ferdinand. *Imperial Hearst: A Social Biography*. New York: Random House, 1936.

Manitowoc (Wisconsin) Herald-News, 24 July 1925.

Map of Walworth County, Wisconsin (Elkhorn: Redding & Watson, 1857).

Map of Walworth County, Wisconsin (Everts: Baskin and Stewart, 1873).

Marin (California) Independent Journal, Nels Johnson, "For Sale: A Mile of Marin County Coastline" 13 March 2011, accessed February 25, 2020: https://www.marinij.com/2011/03/13/for-sale-a-mile-of-marin-county-coastline/.

Marin County, California Assessor, accessed February 9, 2020: https://www.marincounty.org/depts/ar/divisions/assessor/search-assessor-records.

Marshall, H. Snowden: Hearings Before the Committee on the Judiciary, 64th Cong. (1916).

Marshall County, Marshalltown, Iowa, Register of Deaths: O. C. Pell, 3 December 1901.

Marshall v. Gordon, 243 U.S. 521 (1917).

Mason, Jack. *Last Stage For Bolinas*. Inverness, CA: North Shore Books, 1973.

Massachusetts Town and Vital Records, Boston Births 1865, Bertram Mayo, No. 1010.

Mayer, Milton. *Robert Maynard Hutchins: A Memoir*. Berkeley: University of California Press, 1993.
Mcbee, Randy D. *Dance Hall Days*. New York: New York University Press, 2000.
McCollum, Shoshanna. *Fire Island Beach Resort and National Seashore*. Charleston: Arcadia Publishing, 2012.
McDonough, John, ed. *Advertising Age: Encyclopedia of Advertising*, v. 2. New York: Fitzroy Dearborn, 2003.
McHenry (Wisconsin) Plaindealer: 16 October 1924; 9 April 1925; 11 June 1925.
Menasha (Wisconsin) Record: "Inspector Was Drunk at Dance" 17 November 1927.
Michigan Department of Licensing and Regulatory Affairs: Lakewood Street Railway Articles of Incorporation, ID No. 800170911.
Millville (New Jersey) Daily Republican: Display Ad 2 June 1927; "Work Progressing on Laurel Lake Tract," 16 May 1927; "Laurel Lake Is Beautiful Spot" 23 May,1927; "Temporarily Halt Work at Laurel Lake" 5 June 1929; "Laurel and Beach Club Lakes Were Incorporated" 26 November 1929; "Buyers Flooding City with Bids for Laurel Lake Lots" 9 August 1946; "Laurel Lake Dam May Cost $30,000" 13 May 1957.
Milwaukee Journal-Sentinel: "Investigate Lot Sales Plan of Chicagoans" 25 May 1926; "Gets License to Sell Lots on Lake Como" 26 May1926.
Milwaukee Sentinel: "Railroad Sets Terms on Keeping State Run" 28 February 1975.
Minneapolis Daily Star: Display Ads 6 August 1925, 20 August 1925; "Rush Starts for Star's Home Sites on Coon Lake" 6 August 1925; "Star Readers' Resort Grows" 12 August 1925.
Minneapolis Star: Display Ads 5 August 1925, 28 July 1927; "Thousands Visit Daily Star Summer Resort at Coon Lake" 10 August 1925.
Missouri Secretary of State, Articles of Incorporation: Iron Mountain Lake POA, Charter No. 00000214.
Modesto (California) News-Herald: Display Ad 1 February 1929.
Moline (Illinois) Daily Dispatch: Display Ad "The People Who Work with Swift & Company" April 9, 1919, 13.
Montauk Beach Property Owners Association, accessed February 24, 2020: http://www.mbpoa.com/about-us.

Montreal River Miner (Hurley, Wisconsin): "Improve Dance Halls by Inspection" 25 December 1925; "Dance Regulation" 18 February 1927.
Morning Call (Paterson, New Jersey):, Display Ad 25 July 1928.
Morning Herald (Hagerstown, Maryland): Display Ad 24 January 1956.
Morning Post (Camden, New Jersey): Display Ad 11 May 1929.
Muncie (Indiana) Star: Eldon Pitts, "Misunderstanding: Knightstown Lake Won't Be Shut Down" 15 May 1992.
Muskegon (Michigan) Chronicle: Classified Ads 7 June 1913, 1 July 1913, 15 July 1914; "Sells Resorters Lumber" 12 February 1913; "First Street Railway Ever Operated in State Summer Resort Begins Operations" 27 October 1913; "Judge Sullivan Cuts Jury's Verdict, Holds Sum Allowed Excessive," 16 February 1914; "Postal Probe of Lakewood Resort Fizzles," 20 July 1915.
Muskegon (Michigan) News Chronicle: Redfern, C. W., "Lakewood, Transformed Wilderness, Shows Possibilities of Lake Resorts" 3 June 1912.
Nassau Village (New York) Beautification Committee, *The Village Green*, August 2016, accessed February 25, 2020. (http://nebula.wsimg.com/a0d05874ae59450a2ba506a80bd8944c?AccessKeyId=3150E8AC5058496F1B24&disposition=0&allow origin=1).
New Jersey Secretary of State, Corporations, List of Certificates Filed During the Years 1915–16, Beachwood POA.
The (New York) World: "An Incomparable New York Suburb" 22 March 1895.
New York Age: "Real Estate Man for Fair Play," 12 July 1917.
New York City Department of Health, Record of Deaths: Louis Smadbeck, 8 February 1911.
New York City Municipal Archives, Index to Marriages 1866–1937: Certificate No. 27937, 9 October 1883; Certificate No. 7168, 27 March 1911.
New York Department of State, Division of Corporations, Articles of Incorporation: Home Guardian DOS ID 30431; Mirror Holding DOS ID 40805.
New York Evening World: "Sherman Park's Guests" 8 December 1891.
New York Herald: Classified Ad 3 May 1921; "Estates Appraised" 6 April 1921.

New York Post: Alfred G. Aronowitz, "Fire Island" 31 July 1959.
New York State Census 1905, New York County, Borough of Manhattan; 1925, Manhattan County, City of New York.
New York Times: Classified Ads 5 August 1918, 29 March 1922; Display Ads 19 December 1909, 17 June 1928, 12 June 1930, 10 June 1931; "J. Freudenthal Missing" 12 July 1896; "Business Troubles" 15 July 1896; "Wills for Probate" 1 July 1913; "Kill Resolution to Impeach Marshall," July 12, 1916"; Real Estate Transfers" 12 January 1919; "Smadbeck-Shear" 8 October 1919"; H. S. Marshall Dies' Famous as Lawyer" 30 May 1931; "Wills for Probate" 10 January 1935; "Mrs. Fay Wed to Dr. Smadbeck" 19 December 1935; "2-Day Art Auction Realizes $38,038 Here" 16 February 1936; "Subdivision Is Set at Barnes Landing" 13 July 1952; "Coliseum Leader Sold Suburbs, but Stayed in New York Himself" 29 April 1956; "Warren Smadbeck, 80, Is Dead; Suburban Real Estate Developer" 30 July 1965; Peter B. Flint, "Arthur Smadbeck, 90, Ran Coliseum" 7 September 1977; Diane Ketcham, "At the Pines, Sadness Amid the Splendor" 1 August 1993; Lisa W. Foderaro, "Long Island Village Votes to Disband 6 Years After Incorporating" 26 November 2016.
New York Times Book Review: Keith Dixon, "Debt of Honor" 3 June 2012.
New York Tribune: Display Ads 9 March 1916, 11 March 1916, 17 March 1916, 27 July 1919; Masthead 3 January 1915; Notices 31 March 1915, 5 May 1915, 15 December 1916, 12 December 1917, 5 January 1919; Photo 30 May 1913; "Summer Homes Offered Readers" 18 November 1914; "Ad-Visor" 10 September 1915; "Jurors Defend Marshall's Acts," 29 February 1916; "Says Marshall Shields Tribune; Agent of American Attempts to Prove Beachwood a Swindle" and "Attack on Marshall Baseless, Says Wise." 25 April 1916; "Beachwood as It Is" 12 May 1916; "What the Camera Tells of Improvements at Beachwood, The Tribune's Land Project" 14 May 1916; "Rintelen, Lamar and Martin Guilty in Munition Plot" 21 May 1917; "Who's Who Against America: William Randolph Hearst" 14 September 1917, 16 September 1917, 23 September 1917, 30 September 1917; "Coiled in the Flag" 14; September 1917; "Coiled in the Flag" April 28, 1918; "Coiled in the Capital" 21 September 1918; "Arrests Due When O'Leary Comes To-day," 18 June 1918; "'I Do Not Read Hearst Papers' Case is Reviewed" 10 November 1918.
New York Wills and Probate Records 1659–1999, Surrogates Court, Record of Wills, v. 915 p. 111.
News Journal (Wilmington, Delaware): Display Ad 4 June 1925; "Centreville C. of C. Wary of Real Estate Proposal" 29 April 1959.
News-Palladium (Benton Harbor, Michigan): "Deputy Sues Land Holder" 7 December 1925; "New Jersey Firm Buys Farms on Madron Lake" 21 May 1928; "Plat of Madron Lake Filed Today" 28 February 1929; 15 September 1930; 22 September 1930; "There'll Be New Town Up Lake Michigan Beach Way Some Day" 1 January 1938.
News-Press (Fort Myers, Florida): "New Recreation Center" 12 May 1954.
Ninth Annual Report of the Michigan Railroad Commission for the Year Ending December 31, 1915.
North Carolina Death Certificates, Buncombe County, North Carolina. Bertram Chapman Mayo, 12 July 1920.
North Shore Beach Property Owners Association, History, accessed February 24, 2020: http://www.northshorebeach.org/history.
Oakland Tribune: Bolinas Beach Display Ads 11 May 1927, 12 May 1927; "Daniels Named On Prison Board" 10 December 1925.
Ocean County Courthouse Wills and Probate Records, 1917–1921, v. 17, Tom's River, New Jersey.
Official Year Book and Directory of the Lake Como Beach Property Owners Association For the Year 1929.
Omaha World-Herald: Classified Ad 16 July 1926; "Charges King Lake Agent Didn't Aid Kin" 28 July 1925; "Pinto Says King Lake Well Water Is Unfit" 21 July 1925; "King Lake Promoters May Dig Two Wells" 25 July 1925; "King Lake Lots Sold" 24 July 1929; "King Lake Has Water and Bullheads Again" 21 November 1934.
Opinion and Decisions of the Railroad Commission of Wisconsin, Memorandum of Decision, 11 June 1925.
Oregon Daily Journal: "Lots Cost Little; See Picture Show" 25 November 1911.

Orlando Sentinel: Display Ad 25 July 1954.
Oshkosh (Wisconsin) Daily Northwestern: "Areas Are Using More Electricity" 31 December 1929.
Palladium-Item (Richmond, Indiana): "New Castle News" 18 November 1959; 12 July 1961.
Parsipppany Historical and Preservation Society. *Parsippany-Troy Hills*. Charleston: Arcadia Publishing, 1997.
Passenger List of Vessels Arriving at New York, New York: 6 April 1910, SS *Moltke*; 8 November 1910, SS *Kronprinzessin Cecilie*.
Paterson (New Jersey) Evening News: Display Ads 31 August 1928, 17 May 1929; "Exclusive Summer Home Colony in the Making in Monroe Lake Region" 30 August 1928.
Pell Lake, Walworth County: An Inventory With Planning Recommendations, Lake Use Report No. FX-37, DNR, 1969.
Pell Lake Property Owners Association v. Chicago Evening Post, File No. 10547 Walworth County Wisconsin Clerk of Circuit, Elkhorn (1930–1934). Perry, Elisabeth I. "The General Motherhood of the Commonwealth": Dance Hall Reform in the Progressive Era." *American Quarterly* 37, no. 5 (Winter 1985).
Petaluma (California) Argus: "Real Estate Transfers" 25 February 1910; "Told Land is Worthless," 22 August 1923.
Petaluma (California) Daily Courier: "They Will Bite" 4 June 1912.
Phase 1 Inspection Report, National Dam Safety Program, Beaver Dam, NJ 00077. Philadelphia: Department of the Army Corps of Engineers, 1979.
Phelps, Barton. *A Place in the Canyons*. Menlo Park, CA: Sunset Books, 2013, accessed July 11, 2018: http://bpala.com/wp-content/uploads/2012/05/Arroyo-Garden-Book-SM.pdf.
Philadelphia Inquirer: Classified Ad 17 July 1921; Display Ads 20 March 1928, 14 July 1944; "Chester Harbor Selling Fast" 4 October 1959.
Philadelphia Record: Display Ad 12 May 1929.
Pizzitola, Louis. *Hearst Over Hollywood: Power, Passion, and Propaganda in the Movies*. New York: Columbia University Press, 2002.
Plainfield (New Jersey) Courier-News: "Face Charges in Fatality" 24 January 1952.

Presbrey, Frank. *The History and Development of Advertising*. Garden City, NY: Doubleday, Doran & Company, 1929.
Prescott (Arizona) Morning Courier: "Articles of Incorporation" 18 December 1906.
Printers Ink. "No Blanket Ruling on Marking Reading Notices 'Adv.'" (December 28, 1916), 74.
Procter, Ben. *William Randolph Hearst: Final Edition, 1911–1951*. New York: Oxford University Press, 2007.
Procter, Ben. *William Randolph Hearst: The Early Years, 1863–1910*. New York: Oxford University Press, 1998.
Purzycki v. Lake Parsippany, Case No. C-2-17, Superior Court of New Jersey, Chancery Division, Morris County (2017).
Racine (Wisconsin) Journal News: "Shearer Knocks Blaine Tactics" 13 June 1925; "County News: Caldwell" 14 May 1926.
Ramsay, Elizabeth. "The History of Tobacco Production in the Connecticut Valley." *Smith College Studies in History* 15, nos. 3–4 (April 1930–July 1930): 93.
Reno-Gazette Journal: 17 July 1943.
Reynolds, Marie F. *Browns Mills*. Charleston: Arcadia Publishing, 2000.
Rockford (Illinois) Daily Register-Gazette: "Illinois for Hughes" 8 November 1916.
Rockford (Illinois) Morning Star: "Buchanan and Seven Others Are Indicted" 29 December 1915.
Rockford (Illinois) Republic: "From Overalls to Congress and Then Back to Overalls" 8 February 1918.
Rosenbaum v. Sarasohn, Reports of Cases Heard and Determined in the Appellate Division of the Supreme Court of the State of New York, v. 184 (1918): 204–09.
Roy Thompson v. Chicago Evening Post, File No. 10584, Walworth County Wisconsin Circuit Court, Elkhorn (1930–1934).
Rudwick, Elliott. *Race Riot at East St. Louis. July 2, 1917*: Carbondale: Southern Illinois University Press, 1964.
Ruidoso News: Diane Stallings, "Skyland Development Reflects Ruidoso History" 19 September 1991.
Rushville (Indiana) Republican: "Knightstown Will Develop Lake Site Just East of Town" 1 September 1961.
Saint Louis Post-Dispatch: Display Ads 9 June 1939, 8 August 1943; "Mountain Lake Tract in Ozarks To Be Subdivided" 4 June 1939; "Pittsburgh Firm to Begin

Tests of Missouri Iron Ore Tomorrow" 27 March 1942; Michael Shaw, "Brooklyn Goes Broke, Files for Bankruptcy" 15 October 15, 2003.

Saint Petersburg Daily Times: "Rides in Plane to Study Lines for Speed Boat" 25 January 1920.

Saint Petersburg Times: "Avon Park C. of C. Sponsors Low Cost Lot Sales" 6 January 1957.

Salt Lake Tribune: "Diamond Drill at Goldfield District" 16 June 1913.

San Anselmo (California) Herald: 25 February 1927; Display Ad 16 November 1933.

San Francisco Call: "Over Five Hundred Citizens Help to Boom the Interests of Oakland" 4 April 1904; "Realty Company Formed" 17 February 1907.

San Francisco Chronicle, Peter Fimrite, "Bolinas Oceanfront Parcel $3.9 Million, No Building" 29 March 2011, accessed February 9, 2018: https://www.sfgate.com/science/article/Bolinas-oceanfront-parcel-3-9-million-no-2377069.php.

San Francisco Examiner: "Sunbathing in the Buff: Where to Go from Here" 12 September 1979.

Sandburg, Carl. *The Chicago Race Riots July, 1919*. New York: Harcourt, Brace & World, 1919.

Schaefer, Janice L. *The History of Mastic Beach*. Mastic Beach POA. 1994.

Schenectady (New York) Gazette: Display Ad 23 November 1920.

Schneider, Grace, "Lake Louisvilla," *A Place in Time: The Story of Louisville's Neighborhoods.* Courier Journal and Louisville Times, 1989.

Scott, William R. *Scientific Circulation Management for Newspapers.* New York: Ronald Press, 1915.

Sentinel (Chicago): Display Ads 13 May 1927, 27 May 1927.

The Sentinel Presents 100 Years of Chicago Jewry. Chicago: Sentinel Publishing, 1948.

Sheboygan (Wisconsin) Press: "Insure Dance Inspectors—A Risky Job" 20 November 1925; 2 May 1932.

Sheboygan (Wisconsin) Press-Telegram: "Argument Seems To Be All Against 'Pass-out' Checks in the Rural Dance Halls" 26 November 1923.

Shoptaw, John. *Times Beach.* Notre Dame: University of Notre Dame, 2015.

Simmons, James. *Annals of Lake Geneva,* *Wisconsin 1835–1897*. Lake Geneva: The Herald, 1897.

Sixty-Fifth Annual Report of the Chicago and North Western Railway Company, Year Ending December 31, 1924. Chicago: C & NW Railway Company, 1924.

Smadbeck, Warren, Petition, W.P. 211, *Opinion and Decisions of the Railroad Commission of Wisconsin,* v. 29. (1930).

Smirnoff, Leslie E. "A Cultural Resources Inventory and Management Plan for Sonoma Land Trust's Little Black Mountain Property." Master's thesis, Sonoma State University, 2009.

Sonoma County California Archives, Assessor Records 1873–1983, accessed July 13, 2018: http://www.sonoma.lib.ca.us/history/archive/?p=collections/findingaid&id=25&q=&rootcontentid=63 (site discontinued).

Sonoma County California Recorder, Deed Book.

South Bend Daily Tribune: "Mill Creek" 22 September 1899; "Nothing But Muck" 21 August 1903.

South Venice Civic Association. "A History of South Venice Beach," accessed February 25, 2020: http://southvenicebeach.org/a-history-of-south-venice-beach/.

Southtown Economist (Chicago): 9 August 1927; Display Ads 19 June 1928, 10 July 1928, 24 July 1938.

Spear, Allan H. *Black Chicago, the Making of a Negro Ghetto 1890–1920.* Chicago: University of Chicago Press, 1967.

Spence, Gloria Ryan. "The History of Herald Harbor, MD. (1924–1984)," Herald Harbor Citizen's Association, accessed February 25, 2020: https://www.heraldharborcommunity.com/history,.

Staff Report to the Planning Commission, Kidson Appeal. Application No. CC98-02, Marin County Community Development Agency. 10 October 2005.

Star Press (Muncie, Indiana): Display Ad 31 August 1961; Eldon Pitts, "Residents Want County to Take Control of Lake" *Star Press,* 28 September 1996; Eldon Pitts, "Dispute Over Who Owns Raysville Lake in Court" 11 April 1997; "Living Dangerously: Ownership Dispute Has Stymied Repair of Knightstown Dam" 28 December 1999.

Stevens Point (Wisconsin) Daily Journal: "Blaine Signs Bill Giving to Counties Rule of Dance Hall" 7 June 1923.

Strong, Moses M. *History of the Territory of Wisconsin, From 1836 to 1848*. Madison: Democrat Printing Co., 1885.
Sullivan, Mark. *Our Times 1900–1925, The War Begins 1909–1914*, v. 4. New York: Charles Scribner's Sons. 1932.
Sun (New York): "Arrest of Nathan Vidaver" 5 March 1908; "Marshall Escapes Impeachment Trial" 12 July 1916.
Sun (Baltimore): "Shore Lots on Sale" 26 August 1962.
Sunset: Display Ad, v. 25, no. 3 (September 1910).
Surveyor General of Wisconsin and Iowa, *General Instructions* (1846).
Tampa Daily Times: "Send a Car of Oranges to Poor" 20 February 1915; Steve Raymond, "Giant Ad Drive to Launch New Palmetto Development" 31 January 1955.
Tampa Morning Tribune: "Likes Florida's Climate" 10 December 1913; "A Significant Incident," 12 December 1913; "Two Elections Claim Attention of Voters" 1 February 1914; "Tarpon Springs" 8 December 1915; "Tarpon Bank Increases its Capital by Double," 14 January 1916; "Arrested at Tarpon on Incendiary Charge" 15 January 1916; "Tarpon Springs" 27 January 1916; "The Florida Press," 3 May 1917; "Many Realty Deals in Tarpon Springs" 16 March 1920; Walter Powers, "Sarasota Board Seeks Ervin Ruling on Venice Chamber's Part in Realty Promotion" 3 February 1953.
Tampa Sunday Tribune: "Tarpon Springs" 29 June 1919; "Avon Park Chamber Sponsors Realty Project to Encourage New Residents" 6 January 1957.
Tassin, Algernon. "Dollars and Display: The Earnings of Advertising Men." *The Bookman*. (September 1910), 26, https:// www.google.com/books/edition/The_ Bookman/SItHAQAAMAAJ?hl=en&gb pv=1&dq=tassin+dollars+and+display& pg=PR6&printsec=frontcover.
"They Call Him 'The Miracle Man' of the Oil Fields." *National Magazine* 50 (April 1921–May 1922).
Times Herald (Port Huron, Michigan): Display Ad 2 July 1930.
Times Union (Albany): Display Ads 28 May 1920, 24 June 1920.
Trent, Karen Pyle. *Knightstown*. Charleston: Arcadia Publishing, 2010.
Trenton Evening Times: "New Corporations" 5 March 1910; "Pines Resort Sold at Master's Sale" 3 June 1916.
Trenton Sunday Advertiser: "Ex-Senator Pfeiffer Goes in Bankruptcy," 3 December 1905; Proclamation 14 April 1907.
Trenton Times: "Brown's Mills to Be Made Into Summer Resort" 2 March 1903; Editorial 10 March 1903; "Brown's Mills Improvements" 6 January 1905.
Turner, Gregg M. *The Florida Land Boom of the 1920s*. Jefferson, NC: McFarland, 2015.
Tuttle, William M., Jr. *Race Riot: Chicago in the Red Summer of 1919*. Champaign: University of Illinois Press, 1970.
Union Postal Clerk: Display Ad. v. 9, no.10 (October, 1913).
University of Louisville Archives and Special Collections, accessed February 10, 2018: https://digital.library.louisville. edu/cdm/search/searchterm/lake%20 louisvilla/field/all/mode/all/conn/and/ order/nosort/ad/asc/cosuppress/0.
U.S. Bureau of Land Management: General Land Office, Mineral patents.
U.S. Census: 1810, Clarendon, Rutland County, Vermont; 1860, Cromwell, Middlesex County, Connecticut; 1870, Bloomfield, Walworth County, Wisconsin; 1870, Boston, Suffolk County, Massachusetts; 1910, Oakland, Alameda County, California; 1920, Akron, Summit County, Ohio; Cook County, Illinois; Los Angeles, Los Angeles County, California; 1930, New York County, New York; Queens County, New York; 1940, Queens County, New York.
U.S. Foreign Claims Settlement Commission: Warren and Arthur Smadbeck, Claim No. CU 2465, Decision No. CU 967.
U.S. Passport Applications: Warren Smadbeck, No. 134875, 27 January 1921.
U.S. Statutes at Large, Newspaper Publicity Act of 1912, 37 Stat. chap. 389, sec. 2.
U.S. WWI Draft Registration Cards: 1917, Burlington County, New Jersey; New York, New York; Chicago, Illinois.
U.S. WWII Draft Registration Cards: Philadelphia, Pennsylvania.
Vallero, Daniel A., and Trevor M. Letcher. *Unraveling Environmental Disasters*. Waltham, MA: Elsevier, 2013.
Vickers, Raymond B. *Panic in Paradise, Florida's Banking Crash of 1926*. Tuscaloosa: University of Alabama Press, 1994.

Walworth County Board of Supervisors Proceedings for the Year 1923.
Walworth County Register of Deeds, Elkhorn, Wisconsin: Deeds, Farm Names, Mortgages, Plats, General Index Books.
Wandawega Historical Society, Elkhorn, Wisconsin: The Wandawega Hotel (Circa 1925–1942), accessed February 22, 2020: http://www.wandawegahistory.org/index#/the-wandawega-hotel.
Washington (Missouri) Citizen: "Beach on Meramec" 14 August 1925.
Washington Post: Display Ad 11 July 1924.
Washington Post: Daniel de Vise, "Once a Daring Marketing Scheme, Arundel Colony Now a Realtor's Dream" 23 July 2005, accessed February 25, 2020: https://www.washingtonpost.com/archive/local/2005/07/23/once-a-daring-marketing-scheme-arundel-colony-now-a-realtors-dream/b6210f54-832a-4dc3-b1b4-5b15ef59b05a/.
Watertown (New York) Daily Times: "Marshall Loses His Habeas Corpus Writ" 19 July 1916.
Wausau (Wisconsin) Daily Record-Herald: "Twelve Cases Are Scheduled Before R. R. Commission" 21 October 1924.
Weber, Erik. "Building Beachwood Parts I, II, III, and IV." *Riverside Signal* 1, issues 6–9 (February 25–April 21, 2011).
Week (Delevan, Wisconsin): Linda Godfrey, "The Como Clubhouse" 13 June 1993; Chris Schultz, "Voters Reject Pell Lake Incorporation" 25 February 2001.
Who's Who in Advertising. Detroit: Business Service Corporation, 1916.
Wichita Beacon: Display Ad 13 August 1909.
Wichita Daily Eagle: Display Ad 4 September 1909.
Wiese, Andrew. *Places of Their Own: African American Suburbanization in the Twentieth Century.* Chicago: University of Chicago Press, 2004.
Williamson, Leland M., et al., eds. *Prominent and Progressive Pennsylvanians of the Nineteenth Century,* v. 3. Philadelphia: Record Publishing, 1898.
Wilmington (Delaware) Morning News: "Carroll Griffith Ended Own Life, Theory of Police" 11 September 1931; March 4, 1932.
Winnipeg Evening Tribune: Display Ad 2 August 1927; "Dr. Smadbeck, Millionaire, Sends Orphans to Circus" 5 August 1927; "Children Visit Circus, Guests of Millionaire, Dr. and Mrs. Smadbeck, of Sandy Hook Fame, Entertain 137 Tots" 8 August 1927.
Wisconsin Death Records: Nelson Pell, 16 January 1882.
Wisconsin Department of Financial Institutions; Interlaken POA, Entity ID 6I03143; Lake Como Beach POA, Entity ID L012564; Pell Lake POA, Entity ID 6P02082.
Wisconsin Historical Society Archives, Corporate Records: Box 033, File No. L003582, Lake Como Beach Social and Civic Club; Box 044: Pell Lake Social Club, File No. P002835; Pell Lake Friendship Club, File No. P002851; Box 0108, Silver Lake POA File No. S008993; Box 0045, File No. P004120, Pell Lake Businessmen.
Wisconsin Rapids Daily Tribune: "Anti-Klan Bill Meets Death by Governor's Veto" 1 June 1923; "Okeh [sic] Removal," 8 September 1941.
Wisconsin State Journal: Robert S. Allen, "Wisconsin Joins Move to Curb Masked Bodies" 23 January 1923; "State Arrests 6 on Real Estate Count" 17 May 1926; "Badger Real Estate Law Due for U.S. Court Test" 13 October 1929; "Incident at a Lake" 7 August 1950.
Woodbury (New Jersey) Daily Times: "Plan $50,000 Hotel at Brown's Mills" 30 April 1903.
Zaykowski, Dorothy Ingersoll. *Sag Harbor: The Story of an American Beauty.* Sag Harbor: Sag Harbor Historical Society, 1991.

Index

Acker, Marvin 133, 135
Ad-Visor column 73–74, 120
Adams, Samuel Hopkins 73, 120, 124
advertising: content of 3–4, 19, 22, 35, 79–80, 82, 85, 90, 102–3, 107, 109–110, 112–14, 128, 148–49, 162–63, 184; cost of and revenue from 29–30, 32, 38, 40, 71–72, 74–75, 79, 88, 92–93, 101, 117–18, 190; direct mail 69, 72, 75; history of 5, 54–56, 69, 72–73, 75; reason-why 44, 52, 55–56, 68, 75, 79; *see also* advertorials; circulation; display advertisements; individual newspapers; subscription premiums
advertorials 5–6, 56, 62–64, 68–69, 72, 74–75, 81–82, 87–88, 109–10, 117, 175, 183
African Americans *see* Negroes
Albany Evening News 68
"The American Newspaper" 70, 117
Anglin, Frank 147–48
Anne Arundel County, Maryland 90, 125
Anti-Saloon League 159
Asbury Park Estates, New Jersey 12, 29–30, 32, 58, 64, 74, 104, 123, 151–52, 172, 174; advertisements for 29, 32, 52, 55–56, 75, 152
assembly line production of colonies 65–68
Auth, Henry J. 190
Avon Park Lakes, Florida 101

Bach, Jennie 11
Baker's Department Store 95
Bartlett, John Berkley 35–36
Beach Club Lake, New Jersey 81, 108, 132–33; POA 82, 141
Beachwood, New Jersey 44–51, 64, 68, 113, 115, 123, 156, 186; advertisements for 42–43, 44–46, 52–53, 69, 73–74, 118; fraud investigation 45–46, 48, 73–74, 117, 119–23, 125–27, 187; and race 151
Beachwood New Jersey Historical Archive 186
Beachwood Property Owners Association 47–48, 68, 123
Bell, Ivan 128, 148
Bennett, James Gordon, Sr. 71, 119

Bentley, Frank 187
Berlin, Louis S. 108
Betts, H.G. 34–35
Beverly Glen, California 38, 44, 53, 62, 67, 156; Consolidated Utilities 38, 62; Land Company 38
Big Blue River, Indiana 60, 62, 130
Bishop, William 165
Bliss, Russell 176
Bloomfield Town Board 17, 182
Bloomfield Township (Walworth County) 8–10, 22, 133, 182
blue arrows 22, 80
Bolinas, California 86, 138; *see also* literary treatment of colonies
Bolinas Beach, California 85–87, 93, 95–96, 108, 140, 146, 171, 182; *see also* literary treatment of colonies
Bolinas Community Public Utility District 140, 181
Boston Evening Record 57, 93
Boston News-Letter 54
Boston Post 103, 110
Break, Samuel R. 35
Brinkman, George 111
Brisbane, Arthur 18, 125
Brooklyn Citizen 57, 98, 152
Brooklyn Daily Eagle 57
Brow, Florence 153
Brow, Grover 153
Brown, Stanley D. 64, 203n10
Brown's Mills-in-the-Pines, New Jersey 47–51, 56, 66, 151, 156
Brumfield, Jeremiah 147–48
Buchanan, Frank 120–23
Buckshutem Creek and Pond, New Jersey 81–82, 132
Buffalo Courier 58, 93, 191
Buffalo Enquirer 58, 83, 93
Buffalo Times 172
bungalows *see* cottages
Bunting, Henry Stanhope 55
Burdett, Madeline 95
Butler, William Mill 33–34, 38, 47, 151

233

234   Index

C and NW *see* Chicago and North Western Railway
California: climate and health 47, 49–50; land speculation 4, 33, 37, 138
California Penal Code 37
Callenbach, Ernest 179–81
Campbell, Stella 95
Canby, California 34
Carver Beach, Minnesota 76–78, 82, 108, 169
Casler, Richard 58
Catholic Advance 168
Cazadero, California 35
Cazadero Redwoods, California 36–38, 47
Cedarwood Park, New Jersey 113–14, 116
Centers for Disease Control 176
Centerville, New York 8–9
Chagrin Falls, Ohio 153
Chagrin Falls Park, Ohio 152–53, 174
chain of lot ownership 49, 64, 68, 186
Chambers of Commerce 100–1
Chapman, Rufus C. 35
Chesapeake Landing, Maryland 101
Chicago, Illinois 16–18, 23, 27, 40–41, 44, 51–52, 58–59, 108–11, 123, 136, 145, 147–48, 163, 167, 175, 185, 188
Chicago and North Western Railway 10, 17, 22, 166, 185
Chicago Daily Tribune 21, 52
Chicago Evening Post 2, 44, 53, 58–59, 69, 91, 93, 99, 129, 175–76, 183, 187–90; Interlaken 89, 188; Lake Como Beach 80–81, 184, 187; Lake Michigan Beach 58; Lakewood 40, 44; Pell Lake 7, 19–20, 23, 63–64, 66, 146, 152, 175–76, 187, 189–90
Chicago Jewish Chronicle 154
The Chief 104, 152
Childs, Charles R. 185
circulation 30, 71–74, 116–120, 124–25; circulation wars 117
Clear Lake Shores, Texas 87, 108, 140, 157
Cleveland Spectator 153, 215n57
clubhouse 3, 5, 18–19, 21, 38, 41, 45, 63, 67, 79, 88, 96, 103–5, 107–8, 114–15, 124, 139–42, 156, 158, 175; design and location 41, 81, 90, 102, 156–57; functions 68, 83, 85, 101, 156; maintenance of 79, 136, 138, 141, 143, 156, 168; modern uses 141, 157, 183; *see also* Pell Lake
clubs 163–67; *see also* names of individual clubs
Collier's 70, 117
Colonie Estates, New York 57–58, 174
Columbus Dispatch 81
Colvin, Lydia 8
Commercial Tribune (Cincinnati) 66, 93
common interest communities 3, 5, 68, 112, 137–38, 141–42
conditions of purchase and sales of lots 3, 37, 40, 63, 74, 79–80, 88, 90, 109, 112–14, 126, 129, 151, 173

contamination *see* dioxin
Coon Lake Beach, Minnesota 62, 75–76, 78–80, 84, 169
cottages 25, 46, 63, 75, 79, 82–83, 85, 98, 113, 131, 136, 163, 165, 167, 169, 177–78, 183; design and construction of 23–24, 26, 41, 60–61, 62, 79, 82–83, 85, 98, 167, 176, 183, 186
County Ministerial Association (Walworth County) 158, 164
Courier-Journal (Louisville) 178
Crane, Arthur D. 89
The Crisis 151
Crystal Lakes, Ohio 64–65, 115, 156
Cuba 12, 87–88, 94, 174

Daily Appeal (Carson City) 35
Daily Mirror (New York) 90–93, 127
dams 61, 81–82, 92, 103–4, 130–33, 136, 187, 191; *see also* Pell Lake
dance halls 5, 7, 158–65, 182
Daniels, Gilbert Barber 34–35, 37–38, 50–51
Day, Benjamin H. 71
Dayton Daily News 65
Dayton Herald 64–65
Dayton Journal 64
Deal Beach Estates, New Jersey 190
Denver Evening Times 59
Department of Natural Resources (Indiana) 131–132
Detroit Daily 89
dioxin 130, 176–77
display advertisements 5–6, 12, 13–14, 22, 30, 31, 42–43, 44, 56, 67, 69, 73–75, 76–78, 83, 113
drainage 100, 142; of lakes 131–32, 178; *see also* Pell Lake
Duck Lake, Wisconsin *see* Lake Como

East Saint Louis, Illinois 144
Ecotopia Emerging 179–180
Ecotopia: The Notebooks and Reports of William Weston 179
Eddy, C.S. 125–26
El Paso Herald 87, 93
El Paso Times 87, 93
Eller, Morris 110
environmental movement 5, 79, 130, 179, 181, 183
Environmental Protection Agency 130, 176–177
EPA *see* Environmental Protection Agency
Estacada Lake, Oregon 86, 139
Evening World (New York) 12, 29, 57, 119

Fairfield Beach, Ohio 81
Farmer, Mary 8,10
farmland 6, 8, 16, 28, 40, 58, 66, 91, 125, 133, 148, 175, 182
Fay, Devereaux 93–94

Index

Fire Island Pines, New York 105-6
Fish Lake, Indiana 111
Fitchburg Sentinel 103
Florida 4, 20, 50, 94, 100, 145, 166; climate and health 47, 49-50, 53; land boom 20, 81, 91, 100
Florida Speaks 100
Ford, Henry 68
fraud 4, 36, 72, 119, 126, 187-88, 191; *see also* Marshall hearings
Freudenthal, Henrietta 11, 88
Freudenthal, Joseph 88
Freudenthal, Julius 11, 200n2
Freudenthal, Rabbi Koppel 11, 16
Freudenthal, Ludwig B. 16, 64, 96, 200n2

Gann, Kirby 178, 181
Geneva Lake *see* Lake Geneva, Wisconsin
Genoa City, Wisconsin *see* Genoa Junction
Genoa Junction, Wisconsin 147, 185
Ghosting 178, 181
Girdler, Amy 49, 51, 53
Gleason, Charles 133
Gobeil, John A. 191
Golden Gate Bridge and Highway District Act 86
Goldfield Diamond Drilling and Mining Company 34-35, 37
golf courses 22, 49, 63, 67, 85, 97
Gonzales, Samuel 150
Gordon, John J. 188
Great Depression 5, 90, 92-94, 96, 98, 106, 154, 177, 188
Great Lakes Beach, Michigan 90, 92
gridded mesa 86, 180
Griffith, Carroll W. 107-8
Gustavus, Catherine 111

Hackett, Alice 149-50
Hafs, Andrew 22
Hafs, Herman 10
Hagar Shores, Michigan 205n24
Hall, Henry 125-26
Harris, Marguerite 181
Hearst, William Randolph 5, 45, 118; Herald Harbor 116, 125-27; Marshall fraud hearings 120, 123, 127; *Mirror* colonies 126-27; political involvements 117, 121, 124-25; publication practices 116-17, 119, 124-25; *see also* advertorials; newspapers
Heckscher Foundation for Children 94, 145
Henry's Tavern 166, 169
Hepburn, Andrew H. 61-62
Herald Harbor, Inc. 126
Herald Harbor, Maryland 116, 126-27, 171
Hibbard, Harriet 16
Hibbard, Hattie 133
Highlands Sunshine Club 163
Hirshberg, Maximillian 169
Hitchcock, Anderson 153

Holtzheimer, Ed 16
Home Guardian Company of New York 29-30, 32, 58, 64, 68, 74, 105-6, 137-38, 152, 190-91, 213n10
Hotel Presidente, Havana 88, 94
Houston Post Dispatch 87, 93
Hudson Dispatch 113-14
Hudson Lake Beach, Indiana 107-11, 115-16, 171
Hussey, Frank 59, 62, 64, 129, 176, 189-90
Hussey, Russell Blair 59, 128-29, 176, 189-90

ice harvesting 17, 111, 135
Illges, George 108
Indianapolis Star 59, 61-62, 85, 175
infomercials *see* advertorials
Interlaken, Wisconsin 89-91, 129, 146-47, 157
Interlaken Property Owners Association 166
International Association of Bridge and Structural Iron Workers' Union 120, 123
Iron Mountain Lake, Missouri 105-6
Irwin, Will 70-72, 117-18
Ivan Bell Realty 128

Jacoby, Joseph 95-96
Janesville Gazette 149-50
Jewish Daily News (New York) 29-30, 56, 93, 152
Jewish World (Cleveland) 152-53
Jews 32, 104, 108, 110, 147, 151, 153, 215n56; *see also* Yiddish newspapers
Jonap, Matthew 20, 95-96, 99
Judicious Advertising 56

Kamaiky, Leon 30, 32
Kansas Magazine 33
Karbiner, Henry 166, 169
Karbiner, Katie 166, 169
Kaufman, William 134
Kidson, Jeremy 140
Kimball, Lewis 21
King, Arthur 17
King Lake, Nebraska 80, 95
KKK *see* Ku Klux Klan
Knickerbocker Press (Albany) 68
Knightstown Lake, Indiana 59-62, 66, 75, 85, 91, 101, 107, 130-32, 137, 174-75
Knightstown Lake Property Owners Association 85, 132, 137
Ku Klux Klan 146-47, 161
Kull, Charles 16

labor unions 122-23, 144
Lachenbruch, Madeline 93
Lake Carmel, New York 92, 94
Lake Como Beach, Wisconsin 80-81, 91, 129, 146, 157, 184-85, 187, POA 136-37, 168; *see also* sanitation
Lake Como Beach Social and Civic Club 166-67

Index

Lake Erie Beach, New York 58, 62, 75, 82, 84, 95, 137–38, 174, 191; advertisement for 78; POA 137–38
Lake Geneva, Wisconsin 10, 22, 26, 89, 146, 147–48, 167, 175, 182–84
Lake Geneva News Tribune 183–84
Lake Holloway 178, 181
Lake Ivanhoe, Wisconsin 128, 148–50, 154
Lake Louisvilla, Kentucky 67–68, 91, 93, 130–32, 139, 163, 171, 174, 181; POA 131, 139; *see also* literary treatment of colonies
Lake Michigan Beach, Michigan 58–59, 59, 91, 139, 174–75, 185
Lake Parsippany, New Jersey 92, 113, 142, 157; POA 142
Lake Ryan *see* Lake Ivanhoe
Lake Saint Croix Beach, Minnesota 68, 76, 78, 140, 174, 191
Lake Sam-O-Set, Massachusetts 96–98, 102–4, 110, 114
Lake Wandawega, Wisconsin 89–90, 147
Lakehurst, New Jersey 190
Lakewood, Michigan 40–42, 44–46, 51–53, 59, 68–69, 91, 104, 115, 120, 140, 156, 175
Lakewood, New Jersey 104–5, 108, 113, 123
Lakewood Club, Michigan 140
Lakewood Gardens, New Jersey 113–14, 116
Lakewood Pines, New Jersey 104, 107–8, 113, 152, 169, 174
Lakewood Street Railway Company 41, 46, 120
Lakewood Township, New Jersey 104
land boom *see* Florida, Walworth County
Land O Lakes Resort Company 21
Laurel Lake, New Jersey 81–83, 108, 132–33, 141–42, 62–63; POA 82, 141
Laurel Lake Development 133
Lesinsky, Charles 11
Lesinsky, Henry 11
literary treatment of colonies: Bolinas 179–81; Bolinas Beach 179–81; Lake Louisvilla 178–79; Pell Lake 176, 181; Times Beach 176–79
Little Black Mountain Preserve *see* Sonoma Land Trust
Long Island, New York 12, 57, 91–92, 98, 105–6, 139
Long Lake Beach, Massachusetts 102–4, 114
Longfellow copper mine 11
Los Angeles Examiner 117
Los Angeles Herald 38, 62
Los Angeles Times 180
lots 17, 22–23, 27–28, 34, 84, 101; contract to purchase 58, 95, 188; disposal of unsold lots 20, 95–96, 98–99; location of 26, 36, 62, 187; tax forfeiture sales 98–99, 101, 133, 153, 169; *see also* pace of lot sales; plat maps; price of lots; size of lots
Louisville Herald 59, 67, 93
Louisville Post 67, 93
Loveland Park, Ohio 66–67, 174

Lowenthal 86
Lucas, L.L. 51

Macgowan, Kenneth 124–25
Madron Lake, Michigan 154, 156
magazines 36, 38, 100, 118; *see also* names of individual magazines
maps 9, 10, 22, 26, 45–46, 81, 83, 99, 109, 138, 154, 184; *see also* plat maps
Marshall hearings 45–46, 48, 50, 56, 120–24, 127; *see also* Buchanan, Frank; Hearst, William Randolph; Watson, Victor
Marshall, H. Snowden *see* Marshall hearings
Marshfield Estates, Massachusetts 57–58, 139, 156, 174
Mastic Beach, New York 57, 83, 98, 139
Mastic Park, New York 57, 83, 96, 152
Mayo, Amy *see* Girdler, Amy
Mayo, Bertram Chapman: biographies 33–34, 187; business associates 33, 37–38, 41, 50–51, 186; connection with Smadbecks 51–54, 56; personal life 33, 49–50, 53; legal disputes 42–43, 51–52
Mayo, Geoffrey 49, 51, 53
Mayo, Noah 33
McDonald, Earl 21
McIlwain, Cy 187
McManus, William 134, 189
McQuillan, Hugh 45–46; *see also* postal inspectors
Minneapolis Daily Star 76, 78–79, 83
Mirror colonies 91–92, 105, 115, 127
Mirror Holding Corporation 92, 190
Modoc Oil and Development Company 34, 37
Montauk Beach, New York 92, 95
Muncie Star 59
municipal annexation 139, 143
municipal incorporation 105, 123, 131, 138–40, 143, 157, 182
Murphy, Eugene C. 58, 137–38, 191

NAACP *see* National Association for the Advancement of Colored People
naming of colonies 40, 48, 58, 66, 79–81, 126, 148, 171–72, 182
naming of roads 50, 61, 66–67, 81, 86, 88, 92, 148, 152, 154, 156, 169, 183, 190
Nassau Lake Park, New York 68, 157, 174
National Association for the Advancement of Colored People 151, 199n1
Natural Resources and Environmental Protection Cabinet (Kentucky) 131
Negro Digest 153, 215n57
Negroes 5, 144–49, 151–54
New Jersey Courier 44
New York Age 145
New York American 45, 117–22, 124
New York Coliseum 94
New York Times 29, 119, 190

New York Tribune 42–43, 44–47, 50, 52–53, 57, 64, 69–70, 73–74, 117–25, 127, 151
New York University School of Dentistry 12
Newark Star Eagle 190
newsheads *see* advertorials
Newspaper Publicity Act 63, 72
newspapers: effects of Great Depression 5, 92–93; history of development 54–56, 70–72, 90; merger with real estate 4, 54, 92, 190; penny papers 12, 55–56, 70–71; used as insulation 23; *see also* advertising; advertorials; circulation; display advertisements; names of individual newspapers; penny papers; subscription premiums
Newton, Mahlon W. 48–49
Nickerson, Addison Doane 33, 43, 46–47, 49, 64, 186
North Shore Beach, New York 91–92, 142, 157; POA 142
Norton, Frank 95

Oakland Enquirer 33–36, 50
Oakland Tribune 35
Olden, Arthur 133, 135
Omaha Daily News 80
Omaha World-Herald 80
Orienta Park, Kansas 33, 37, 114, 168
Osborne, Clifford 21
outhouses 20, 23–24, 128–29, 173, 182; *see also* sanitation

pace of lot sales 19, 23, 38, 58, 63, 78, 85, 100, 152–53
Palmetto Point, Florida 101
Panic of 1893 12, 14, 12, 94
paper roads 126, 138, 154
paper subdivisions *see* wildcat subdivisions
Pardee, George 37–38, 50–51
Patchogue Lakes, New York 57, 70, 75, 82, 123, 152, 174
Paterson Evening News 112
Paterson Press Guardian 89
La Patrie (Montreal) 88
pavilions *see* dance halls
Pel-Lakens 163
Pell, George 171
Pell, Ira Allen 8–11, 133; location of acreage 9, 169–170; naming lake after him 10
Pell, Lydia *see* Colvin, Lydia
Pell, Mary *see* Farmer, Mary
Pell, Oren 10
Pell, Sanford 10
Pell, Thomas 8
Pell City, Alabama 171
Pell Farm Annex to Pell Lake Summer Resort 22, 140
Pell Lake, Wisconsin 3, 5–7, 16, 18, 20, 23, 26, 27, 95, 128, 170; advertisements 19, 22, 76–77, 97, 128–29, 183; advertorials 62–63, 183; churches 18, 165–66, 169–70; clubhouse 150, 157–58, 157–58, 158, 170, 175, 182–83, 189; clubs 163–64, 166–67; dam 17, 96, 133–35, 174, 182, 184, 188; dance hall 161–62, 164–65, 182; depot 17, 18–19, 166, 167–68, 185; drainage 7, 17, 133–35, 182, 188–89; dredging 17, 96, 134, 136, 182, 184; marshland 7–8, 17, 103, 133–35, 175, 182, 184, 188–89; name of lake and colony 7–8, 10, 16, 143, 171–72, 182, 186; POA; 20, 96, 134, 140–41, 143, 149–50, 152, 161, 165, 168, 170, 174, 182–84, 189–90; post office 19; racial attitudes 146, 149–51; roller rink 165, 169, 182; rubber bridge 135; *see also* cottages; ice harvesting; literary treatment of colonies; municipal incorporation; naming of roads; outhouses; postcards; roller rink; sanitation; taverns; taxation; water level
Pell Lake Addition 21–22, 97, 97, 99, 128, 140, 146; golf club 22
Pell Lake Development 128
Pell Lake Highlands 22, 67, 98–99, 140, 146; golf club 21
Pell Lake Hotel 21–22, 97
Pell Lake Sanitary District 182
Pelladium *see* roller rink
Pells Lake, Wisconsin *see* Pell Lake
Penn Beach, New Jersey 79–81
Pere Marquette Railroad 41
Pfeiffer, George, Jr. 48
Philadelphia Inquirer 83, 152, 190
Philadelphia Jewish Morning Journal 104
Philadelphia Press 49
Philadelphia Record 79, 81–82
Pickwick Stage 87
Plage Laval, Quebec 88, 163, 171, 174
plat maps 17, 20, 29, 49, 56, 84, 86, 101, 138, 140, 148, 169, 174, 182, 184, 187
POAs *see* Property Owners Associations
Portland Telegram 86
Post Office Colony, Indiana 51
postal inspectors 45–45, 120–21
postcards 26, 185–86
Potawatomi 7–8, 109
The Premium System of Forcing Sales: Its Principles, Laws and Uses 55
price of lots 30, 46, 57, 73–74, 85, 95–98, 107, 111
Prohibition 4, 110, 144, 158, 162–64, 184; *see also* dance halls
Property Owners Associations 68, 85, 95–96, 108, 136–37, 140–41, 163, 167–68; *see also* individual colonies'
Public Land Survey System 8
Public Service Commission *see* Railroad Commission of Wisconsin
Public Trust Doctrine 142
Putnam County, New York 91, 105
Putnam Lake, New York 92

238　Index

Radio Corporation of America 91
Railroad Commission of Wisconsin 133–34, 189
railroad depots 41, 45, 57, 175, 185; *see also* Pell Lake
railroads 4, 11–12, 16, 22, 24, 27, 33, 40–41, 44, 57, 86, 135, 144, 185; *see also* Iron Mountain Lake; names of individual railways
Rapid Transit Real Estate Co. 12
reading notices *see* advertorials
Real Estate Brokers Board 129, 173, 187–88
Reeves, James 16, 148
Reid, Ogden 119
Reid, Whitelaw 119
Reilly, James B. 48
reversion clause 140
Ridgway, Eldo T. 159, 162
Ridgway Dance Hall bill *see* dance halls
roads 22, 38, 47, 60, 101, 121, 130–31, 153, 158, 174, 176, 180, 187; ownership of 105, 109, 114, 137–38, 141; *see also* naming of roads; paper roads
Roaring Twenties 4, 27–28, 110, 191
Rocker, Samuel 152–53, 215n57
Rocky Mountain News 59
Rodriguez, Violeta 94
roller rink 165, 169, 182
Rosenbaum, Irving 29–30, 32
Rosenbaum v. Sarasohn 32, 64
Round Island Lake, New York 112–13, 116
Route 66 State Park 130, 177
rubber bridge *see* Pell Lake
Rushville Republican 187

Saint Augustine South, Florida 100
Saint Louis Times 78
Saint Paul News 68, 191
sales staff 38, 45, 83–85, 84, 156, 175–76
Sampson, Frank 21
San Francisco Bulletin 85, 93
Sandy Hook, Manitoba 88–89, 174
sanitation 5, 128–29, 172–73, 182
Sarasohn, Ezekiel 30, 32
Sarasota County Commission, Florida 100
Schaeffer, Oliver 45–46; *see also* postal inspectors
Schmadbeck, Henrietta *see* Freudenthal, Henrietta
Schmadbeck, Jacob 11
Schmadbeck, Louis *see* Smadbeck, Louis
Schow, Herbert 164
Schulze, Gustave 99–100
Sea Isles Estates, New Jersey 107–9, 116
The Sentinel (Chicago) 108, 110
Sentinel Beach, Indiana 107–10, 115–16, 171
Sex, Leon 21
The Shades, Indiana 51–52
Shaffer, Carroll 129, 190
Shea, Thomas 58
Shear, Ruth 94, 145

Shelton, William 125–26
Sherman Park, New York 11–12, 29–30, 89, 91, 94; advertisements for 12, 30
Sherman Park Savings and Building Association 12
Shoptaw, John 177, 181
Silver Lake, Wisconsin 89
Silver Lake Property Owners Improvement Association 166
Sitterle, George 18, 21–22, 133
Sitterle's Subdivision and Addition 21–22, 99, 140
size of lots 3, 17, 19, 22, 30, 33, 49, 80, 83, 107, 129, 168
Skyland, New Mexico 86–87, 95, 139, 157, 171; dance hall 87
Smadbeck, Arthur: civic service 88, 94; racial attitudes 145, 152, 154; wealth and personal life personal 11–12, 94–95, 99
Smadbeck, Devereaux *see* Fay, Devereaux
Smadbeck, Evelyn 11
Smadbeck, Jennie *see* Bach, Jennie
Smadbeck, Louis 11–12, 15, 29, 40, 51, 57, 88–89, 94; advertising 12, 29, 13–14; copper mining 11; Cuba 12
Smadbeck, Madeline *see* Lachenbruch, Madeline
Smadbeck, Ruth *see* Shear, Ruth
Smadbeck, Violeta *see* Rodriguez, Violeta
Smadbeck, Dr. Warren: civic service 89; racial attitudes 144–45, 152, 154; wealth and personal life 11–12, 93–95, 99, 173
Smith, Alfred E. 94
Snodgrass, Rhey 125–26
social clubs *see* clubs
Sonoma County, California 34–37
Sonoma Land Trust 37
Sound Beach, New York 91
South Shore electric rail line 109
South Venice, Florida 100
Southern Pacific Railroad 36–38
Southern Wisconsin Electric Light Company 18
Southtown Beach, Indiana 111–12, 116
Southtown Economist (Chicago) 108–12
Sparta Lake, New Jersey 89, 113
Stacy, Loren 9
Stead, Frank 112
Steffens, W.O. 164, 166
Stocker, John 58
subscription premiums 44, 55–56, 71, 74, 116–117; lots sold as 4, 16, 30, 32–34, 37–38, 40, 51–52, 56, 68, 106, 126, 176
Summer Bungalow Corporation 83
Summerill, Joseph J. 48
The Sun (New York) 12, 29, 71, 119
Sunday Star (Wilmington) 107
Sunrise Magazine of Southern Living 100
Sunset 36–38
Superfund 130, 177

Index 239

Sur, F.J.S. *see* Swears, Forest J.
Swears, Forest J. 35
Swears, William B. 34–35, 37
Swift & Company 111, 147

Taggart, Sturges P. 17
Tarpon Springs, Florida 49–51, 53
Tarpon Springs Board of Trade 50
Tarpon Springs Leader 51, 53
Taussig, Theodore 106
taverns 164–66, 169; *see also* dance halls
taxation 5, 27, 47–48, 98–99, 101, 132–33, 138, 143, 169, 184, 189
tents 23, 24, 41, 106
Terre Haute Star 59
Thorson, Arthur 99, 187, 189–90
Times Beach (book) 177–78
Times Beach, Buffalo, New York 172
Times Beach, Missouri 79, 96, 130, 171–72, 181–82; *see also* literary treatment of colonies
Toms River, New Jersey 42, 44–45, 124
Town of Bloomfield *see* Bloomfield Township
Town of Evans (Erie County, New York) 138
Treaty of Chicago 8
Trend Magazine 51–52
Troy Record 75

Union Postal Clerk 51
US House of Representatives *see* Marshall hearings
US Post Office Department 63; *see also* postal inspectors
Upper Greenwood Lake, New Jersey 91, 113
urban renewal 168–69, 182
utilities 18, 38, 46, 62, 65–66, 68, 136, 139, 153, 181, 187

Van Winkle, Noah A. 50–51
Van Winkle Island, Florida 50–51
Village of Bloomfield (Walworth County, Wisconsin) 143, 182

Wachtel, August E. 18
Wadsworth, Philip C. 112–13
Walby, Stanley 164
Walton Lake, New York 112–13, 116
Walworth County, Wisconsin 8, 10, 80, 89,
96, 163, 167, 173, 184, 187–88; land boom 19–20; *see also* dance halls; Ku Klux Klan; maps; Prohibition; Real Estate Brokers Board; sanitation; taxation
Walworth County Board of Supervisors 159–62, 164
Washington Herald 125, 127
Washington Post 9
Washington Times 125
water level 17, 132–35, 137, 175, 182, 187–89, 191
Water Power Law 133
Watson, Bradford 147–48
Watson, Victor 45–47, 119–24, 127, 187; relationship to Hearst 118–19, 123; testimony at Marshall fraud hearings 121–23
Waynesburg Lakes, Pennsylvania 101
Welter, Mathew 165
Wendell, Adele 99
Wendell, Charles H. 99
Westchester County, New York 11, 91
White, Peregrine 156
Whitney, Francis A. 102–3
Wichita, Kansas 33, 168
Wiese, Andrew 153
wildcat subdivisions 36, 138; *see also* California land speculation
Wilkes, Paul 149–50
Williams, Morris 111
Winnipeg Evening Tribune 88–89
Wisconsin State Journal 128, 149
Wise, Henry A. 120–23
Wolberg, Enoch 30, 32, 64
Woman's Christian Temperance Union 159, 164
Woodland Beach, Maryland 92, 115, 125
working class 12, 16, 40, 47, 92, 126, 155, 177, 183
World War I 4, 28, 46, 53, 56, 73, 105, 119, 121, 124, 144, 172
World War II 100, 105–6, 112, 165, 177
World-Herald (Omaha) 80

Yiddish newspapers 30, 104, 152, 173
Yidishe Velt see *Jewish World*
Yidishes Tageblatt see *Jewish Daily News*
Young, Dan 149

www.ingramcontent.com/pod-product-compliance
Lightning Source LLC
Chambersburg PA
CBHW032039300426
44117CB00009B/1112